A Line Drawn in the Sand

A Line Drawn in the Sand

Responses to the AIDS Treatment Crisis in Africa

Editors

PHYLLIS J. KANKI, DVM, DSc

Director, AIDS Prevention Initiative in Nigeria

Principal Investigator, Harvard PEPFAR

Professor of Immunology and Infectious Diseases, Harvard School of Public Health

Boston, Massachusetts

RICHARD G. MARLINK, MD

Bruce A. Beal, Robert L. Beal, and Alexander S. Beal Professor of the Practice
   of Public Health, Harvard School of Public Health

Executive Director, Harvard School of Public Health AIDS Initiative

Vice President, Technical Implementation, Elizabeth Glaser Pediatric AIDS Foundation

Boston, Massachusetts, and Los Angeles, California

HARVARD SERIES ON POPULATION AND DEVELOPMENT STUDIES

Distributed by Harvard University Press

Published by:
HARVARD CENTER FOR POPULATION AND DEVELOPMENT STUDIES
9 Bow Street, Cambridge, MA 02138 USA

Sponsored by the AIDS Prevention Initiative in Nigeria (www.apin.harvard.edu), through
a generous grant from the Bill & Melinda Gates Foundation

A copy of Cataloging-in-Publication data is available from the Library of Congress.

ISBN 978-0-674-03345-0

The material contained in this volume was submitted as previously unpublished material, except
in the instance in which some of the illustrative material was derived.

Great care has been taken to maintain the accuracy of the information contained in this volume.
Neither the publisher nor the editors can be held responsible, however, for errors or for any
consequence arising from the use of the information contained herein.

9 8 7 6 5 4 3 2 1

Photography by Dominic Chavez

Design by Lisa Clark

To our many colleagues in Botswana, Nigeria, Senegal, and Tanzania
who have inspired us with their courage and devotion.
Through HIV research, prevention, treatment, and care,
they have saved hundreds of thousands of lives.

PREFACE

The global inequity was stark: people with HIV/AIDS in the industrialized world were living while those in Africa were dying. HIV disease had largely become a chronic condition in the developed world, yet in Africa, where nearly 70 percent of those with HIV lived, antiretroviral therapy remained out of reach for most. Without treatment, adults with HIV in Africa died within an average of eight years; with the drugs, they could live at least twice that long. Without treatment, infected babies in Africa often died before their second birthday.

For years we had been hearing justifications. Providing treatment to people with AIDS in Africa and other developing regions was simply impossible. The drugs were too expensive; the health care infrastructures were too weak. Africa's best hope was a preventive vaccine. But as the years wore on, a vaccine remained elusive, and other prevention efforts were hampered by denial, discrimination, and despair.

Festus Mogae, then the president of Botswana, became one of the first to draw a line in the sand. "We are threatened with extinction," he told other heads of state at a United Nations special assembly on AIDS in June 2001. "People are dying in chillingly high numbers. It is a crisis of the first magnitude." President Mogae followed his words with action. That same month, he launched a feasibility study for Africa's first national antiretroviral therapy program, which began just seven months later.

This book tells the stories of many who drew lines in the sand—researchers, doctors, funders, political leaders, community advocates, people with HIV/AIDS. Together they have rewritten the history of AIDS in Africa, ensuring that those already infected would not be denied the treatment that could grant them the chance to live.

Phyllis J. Kanki, DVM, DSc
Richard G. Marlink, MD

CONTENTS

Preface   VII

Part I: BOTSWANA

INTRODUCTION   The War Has Started   3

OVERVIEW   The Challenge and Response in Botswana   7
by Richard G. Marlink

ON THE FRONTLINES   Dream Team   29
by John Donnelly

FIELD NOTES   Home Truths   39
by John Donnelly

EPILOGUE   Life After Death   45
by John Donnelly

PHOTO ESSAY   *by Dominic Chavez*   48

Part II: NIGERIA

INTRODUCTION   An Endangered Nation   61

OVERVIEW   The Challenge and Response in Nigeria   65
by Phyllis J. Kanki

ON THE FRONTLINES   The Chance of a Lifetime   95
by John Donnelly

FIELD NOTES   The Burden of Proof   105
by John Donnelly

EPILOGUE   A Gift of Time   113
by John Donnelly

PHOTO ESSAY   *by Dominic Chavez*   116

Part III: SENEGAL

INTRODUCTION   The Magic of Realism   131

OVERVIEW   The Challenge and Response in Senegal   135
by Phyllis J. Kanki

ON THE FRONTLINES   A Bearer of Gifts   163
by John Donnelly

FIELD NOTES   A Mine of Information   173
by John Donnelly

EPILOGUE   Strong Medicine   179
by John Donnelly

PHOTO ESSAY   *by Dominic Chavez*   182

Part IV: TANZANIA

INTRODUCTION   Touched by a Ghost   193

OVERVIEW   The Challenge and Response in Tanzania   197
by Guerino Chalamilla and Wafaie Fawzi

ON THE FRONTLINES   Life Support   217
by John Donnelly

FIELD NOTES   A Power of Good   225
by John Donnelly

EPILOGUE   The Bridge of Goodwill   231
by John Donnelly

PHOTO ESSAY   *by Dominic Chavez*   236

Part V: THE VIRUS

OVERVIEW   HIV Variability in Africa   247
by Max Essex

AFTERWORD   263

EDITORS AND CONTRIBUTORS   267

ACRONYMS   273

ACKNOWLEDGMENTS   275

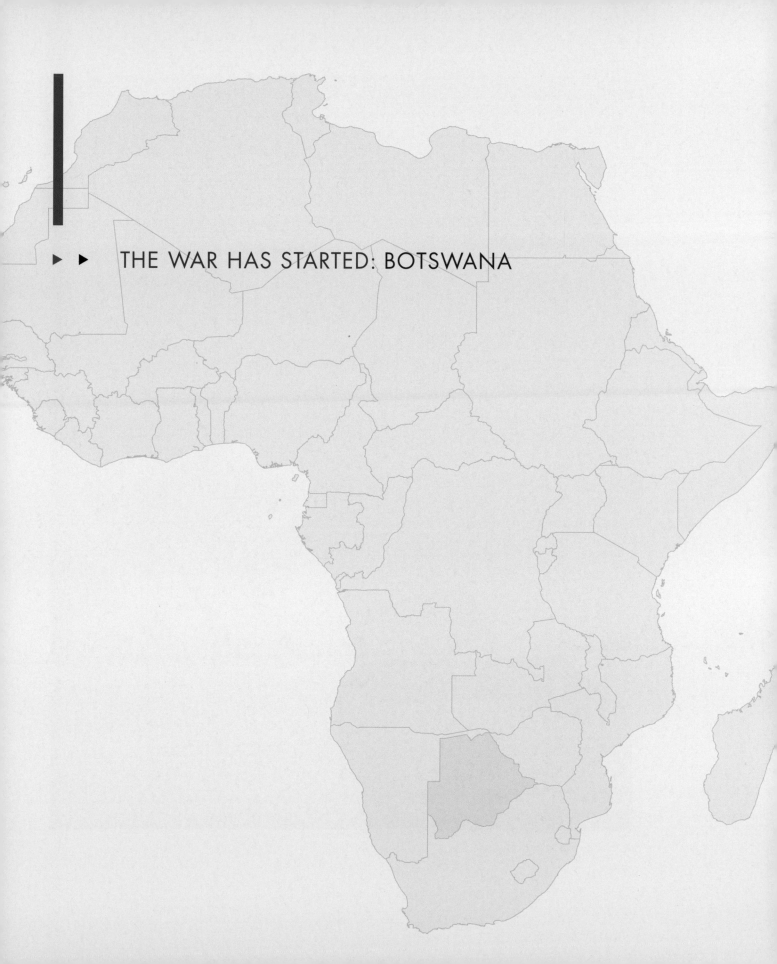

THE WAR HAS STARTED: BOTSWANA

A lone gravesite in Botswana

The War Has Started

AIDS CAME RELATIVELY LATE to Botswana, a peaceful and prosperous country in southern Africa. For nearly a decade, the country's HIV infection rates seemed nearly insignificant compared with the epidemics devastating other African nations. Yet the virus spread in stealth, and by 2001, the country of less than two million people faced the highest rates of HIV infection in the world.

Nearly 40 percent of all adults in Botswana were infected. An estimated 120,000 children had lost at least one parent to AIDS. In less than a decade life expectancy had plummeted by more than 25 years. And each weekend Batswana found themselves attending funerals, sometimes several in a single day. AIDS was erasing the country's past gains, stealing its present, and threatening its future.

Festus Mogae, then the president of Botswana, decried the possible extinction of the Batswana and issued a battle cry. *"Ntwa e bolotse!"* he declared. *The war has started.*

President Mogae launched aggressive prevention, treatment, and care initiatives. To help remove the stigma of testing, for example, he appeared on national television to declare that he had personally been tested for HIV. In 2004, he announced that, unless a patient refused outright, anyone seeking medical care at any health facility for any reason would receive an HIV test. That policy raised the testing rate to more than 90 percent.

Yet the decision that would carry the most far-reaching consequences for the continent was a commitment President Mogae had made several years earlier: to provide every citizen in need with free, lifesaving antiretroviral drugs.

President Mogae enlisted help in his war. As part of the preparation for a national antiretroviral therapy program, the African Comprehensive HIV/AIDS Partnerships, or ACHAP—a country-led public–private partnership among the government of Botswana, the Bill & Melinda Gates Foundation, and Merck—conducted a feasibility study. Based on the findings of that study, in 2001 President Mogae announced that the government would provide antiretrovirals without cost to qualifying patients. The national program, named *Masa,* the Setswana word for "new dawn," launched in 2002 with the opening in Gaborone of Africa's first public antiretroviral clinic.

The challenges were enormous. The country had no model on which to base its program; it would have to *become* the model. And the stakes were high; the Masa Program needed to succeed not only to help Batswana in need of lifesaving treatment, but also to disarm the skeptics who believed AIDS treatment in Africa was simply not feasible.

The government of Botswana activated a national emergency fast-track system to build the country's capacity for launching and maintaining the program. Government officials also formed a dedicated team to implement the program by adopting a phased approach. Such strategic policies have helped the Masa Program flourish.

The program now operates at 32 principal sites throughout Botswana. Six years after the Masa Program began, more than 100,000 Batswana have received antiretroviral therapy. Notably, many of the program's earliest patients are still alive and receiving treatment.

"We see before us the most dramatic experiment on the continent," Stephen Lewis, then the UN Special Envoy for HIV/AIDS in Africa, had said when the Masa Program launched. "If it succeeds, it will give heart to absolutely every country worldwide."

The program's success *has* given heart; a dozen other African nations are creating programs based on Botswana's model.

Since stepping down in April 2008 after two terms in office, President Mogae has continued his work to prevent the spread of HIV through Champions for an HIV-Free Generation, a group of former African presidents and others who share the same goal. In October 2008 he received the Mo Ibrahim Prize for Achievement in African Leadership for his commitment to AIDS.

"Even if you are not infected," President Mogae says, "you are still affected by this disease." ∎

▶ OVERVIEW

The Challenge and Response in Botswana

Richard G. Marlink

BOTSWANA HAS LONG ENJOYED THE REPUTATION OF BEING A STABLE, SAFE, prosperous, and democratic country. Stability and relative wealth could prove no match for the insidious spread of HIV, however. In 2001, Botswana had the highest rates of HIV in the world, with estimates as high as 40 percent of all adults. Not only was the epidemic destroying lives and decimating families, but it was also threatening to reverse the country's hard-earned political and socioeconomic gains of the previous decades.

Economic and Social Background

A landlocked country in southern Africa, the Republic of Botswana borders Namibia, South Africa, and Zimbabwe. Current estimates record the population at approximately 1.8 million people, mostly concentrated in the eastern part of the country.

Compared with many other African nations, Botswana is ethnically, linguistically, and religiously homogenous, with nearly 80 percent identifying as Tswana and more than 70 percent as Christian. Nearly 80 percent list Setswana as their primary language. Batswana, the term for people from Botswana, attend formal school for an average of 12 years. In 2005, the adult literacy rate was approximately 81 percent.

Formerly the British protectorate of Bechuanaland, Botswana gained independence in 1966 and became a parliamentary democracy, dividing itself into nine districts and five town councils. Since independence, presidents have been indirectly yet peacefully elected for a five-year term, with the possibility of one repeat five-year term. The president serves as both the chief of state and the head of government.[1] Seretse Khama served as the first president, followed by Ketumile Masire, then Festus Mogae, each of whom served two terms. The current president is Seretse Khama Ian Khama, who took office in April 2008.

Botswana's economy draws its strength from mineral extraction, tourism, and financial services. The combination of the discovery of diamonds in 1967, more than four decades of civilian leadership, and progressive management policies has transformed Botswana's economy from one dependent on limited agricultural resources into one of Africa's fastest growing economies.

Botswana's small population and significant diamond resources are major factors in its high ranking in the United Nations Development Programme (UNDP) health and economic indicator scale. Botswana is considered a medium-development country—one of the few sub-Saharan African nations in this category. The UNDP ranks Botswana 124 out of 177 member states in its *2007/2008 Human Development Report*.[2]

The World Bank estimates Botswana's gross national income—which takes into account gross domestic product as well as net flows of income from abroad—at US$5,820, which is at least 6- to 12-fold higher than those of Nigeria, Senegal, and Tanzania.[3] Botswana spends US$362 per capita on health, which is significantly higher than what most sub-Saharan African nations can commit (Table 1).

Botswana depends entirely on imports for electricity, oil, and natural gas, and it has only a limited capacity to produce foodstuffs, wood, paper products, textiles, machinery, electrical goods, transport equipment, and metal products. With its current wealth predominantly a result of diamond mining, natural fluctuations and the eventual exhaustion of this finite resource may significantly affect Botswana's economic future.

Botswana's strong economy and high per-capita gross domestic product (GDP) mask significant rates of unemployment. An increase in the migration of people escaping economic and social turmoil in Zimbabwe has helped to raise the unemployment

Table 1. Selected Indicators of Development, Health Expenditures, and Outcomes

Indicator	Botswana	Nigeria	Senegal	Tanzania
Human development index ranking, out of 177	124	158	156	159
Human development category	medium	low	low	low
Population (in millions)	1.8	150	12.9	38.5
Population under the age of 15 in 2005	35.6%	55.9%	44.7%	28.9%
Annual population growth (1975–2005)	2.7	2.8	2.8	2.9
Annual population growth (2005–2015)	1.2	2.2	2.3	2.4
Average life expectancy at birth (in years)	46.1	46.5	62.3	51
Under-five mortality rate per 1,000 live births	120	194	136	122
Incidence of tuberculosis per 100,000 people	556	536	466	496
Adult literacy rate	81.2%	69.1%	39.3%	69.4%
Physicians per 100,000 people	40	28	6	2
Gross national income per capita for 2007 using the Atlas method	US$5,840	US$930	US$820	US$400
Population below the income poverty line (% on US$1 a day), 1990–2005 (World Bank, 2007)	28%	71%	17%	58%
Health expenditure per capita (current US$)	US$362	US$27	US$38	US$17

Sources: Gross national income: World Bank. Gross national income per capita 2007, Atlas method and PPP. World Development Indicators Database of July 1, 2008, accessed at *http://siteresources.worldbank.org/DATASTATISTICS/Resources/GNIPC.pdf* on August 21, 2008. Health expenditure per capita (current US$): World Bank. "HNP at a Glance" database, accessed at *http://go.worldbank.org/MALQ9X8AS0* on August 21, 2008.

Note: GNI for Tanzania refers to the mainland only

rate in Botswana. As of 2007, approximately 28 percent of the population lives below the poverty line, as defined by an income of less than US$1 per day.[2]

Economic models have suggested that the HIV epidemic will have a substantially negative impact on Botswana's economic growth rate from 2003 through 2021.[4] One group of economists estimated that the rate of GDP growth has fallen from a projected 4.5 percent a year if the country had no AIDS epidemic to an estimated 2.8 percent under a scenario of AIDS with antiretroviral therapy (ART). Based on this estimate, after 20 years the economy will be 30 percent smaller than it would have been without AIDS. The impact on the growth of average real incomes—as measured by per-capita GDP—is also negative, if investment is strongly affected, averaging 1.4 percent a year under the AIDS-with-ART scenario, compared with 2.2 percent annually without AIDS. After 20 years, the income growth will be 14 percent lower than it would have been in the absence of the epidemic.[4]

This estimate contrasts, however, with the results of other studies that found—based on the assumption that the reduction in GDP growth could be smaller than the reduction in population growth—that the per-capita GDP could rise as a result of HIV/AIDS. Without AIDS, underemployment falls from 32 percent to 24 percent of the labor force. With AIDS there is no such decline, and underemployment remains at 30 percent in the AIDS-with-ART scenario and rises to 35 percent in the AIDS-without-ART scenario, as the slower growth of the labor force is offset by the effect of lower investment and slower economic growth.[4]

Botswana's population grew by more 2.5 percent from 1975 to 2005. Since 2005, however, the rate has fallen to 1.2 percent, largely because of the HIV epidemic. The population is expected to continue growing, albeit at a lower rate than in the past.

HIV/AIDS has contributed to the dramatic decrease in life expectancy from birth to 46 years, whereas previously the life expectancy for the country exceeded 60 years. In 2007, Botswana had more than 53,000 AIDS orphans.

The Botswana Health Care System

Overview of Botswana Health Infrastructure

Botswana's health care system is under dual jurisdiction; the Ministry of Health oversees national health care policies and care within the country's hospitals and hospital-associated clinics, and the Ministry of Local Government oversees the care provided at the other clinics, health posts, and mobile stops. The country has been divided geographically into 24 health districts, containing a range of health care facilities from basic mobile stops to hospitals.

Botswana's two regional referral hospitals are located in the two largest cities, Gaborone and Francistown, and provide a full complement of specialist care at the most modern medical facilities in the country. In addition to the referral hospitals, there are 13 district hospitals that provide x-ray, laboratory, general surgery and medicine, and obstetric services. An additional 16 primary hospitals offer limited health care services, and 230 clinics, 326 health posts, and 810 mobile stops provide basic services throughout the country.

Nurses and nurse practitioners provide the backbone of the country's medical care. Botswana has approximately 120 medical specialists who offer services in oncology, surgery, and other fields, but these specialists are concentrated at the regional level. Approximately 360 medical doctors (also known as medical officers) provide services at the district level. With no medical school operational in-country as yet, fewer than 10 percent of these doctors are from Botswana.

In contrast, approximately 3,556 of the 4,090 nurses who provide medical care in Botswana are Batswana. Nurses run most clinics and manage mobile facilities in remote areas. In addition, the country has 95 dentists, 42 of whom are Batswana; 1,018 family health educators, all of whom are Batswana; 252 pharmacists, 59 of whom are Batswana; and 135 environmental health officers, 107 of whom are Batswana. The Ministry of Health offers training in nursing and allied health programs in laboratory technology, dental therapy, health education, pharmacy technology, and environmental health.

An estimated 2,000 traditional doctors practice in Botswana, including herbalists, faith healers, and diviners. Communication and interaction are increasing between the Ministry of Health and traditional healers. At the regional level, traditional healers participate in health seminars and workshops. In addition, several associations have been formed to represent the traditional healers and their medicine.[5]

Health Care Personnel Status and Needs

Much of the training of nurses and family nurse practitioners takes place in Botswana's Institutes of Health Sciences, which have several locations in the country. With funding from the government of Botswana, the University of Botswana is creating a medical school, and an "innovation hub" is being planned to accommodate expanded laboratory training and new health-related programs.

Botswana benefits from having 8 to 10 times as many physicians per capita than most other African countries (Table 2). The turnover rate among Botswana's health care professionals has been dramatic, however. Nurses often leave the country for employment opportunities in South Africa, Europe, Australia, or the United States. Physicians in the public health services are not usually citizens of Botswana. They tend to be on three-year contracts; once their contracts expire, they often leave the country or enter private practice.

Table 2. Health Care Workers per Population in Various African Countries

Staff Type	Botswana (2004)		Ethiopia (2003)		Uganda (2004)		Zambia (2004)	
	Number	Density per 1,000 People	Number	Density per 1,000 People	Number	Density per 1,000 People	Number	Density per 1,000 People
Physicians	715	0.40	1,936	0.03	2,209	0.08	1,264	0.12
Nurses	4,753	2.65	14,893	0.21	16,211	0.61	19,014	1.74

Even though health care personnel may be present in relatively high proportions in Botswana, with the scaling up of ART programs the country's need for additional staffing is still acute. The Ministry of Health estimates that a 45 to 50 percent increase in the number of physicians, a 55 percent increase in the number of laboratory technicians, and at least a 12 to 14 percent increase in the number of nurses are needed immediately to meet the increased demand for health care services that AIDS has created.[6]

Pharmacists and pharmacy technicians are also in short supply. In fact, the government of Botswana recently decreed a scarce-skills refurbishment of the salary scales offered in the public health sector to raise the pay of physicians, pharmacists, and laboratory technicians by as much as 40 percent above the usual annual increases.[6]

The History of HIV/AIDS in Botswana

Dr. Banu Kahn—who, some 15 years later, would become the country's first coordinator of the National AIDS Coordinating Agency—described the first clinical case of AIDS in Botswana in 1985. Other AIDS cases were rare for the rest of the decade. It was only during the mid-1990s that government officials began to realize how significant the HIV/AIDS prevalence rate had become.[7]

Botswana instituted yearly sentinel HIV/AIDS surveillance among pregnant women in 1992. The surveillance expanded in geographic scope throughout the 1990s to include all health districts by the 2001 sentinel surveillance. Initially the sentinel surveillance effort also included men who attended sexually transmitted infection (STI) clinics. Obtaining adequate and consistent sample sizes from men with STIs proved difficult, however, and the national survey stopped including the men in 2002. To better understand the dynamics of the epidemic, that same year the country introduced the second-generation antenatal clinic sentinel surveillance program.[8]

HIV/AIDS has affected both urban and rural communities throughout Botswana with great intensity. Certain health districts, though, have somewhat higher HIV prevalence rates. These districts are along the country's eastern corridor, where the population centers and main highways and commerce routes lie (Figure 1).

From 2001 to 2007 the HIV prevalence rate decreased somewhat, but it appears to have been stable since 2005 (Figure 2).[9] There has been a slight decline in HIV prevalence among 15- to 29-year-olds, but

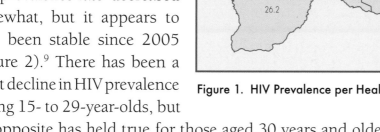

Figure 1. HIV Prevalence per Health District

the opposite has held true for those aged 30 years and older.[10] Notably, the prevention-of-mother-to-child-transmission efforts that began in 1999 have now helped the rate of new infections among children to drop dramatically (Figure 3).

The government of Botswana established the National AIDS Council in 1989 under President Masire and the National AIDS Coordinating Agency (NACA) in 2000 under President Mogae. NACA was given the role of mobilizing and coordinating a multisectoral national response to HIV/AIDS. The agency is ceremoniously chaired by the president of the country and serves as the secretariat for the National AIDS Council.

Botswana completed a National Multisectoral Second Medium-Term Plan for HIV/AIDS, which covered 1997 to 2002. This medium-term plan was followed by a new National Strategic Plan on HIV/AIDS, 2003–2009, which was developed to expand on the previous advances in prevention, treatment, and care in addition to attempting to address the overall impact of the epidemic on the country.[11]

Of note, Botswana was the only African country to have achieved its five-year goals jointly established as a result of the United Nations General Assembly Special

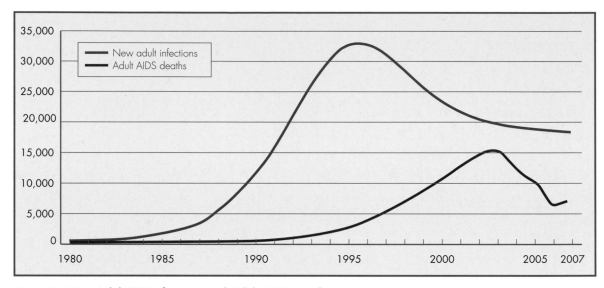

Figure 2. New Adult HIV Infections and Adult AIDS Deaths
Source: National AIDS Coordinating Agency, Botswana. *HIV/AIDS in Botswana: Estimated Trends and Implications Based on Surveillance and Modelling.* Gaborone: National AIDS Coordinating Agency, 2008.

Session on HIV/AIDS, which were pledged in 2001 and reported upon by the member states of the United Nations General Assembly in 2006.[12]

The History of HIV/AIDS Treatment and Care in Botswana

During the 1990s, Botswana's private health care sector began treating people with AIDS, primarily those who could afford the ART services and expensive medications or whose health insurance plans provided appropriate coverage. Those individuals numbered only in the hundreds through 2000 and 2001.

Early in 2001, the Botswana–Harvard Partnership for HIV Education and Research, or BHP, which had been established five years earlier, began a pilot HIV/AIDS treatment and care program in conjunction with the main referral hospital, Princess Marina Hospital in Gaborone. Throughout the latter half of 2001, more than 350 patients began ART after completing the required testing, counseling, and adherence planning.[13] These initial patients in the public health care sector did well, and by the end of 2001, the Ministry of Health and the office of President Mogae were completing preparations to launch a national rollout of ART in public clinics across the country.

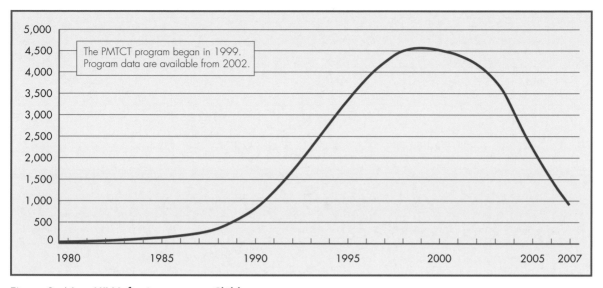

Figure 3. New HIV Infections among Children

Abbreviation: PMTCT: prevention of mother-to-child transmission

A New Dawn: The Masa Program

As part of the preparation for a national ART program, the African Comprehensive HIV/AIDS Partnerships (ACHAP), a country-led public–private partnership of the government of Botswana, the Bill & Melinda Gates Foundation, and Merck and Co., Inc—conducted a feasibility study for a national ART program. Based on the findings of that study, President Mogae announced at the end of 2001 that the government of Botswana would provide ART without cost to all qualifying patients.

The national ART program launched in January 2002, starting at the Harvard clinic and among the group of pilot patients at Princess Marina Hospital and expanding in the first year to include three other large clinic sites in Francistown, Maun, and Serowe. The program was named *Masa*, the Setswana word for "new dawn."

Through its distinct partnership with the government of Botswana, ACHAP was instrumental in the creation of the Masa Program and continues to contribute to its expansion, through secondment of key staff to the government, long-term training and preceptorship programs, and site-by-site infrastructure development. The Masa Program expanded fairly quickly after its launch.

From the outset, ACHAP worked with the government of Botswana and with local partners to expand a comprehensive approach to the epidemic. In those early stages,

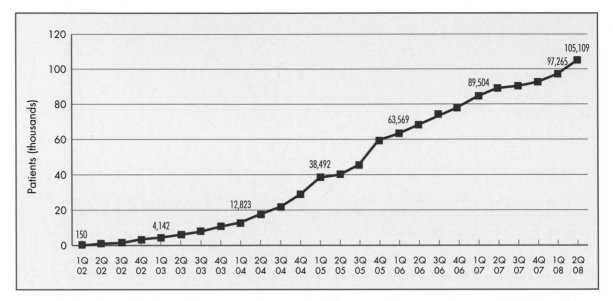

Figure 4. Cumulative Number of Patients on Antiretroviral Therapy in Botswana, January 2002 through June 2008

ACHAP and the government of Botswana initiated patient and family support group organizations, HIV testing services, and various national and local prevention programs. The U.S. government and other collaborators with the government of Botswana also began to expand their efforts.

The Masa Program was developed with attention to nine major areas that would need to be strengthened, expanded, or reorganized to support the provision of ART to all qualifying patients. Those areas were:

- Policy, planning, and project management;
- Information, education, communication, and community mobilization;
- Training of health care professionals;
- Staff recruitment and retention;
- Drug logistics;
- Laboratory and testing logistics;
- Information technology for national tracking and monitoring of patients, laboratory samples, and medication utilization;
- Procurement and upgrading of space; and
- Monitoring, evaluation, and operational research.

During its first year of operation, to allow adequate time to hire key staff, provide training, and build infrastructure, the Masa Program was limited to four ART sites: Gaborone, Maun, Francistown, and Serowe. The following year, seven additional treatment sites were launched, as capacity development increased the resources available to the program.

The Masa Program now operates at 32 principal sites throughout Botswana and has expanded to satellite clinics that use the hospital-based ART sites for referral, training, and pharmacy support. Efforts continue to decentralize ART to more rural locations, with the goal of ensuring that all health clinics in the country are capable of administering ART. To date, 160 clinics have this capacity. Another national goal is to have all of the small health posts—which are usually facilities with only one or two nurses or nurse aides—be upgraded to become fully functional health clinics (Figure 4).

By the end of July 2008, a total of 107,682 patients were receiving ART in Botswana. This figure includes 87,173 patients who had

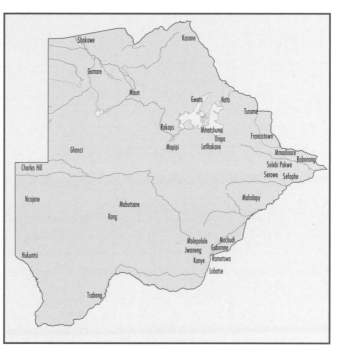

Figure 5. Antiretroviral Therapy Centers in Botswana

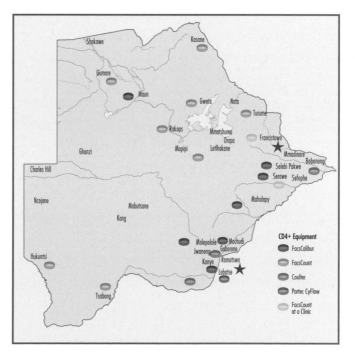

Figure 6. Laboratories with CD4+ Count Capabilities

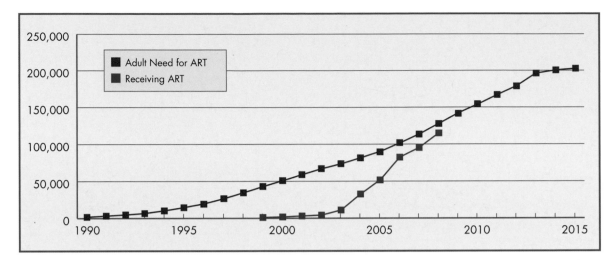

Figure 7. Estimate of Those Needing Antiretroviral Therapy (ART) in the Future in Botswana Compared with Those Already on ART

been initiated on treatment in the public sector (of whom 61 percent were female and 7.7 percent were children); 10,284 patients who had been outsourced from the public sector to the private sector under the government's Public–Private Partnership outsourcing program; and 10,225 patients who were being treated in the private sector. These patients are monitored on a monthly basis by the Monitoring and Evaluation Unit within the Masa Program. This unit uses an electronic application that it developed and evaluates reports from its data warehouse.

Since the inception of the Masa Program, 11,150 patients—including private-sector patients—have died while on ART. Yet many of the patients enrolled since the beginning of the Masa Program have been on ART for at least five years.[14] As has been shown in other settings, the likelihood of a patient's dying while on ART has been found to be much higher within the first few months of his or her enrollment in the Masa Program. After those initial months, the likelihood of morbidity and mortality drops, however, and many long-term benefits begin to accrue. These results have been encouraging not just for enrolled patients and their loved ones and communities, but also for the long-term national impact of the Masa Program (Figures 5 and 6).

To improve laboratory and testing logistics, the Masa Program has begun to decentralize the laboratory infrastructure. When the program began, only the two major government laboratories in Gaborone and Francistown were able to perform

Table 3. Number of People in Need of ART, 2008–2016									
Year	2008	2009	2010	2011	2012	2013	2014	2015	2016
Number of adults in need of ART	137,000	153,000	167,000	178,000	186,000	193,000	198,000	203,000	207,000
Number of children in need of ART	8,000	8,700	9,200	10,000	10,800	11,600	12,300	12,900	13,500

Abbreviation: ART: antiretroviral therapy
Source: National AIDS Coordinating Agency, Botswana. *HIV/AIDS in Botswana: Estimated Trends and Implications Based on Surveillance and Modelling.* Gaborone: National AIDS Coordinating Agency, 2008.

all the tests required for HIV/AIDS monitoring and treatment. Since then, the government of Botswana—with help from both ACHAP and the U.S. President's Emergency Plan for AIDS Relief, or PEPFAR, program—has expanded and decentralized the laboratory infrastructure to secondary sites in order to increase the overall monitoring capacity.

Current Masa Program eligibility guidelines include HIV-infected people with one or more of the following: CD4+ cell counts of 250 or below; the presence of an AIDS-defining illness; or age 13 years or younger. In addition, several groups have been identified for high-priority access to treatment, including pregnant women and their partners who meet the eligibility guidelines; HIV-infected children six months or older who receive inpatient care; patients who are co-infected with tuberculosis and have a CD4+ count of 250 or below; and adult inpatients with a CD4+ count of 250 or below or who have an AIDS-defining illness.

The Masa Program also includes a national HIV/AIDS education component. Before 2001, the culture of silence that surrounded the epidemic contributed to a general lack of knowledge about the virus, its transmission, and prevention. As part of the public education campaign, Masa began to produce and distribute booklets, posters, flip charts, videos, and newsletters, available in both English and Setswana.

To meet demand as quickly as possible, program managers implemented Masa using a phased approach. This approach allowed for capacity development as the program extended out from the highest priority patients to the rest of the population. As of mid-2008, more than 100,000 people receive ART through the Masa Program, or approximately 80 percent of those eligible for treatment at the 32 operational sites and various satellite clinics throughout Botswana (Figure 7).

Table 4. KITSO AIDS Training Program: BHP Training Numbers for Health Care Workers (2001–2008)									
Training Course	2001	2002	2003	2004	2005	2006	2007	2008 (as of September)	Total
AIDS Clinical Care Fundamentals (4½ days)	93	267	692	1,059	1,986	860	561	606	6,124
AIDS Clinical Care Fundamentals Refresher/Update (2½ days)								694	694
Medication Adherence Counseling (3 days)			7	23	100	136	236	154	656
Advanced HIV/AIDS Care and Treatment (5½ days)					90	151	141	49	431
Introduction to AIDS Clinical Care						378	672	237	1,287
Laboratory Fundamentals			103	434	16				553
Introduction to HIV and Biosafety			98	548	41				687

Abbreviation: BHP: Botswana–Harvard Partnership for HIV Research and Education

ART adherence rates have been reported to be as high as 85 percent, with approximately 86 percent of patients attaining undetectable viral loads—measured at levels below 400 copies/mL based on the viral load detection limit of currently used assays—within six months of ART initiation. Program staff also report successful and consistent follow-up with nearly 90 percent of patients. At one time the Ministry of Health had projected that 130,000 qualifying patients would be receiving ART through the national program by 2009.[15,16] Those numbers are expected to climb, with a projected 207,000 adults and 13,500 children needing ART in 2016 (Table 3). Key to the Masa Program's continued success will be training programs for current and new health care workers in Botswana.

The KITSO AIDS Training Program

In 2000, the Botswana Ministry of Health and what is now the Harvard School of Public Health AIDS Initiative, or HAI, conducted a countrywide needs assessment to determine existing training resources and infrastructure, ascertain available technology, and identify gaps in HIV/AIDS training. The needs assessment and subsequent reference group recommendations culminated in a five-year plan for developing and implementing an HIV/AIDS treatment and care training program tailored to the needs of the Botswana health care sector. This effort resulted in the KITSO AIDS

Table 5. KITSO AIDS Training Program: BHP Projections of Health Care Workers Needing Training (2009–2013)

Training Course	2009	2010	2011	2012	2013	Total
AIDS Clinical Care Fundamentals (4½ days)	700	650	650	650	650	3,300
AIDS Clinical Care Fundamentals Refresher/Update (2½ days)	700	650	650	650	650	3,300
Medication Adherence Counseling (3 days)	200	200	200	200	200	1,000
Advanced HIV/AIDS Care and Treatment (5½ days)	100	100	100	100	100	500
Introduction to AIDS Clinical Care	250	250	250	250	250	1,250
HIV and Sexual/Reproductive Health	50	150	200	200	200	800

Abbreviation: BHP: Botswana–Harvard Partnership for HIV Research and Education

Training Program. KITSO, which serves as an acronym for Knowledge, Innovation, and Training Shall Overcome AIDS, is also the Setswana word for "knowledge."

In 2001, a collaboration among the Ministry of Health, the Botswana–Harvard Partnership, HAI, and ACHAP resulted in an expansion of the KITSO AIDS Training Program that allowed it to serve as the national AIDS training program. Since its first course in July 2001, KITSO has trained more than 7,500 health care professionals through its standardized, comprehensive HIV/AIDS courses and training modules.

The module-based training curriculum development and course implementation have been driven by the immediate need to train Botswana's health care professionals in HIV/AIDS care using formats that provide ample grounding in clinical practice without requiring long periods of staff release for training. Current modules include: AIDS Clinical Care Fundamentals, Medication Adherence Counseling, Advanced HIV/AIDS Care and Treatment, Introduction to AIDS Clinical Care, and HIV and Sexual/Reproductive Health. An audio-enhanced CD-ROM of the entry module, AIDS Clinical Care Fundamentals, was produced in 2006 and distributed throughout the health care sector for refresher teaching and long-distance education.[17]

Table 4 lists courses that BHP has developed and implemented in coordination with the Ministry of Health since 2001. The table also breaks down the number of health care workers completing the courses during the first eight years of the program. Table 5 shows projected numbers of health care workers who will need to take each training course, based on attrition rates of health care workers from the Botswana workforce and the expanded need for their expertise. Other partnerships with the government of Botswana have contributed greatly to the training efforts both within and beyond the KITSO AIDS Training Program, such as the efforts with the Baylor College of Medicine and the University of Pennsylvania.

The Master Trainer Program and Monitoring and Evaluation Efforts

The U.S. government launched PEPFAR in Botswana in 2004. This program has brought numerous avenues of partnership and infrastructure support to the country from the start. Two such efforts have been the creation of the Master Trainer Program and the expansion of the Monitoring and Evaluation Unit within the Ministry of Health.

With the advent of PEPFAR, the Ministry of Health and BotUSA—the U.S. Centers for Disease Control and Prevention program in Botswana—helped evaluate the needs of the Masa Program in 2004. This evaluation revealed that Masa needed a clinical site support program that offered mentoring by local experts; the identification of site-specific needs, such as support, linkages to other health programs, and community outreach; the creation of a Laboratory Master Trainer Program to accommodate the expansion and decentralization of the HIV/AIDS-related laboratory system; and a solid monitoring and evaluation system. The Ministry of Health and BotUSA requested that the BHP–PEPFAR program respond to these needs.

The Botswana master trainer and site-support program was developed in 2004 and 2005 to provide site-specific mentoring and support throughout the country's expanding number of ART sites. The program now includes master trainer physicians, nurses, nurse-midwives, and pharmacists. These master trainers help conduct site-readiness assessments, help open new clinical sites and satellite sites, and monitor progress in quality of care through chart reviews, patient satisfaction through exit interviews, and overall clinical training activities. The master trainers provide telephone support to all sites 24 hours a day and maintain a regular schedule of site visits that last from several days to two weeks.

The Master Trainer Program complements the work of the KITSO AIDS Training Program. The BHP–PEPFAR Clinical Master Trainer physicians, nurses, and pharmacists support most of the Masa Program sites. All master trainers are from Botswana or are permanent residents of Botswana, a critical factor given how highly transient Botswana's health care workforce has been.

The BHP–PEPFAR ART Training and Site Support initiative is a multipronged project aimed at developing a sustainable training capacity in the treatment and care of HIV/AIDS patients, expanding CD4+ and viral load laboratory testing to decentralized laboratories, and strengthening the Botswana Ministry of Health's capacity to monitor and evaluate the efficacy of the Masa Program. The initiative encompasses the Clinical Master Trainer Program, the Laboratory Master Trainer Program, and the Monitoring and Evaluation Unit.

The Clinical Master Trainer Program provides ongoing training, mentoring, and on-site and telephone support to ART sites designated by the Ministry of Health. These activities ensure that health care professionals are up-to-date in all aspects of HIV/AIDS treatment and care, that they have continual opportunities to strengthen and reinforce their clinical skills, and that they receive sufficient technical support. BHP–PEPFAR has established a Clinical Master Trainer Corps, consisting of six physicians, two pharmacists, and four nurse-midwives who are all highly experienced in HIV/AIDS treatment and care of both adults and children. These core master trainers educate the site-level master trainers using an integrated approach to ART based on the WHO Guidelines for Integrated Management of Adolescent and Adult Illness. The core master trainers also provide the site-level master trainers with ongoing site and telephone support.

The Laboratory Master Trainer Program was developed to enable the decentralization of CD4+ and viral load testing to newly developed laboratories outside the two National HIV Reference Laboratories in Gaborone and Francistown. As a result of the efforts of the Laboratory Master Trainer Program, 17 sites perform CD4+ counts and seven perform viral load testing. More than half of the CD4+ tests performed countrywide are now run at decentralized laboratories, which both lifts a great burden from the two reference laboratories and significantly decreases the turnaround time of results. Under BHP–PEPFAR's national laboratory director, eight laboratory master trainers provide training in conducting these tests, using the same site-support approach that the Clinical Master Trainer Program takes.

The establishment of the expanded Monitoring and Evaluation Unit within the Department of HIV/AIDS Prevention and Care at the Ministry of Health began with the recruitment of monitoring and evaluation specialists in 2005. The unit developed standardized indicators, reporting instruments, and a uniform reporting schedule. These efforts are supported by electronic medical records and upgraded reporting tools. Data quality is emphasized and data audits are conducted on a regular basis at ART sites. The Monitoring and Evaluation Unit has been involved in many operational research activities as well and provides data management support for these projects. Unit leaders have asked to be able to expand its mandate to provide services to the entire Department of HIV/AIDS Prevention and Care and to incorporate more quality-improvement efforts into the Masa Program.

A National Policy of Routine HIV Testing

During the first years of the nation's response to AIDS—and even of the Masa Program—HIV testing occurred at a much slower rate than was desirable, given the wisdom of having those infected with HIV know their status, both to help prevent the spread of the virus and to be able to extend treatment and care to those who need it most. In response, BotUSA developed free-standing voluntary counseling and testing centers, which became known as Tebelopele centers; in Setswana, *tebelopele* means "look to the future."

In January 2004, the government of Botswana initiated another bold national HIV/AIDS policy—a national opt-out testing policy, which strove to make HIV testing part of all medical appointments unless the patient specifically requested that the test not be performed. Coupled with treatment options, the opt-out policy not only greatly increased the number of tests performed in Botswana, but it is also credited with helping reduce the stigma of HIV testing and altering the culture of silence surrounding HIV/AIDS.[18–20]

Extending the Masa Program to Satellite Clinics

By January 2005, within three years of becoming operational, the Masa Program had enrolled more than 32,000 patients across the country in the 32 hospital-based treatment and care clinic sites, which are also known as infectious diseases care clinics. An estimated 100,000 people still urgently needed ART. For the program to succeed and be fully functional within Botswana's health care system, its human and physical infrastructure capacity needed to be increased beyond the existing 32 sites. Another dramatic health care policy change was proposed to help achieve this expansion.

The Ministry of Health and the Ministry of Local Government jointly proposed this policy change at the end of 2005, with guidance from NACA and ACHAP. The goals of the proposal were not made operational, however, until the Masa Program and the PEPFAR-supported Master Trainer Program could begin to organize in 2007 and 2008 a task-shifting training program for nurses to learn to prescribe and dispense antiretrovirals in clinical settings outside the original hospital-based Masa Program sites.

Since its pilot beginnings in 2007, this new program has trained more than 213 nurses in dispensing antiretrovirals and more than 105 nurses in prescribing the drugs for stable patients already on ART. Appropriately trained nurses dispense antiretrovirals to all patients, whether clinically stable or unstable, and account for all medicines dispensed. Their duties resemble those of pharmacists and pharmacy technicians, both of which are in extremely short supply in Botswana.

Nurses trained to prescribe antiretrovirals assess each patient's clinical status, review the treatment history, and then prescribe antiretrovirals to stable patients already on therapy. These nurses also train other nurses to triage patients to facilitate referral of patients to appropriate services, such as the tuberculosis service, prevention counseling, and family planning.

Conclusion

The government of Botswana estimates that 90 percent of the country's AIDS costs are borne by the government and the people of Botswana. The Masa Program accounted for more than half the national government's spending on HIV/AIDS between 2003 and 2006.[21] These efforts have kept more than 100,000 Batswana alive. This number represents almost one-third of all those estimated to be living with HIV in the country.

Despite these successes, Botswana still has a long way to go to curb the HIV epidemic and mitigate its impact. Improved linkages and coordination with other related public health programs—such as the tuberculosis program, reproductive health efforts, and pre-service training—are all needed. Government officials are also aware that much more intensive national efforts are needed in HIV prevention. To that end, the government of Botswana has created a National Operational Plan for Scaling Up HIV Prevention, which includes the scaling up of adult and infant male circumcision, along with other intensified national prevention efforts.[22]

In July 2008 delegates convened to discuss the initiative, which has been dubbed *Thebe le Segai*, or Shield and Spear. With a budget of more than US$102 million, the prevention program is expected to invest heavily in information, education, and communication efforts, with the goal of preventing all new cases of HIV infection by 2016.

The Masa Program and other successful efforts such as the national PMTCT program have provided many thousands of individuals and families in Botswana with a new dawn—and new hope. In addition, these successful national programs have inspired confidence that the further efforts needed in HIV prevention and in linkages with other health services can also achieve nationwide success.

REFERENCES

1. U.S. Central Intelligence Agency. *The World Factbook: Botswana.* https://www.cia.gov/library/publications/the-world-factbook/geos/bc.html; accessed September 29, 2008.

2. United Nations Development Programme. *Human Development Report 2007/2008.* New York: United Nations Development Programme, 2008.

3. World Bank. *Gross National Income 2007, Atlas Methods and PPP.* World Development Indicators Database of July 1, 2008. Washington, DC: World Bank, 2008. http://siteresources.worldbank.org/DATASTATISTICS/Resources/GNIPC.pdf; accessed October 28, 2008.

4. Jefferis K, Kinghorn A, Siphambe H, Thurlow J. Macroeconomic and household-level impacts of HIV/AIDS in Botswana. *AIDS*, 2008;22(Suppl 1): S113–S119.

5. Ministry of Health, Botswana. *KITSO AIDS Care Training Program Long-term Evaluation Report, 2007.* Gaborone: Ministry of Health, 2007.

6. Ministry of Health, Botswana. *Scarce Skills and Salary Structure.* Gaborone: Ministry of Health, 2008.

7. UNAIDS. Report on the Global AIDS Epidemic. Geneva: UNAIDS, 2008.

8. Ministry of Health, Botswana. *2002 Second Generation HIV/AIDS Surveillance, Technical Report.* Gaborone: Ministry of Health, 2002.

9. Stover J, Fidzani B, Molomo BC, Moeti T, Musuka G. Estimated HIV trends and program effects in Botswana. *PLoS One*, 2008;3(11):e3729.

10. Ministry of Health, Botswana. *2007 Second Generation HIV/AIDS Surveillance, Technical Report.* Gaborone: Department of HIV/AIDS Prevention and Care, 2007.

11. National AIDS Coordinating Agency, Botswana. *National Strategic Plan on HIV/AIDS (2003–2009).* Gaborone: National AIDS Coordinating Agency, 2004.

12. Republic of Botswana. *2008 Progress Report of the National Response to the UNGASS Declaration of Commitment on HIV/AIDS.* http://data.unaids.org/pub/Report/2008/botswana_2008_country_progress_report_en.pdf; accessed November 11, 2008.

13. Wester CW, Kim S, Bussmann H, et al. Initial response to highly active antiretroviral treatment in HIV-1C infected adults in a pilot programme in Botswana. *J AIDS*, 2005;40:336–343.

14. Bussmann H, Wester CW, Ndwapi N, et al. Five-year outcomes of initial patients treated in Botswana's national antiretroviral treatment program. *AIDS*, 2008;22(17):2303–2311.

15. African Comprehensive HIV/AIDS Partnerships in Botswana. Programmes. http://www.achap.org/programmes/masa.html; accessed November 11, 2008.

16. Ministry of Health, Botswana. http://www.moh.gov.bw/index.php?id=192; accessed November 11, 2008.

17. Bussmann C, Rotz P, Ndwapi N, et al. Strengthening healthcare capacity through a responsive, country-specific, training standard: the KITSO AIDS Training Program's support of Botswana's national antiretroviral therapy rollout. *Open AIDS J*, 2008;2:8–20.

18. Weiser SD, Heisler M, Leiter K, et al. Routine HIV testing in Botswana: a population-based study on attitudes, practices and human rights concerns. *PLos Med*, 2006;3(7):e261.

19. Steen TW, Seipone K, de la Hoz Gomez F, et al. Two and a half years of routine HIV testing in Botswana. *J Acquir Immune Defic Syndr*, 2007;44(4):484–488.

20. Creek TL, Ntumy R, Seipone K, et al. Successful introduction of routine opt-out HIV testing in antenatal care in Botswana. *J Acquir Immune Defic Syndr*, 2007;45(1):102–107.

21. National AIDS Coordinating Agency, Botswana. *2006 Report.* Gaborone: National AIDS Coordinating Agency, 2006.

22. National AIDS Coordinating Agency, Botswana. *National Operational Plan for HIV Prevention in Botswana: 2008–2010.* Gaborone: National AIDS Coordinating Agency, 2007.

Ndwapi Ndwapi oversees the national AIDS treatment program in Botswana.

Dream Team

John Donnelly

T HEY FIRST MET at age four. Their families lived on Hospital Way in Gaborone, just a few doors down from each other, right across from Princess Marina Hospital. Their fathers, members of the political elite, were good friends. And their playground was the hospital grounds. They explored every corner of it, even daring each other to peek into the window of the hospital morgue in hopes of seeing something scary, like a body.

More than three decades later, Dr. Ndwapi Ndwapi and Dr. Tendani Gaolathe are still friends, and they are still following each other around. Now, instead of circling the exterior of the country's largest hospital, they have become critical players inside Botswana's health care system, helping lead the nation's fight against AIDS.

They assumed their roles at an early stage in the country's response to the deadly virus—just as Botswana prepared to make antiretroviral drugs available for free to all who needed them. It was around 2002, and the doctors stood at ground zero of the AIDS epidemic in sub-Saharan Africa, shouldering an immense amount of pain and suffering from all the death around them. Back then, before the drugs became widely available, they could do little to save the lives of those infected, and the two doctors found themselves far too often sending bodies to the same morgue of their youth.

During those years, Botswana registered the highest HIV prevalence rate of any country in the world, soaring by 2004 to well over 30 percent among those aged 15 to 49. But from the year 2000 onward, the country, led by then-President Festus Mogae, mounted one of the world's most vigorous responses to the epidemic, scaling up treatment, care, testing, and prevention programs. Botswana's response was characterized by strong political determination, a willingness to seek partners to stem the toll and speed the healing, and a belief that the country's systems—especially its health care system—would stand up to the worst epidemic they had ever known.

By mid-2008, Ndwapi was overseeing the country's AIDS therapy programs as head of Masa, the National Antiretroviral Treatment Program, while Gaolathe was both an AIDS doctor and director of the Botswana–Harvard Partnership's efforts to train the country's health workers to provide better care for AIDS patients.

They work separately now, in different buildings, fulfilling complementary tasks. But at the beginning of Botswana's response to AIDS, they labored side by side as doctors, as close together as when they were kids—only this time, their running around was done with supreme purpose.

Tandem Acts of Kindness

In 2001, Gaolathe called Ndwapi in the United States. She had just begun to work on the country's fledgling AIDS treatment program. Gaolathe told him his country needed him, patients needed him, and he should come home. By that time, Ndwapi had been in the United States for 11 years, as an undergraduate at George Washington University, a medical student at the Medical College of Pennsylvania in Philadelphia, and a specialist in internal medicine at the Robert Wood Johnson University Hospital in New Jersey. Gaolathe, too, had spent years living abroad—also as an undergraduate

Tendani Gaolathe found herself on the frontlines of the worst health crisis in Botswana's history.

at George Washington; a medical student at St. Georges University School of Medicine in Grenada, West Indies; and a medical resident at St. Michael's Medical Center in Newark, New Jersey.

Ndwapi couldn't resist his friend's pleas for help. In October 2001, he returned home to see what he could do.

Within his first hour, he felt shell-shocked, just as he had a month earlier during the terrorist attacks on the United States.

"It was like 9/11 all over again for me," he said. "I had been away 11 years, 9/11 had just happened in the States, and then it was 9/11 here a second time. The hospital corridors were crowded. The morgue was so full they sent bodies to private mortuaries. The hospital was operating at 200 percent capacity."

Gaolathe remembered her friend's reaction well; he seemed caught in a sense of disbelief.

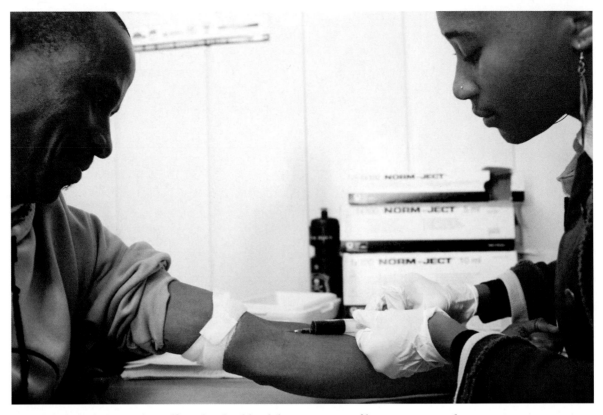

Emmanuel Tawana, a police officer, has his blood drawn as part of his treatment and care regimen.

"He used to ask me, after long days, 'Is this the way it is going to be?' I told him, 'This is the life, my friend. Better get used to it.'"

In particular, she recalled one early morning when they entered a large waiting room completely filled with patients.

"Who is going to see all these patients?" Ndwapi asked her.

Gaolathe looked at him sideways.

"Me and you," she said.

They were working out of a Princess Marina Hospital wing that was dedicated to seeing outpatients; they called it the home-based care program. In early 2002, in practice, it served as an AIDS triage unit.

Ndwapi, six years later, still couldn't get the sight out of his mind. "The parking lot outside the clinic was full of people on stretchers," he said. "There was no room for them inside. So we moved them in as we could see them. Half of the people—those who could walk—sat on benches inside. The other half would lie on stretchers outside."

By that point, he remembered, the country's politicians, led by President Mogae, and its doctors and nurses made several critical decisions. One was that since they would be offering HIV testing to everyone, they would also have to provide free treatment for those who tested positive and had CD4+ counts below 200. Another was that even those nearing death would receive treatment. There would be no giving up on anyone.

"We couldn't say you were too sick," Ndwapi said. "As long as you could swallow the pills, we were treating you."

Creative Sparks

From the start, the Botswana government had outside help. Part came from Harvard University, which had already joined forces with the government in 1996 to form what is now known as the Botswana–Harvard Partnership for HIV Research and Education. In 2000, another critical joint effort began—the African Comprehensive HIV/AIDS Partnerships, or ACHAP, a country-led, public–private initiative among the Botswana government, the Bill & Melinda Gates Foundation, and Merck Company Foundation/Merck & Co., Inc.

The efforts also benefited from Botswana's still-intact health care system, which had been built on a primary health care model since the country's independence in 1966. "When we had to start dealing with antiretroviral drugs, we were fortunate that we had such a robust system in place," Ndwapi said. "AIDS was a big blow to our system, but we were able to stay standing."

Barely—the system wobbled at times, and the professionals suffered from burnout. In those early treatment days, doctors, nurses, counselors, lab technicians, and support staff faced long lines of people waiting for help. It was first come, first served, day after day; sometimes the clinics were crammed with patients by five in the morning.

The hospital personnel began to get creative—and to challenge outsiders' notions of what they should be doing. Ndwapi remembers late-night sessions with others, including Gaolathe and Dr. Ernest Darkoh, the operations manager of Botswana's

AIDS treatment program, trying to figure out ways to move patients through the system without sacrificing quality of service.

"We needed to create a conveyor belt of people going through antiretroviral therapy," Ndwapi said. "We had to create a physical structure that was exclusively designed for antiretroviral therapy. That was a radical concept at the time. Everyone was trying to fight stigma. Here we were building a special entrance to the hospital for AIDS patients. We decided this was appropriate; if we wanted an efficient factory, we needed to build a tight infrastructure. The argument I made to my colleagues was, 'Let's do what makes medical sense, and forget about stigma, because stigma is driven by considerations that do not make medical sense.'

"We needed to respond to this epidemic the way people responded to epidemics in the past," Ndwapi added. "They built everything under one roof."

In time, the program developed an elite corps of nurses and doctors. They amassed huge workloads, with doctors sometimes seeing up to 50 patients a day.

But they also had a few things going for them. One was the patients; another was the drugs. The vast majority of patients adhered to the drug regimens, and the drugs worked for most. "It meant that our subsequent visits with patients became less and less labor intensive," Ndwapi said. "What happened in those early times was either the patients died, or they improved really quickly."

Innovation continued. Program managers created two lines of patients—Darkoh, who excelled at systems management, called it "splitting the queue"—one for the healthier return patients, and one for new patients. The logjam of patients started to clear after Botswana decentralized its AIDS treatment services, offering antiretrovirals in more than two dozen centers around the country. After President Mogae announced in January 2004 that every patient entering a hospital would have an HIV test, unless they opted out, many more people started seeking treatment because they knew their status. But by then decentralization had allowed the system to absorb better the growing numbers of people on treatment.

From 2006 onward, doctors and nurses also began to see the patients who were well far less often: every three or six months, instead of monthly. Those patients' lab tests also were at greater intervals, as long as they remained well.

Sitting in his ministry office in mid-2008, Ndwapi could smile at the thought—AIDS patients who were well. It was a dream he couldn't have envisioned in late

A pharmacy expert trains her fellow pharmacists in the intricacies of antiretroviral treatment.

2001, but across town, at Princess Marina Hospital, the AIDS clinic was no longer crowded with desperately ill people. People were living with the virus.

Alive and Well

By 7:30 one mid-winter morning in 2008, a dozen AIDS patients waited for nurses to open the Infectious Disease Care Clinic, which serves as Princess Marina Hospital's AIDS treatment center. Within a half hour, when nurses started seeing patients, roughly 30 people had taken seats in the main waiting room.

One patient was Emmanuel Tawana, 42, a police officer. Tawana, at five-foot-six, weighed in at 59.5 kilograms, or 130 pounds, up a pound from two months before. He was waiting for Gaolathe, and he looked great. In fact, everyone in the waiting room—save one gaunt man who shuffled his feet—seemed in good condition.

Nearby in the waiting room sat Patient No. 19, the thinnest woman in the room. But unlike past years, when the thinnest people in the AIDS clinic were so fragile they needed assistance to walk, the five-foot-one Marea Maroku bounded up to the nurses' scale, weighing in at 41 kilograms, or 90 pounds. That was up from 38 kilograms, or 83 pounds, three months earlier. The 35-year-old mother of three looked healthy. She was smiling and looking forward, she said, to seeing her doctor, Gaolathe.

When Maroku tested positive for HIV, in late 2002, her CD4+ count had registered at 63. Her sister knew Gaolathe, and the doctor made a point of finding Maroku just before the new year. Maroku still remembered the doctor's words.

"She was counseling me," Maroku said, sitting outside Gaolathe's office. "I was very sick and worried. She told me I needed to take the pills every day, and if I did, I would get better."

Gaolathe's door opened and she saw Maroku. The two smiled and hugged. "Are you well?" Gaolathe asked.

"I am, I really am," Maroku answered.

"You are looking very well," the doctor said. "I'm happy to see it."

Maroku, who lived in Serowe, a four-hour bus ride from Gaborone, was a model patient. She said she hadn't missed taking her antiretrovirals even once in more than five years; her children often remind her when it's time to take her medicine. But the drugs haven't always been that effective. On first-line therapy, Maroku didn't improve significantly; tests done at the Botswana–Harvard laboratory found that her virus was resistant to that drug combination therapy. A second combination didn't work as well as the doctor and patient had hoped either; further tests showed resistance. But a third combination of lopinavir/ritonavir, didanosine, and abacavir was working much better. Maroku's most recent CD4+ count was 203.

Gaolathe recommended that Maroku transfer to an AIDS clinic in Serowe, saving her the expense and wear and tear of the bus ride. Maroku agreed with her doctor. "You won't have to go in for another three months," Gaolathe told her. "You should always feel free to come back here as well."

The two hugged goodbye. Walking toward the pharmacy, Maroku said she felt sad about leaving her doctor and starting at a new place, with a new physician. "I am going to miss this place," she said, looking around. "But it's a long drive. It's time for a change."

Gaolathe later saw Tawana, the police officer who was doing so well he didn't need to return to see a doctor for six months. By noon, she had finished with her dozen morning patients, and she started walking back to her office.

"We're transferring many patients to private doctors, who are distributing our drugs for free, or to clinics closer to their homes," she said. "Most of these patients are really doing well. I saw only one today who wasn't. Now it's just a matter of managing the flow of patients, reinforcing the messages, making sure they get their drugs, and checking that they take their drugs every day."

Her experience now as an AIDS doctor significantly differed from those early days. New thorny problems had arisen in recent months and years—drug resistance was emerging as a major worry, for instance—but overall the work had become so much easier for everyone.

"The visits with patients are no longer as intense," she said. "The clinic, at least by our old standards, is not busy anymore. All this decentralization has really helped. AIDS is just like any other chronic disease."

Gaolathe still had a full day ahead of her—meetings with out-of-town nurses who were being trained on AIDS care, a long list of emails to read, and a work dinner that night. Still, she didn't seem in a hurry as she walked past hospital buildings and courtyards. She seemed happy, and why not? The winter sun was warm, and her AIDS patients were well. ∎

Harriet Okatch lost her parents to AIDS—and found strength in her own efforts to defeat the virus.

Home Truths

JOHN DONNELLY

HER WORK, like that of her colleagues at the Botswana–Harvard Partnership laboratory in Gaborone, was being done with painstaking care. Harriet Okatch was hunting for drug-resistance mutations in the DNA samples of people infected with HIV-1 subtype C, the most common type in southern Africa.

She needed to replicate the DNA in order to do a sequence analysis, which would help her clearly determine the effects of medication on the virus. And so she concocted a stew of enzymes and other materials drawn from color-coded tubes with a pipette that took in quantities measured by the microliter. She looked like a doctor in her white lab coat, doing her work with the same precision that a surgeon would use in making an incision.

If only her mother and father could see her now.

Both died of AIDS-related illnesses—her father, Bethuel, in 1990, and her mother, Susan, in 2000. Since then, the story of their daughter has become one of determination, focus, ambition, and overcoming obstacles—including the extraordinary challenge of coping with both of their deaths. There's a broader story here, too—of how the impact of AIDS in Africa has touched several generations already, causing unforeseen impacts that often motivate people to help others.

For Okatch, it is not purely circumstance that she has become a laboratory scientist working to resolve mysteries surrounding AIDS. "I believe," she said, "it's a tribute in some small way to my parents and to all the people who are enduring what my family experienced."

Okatch was born in the Tororo region of Uganda. Her father was a university lecturer, her mother a dressmaker and secretary. During the political upheavals in the mid-1980s, Okatch's father fled to Kenya after receiving death threats. His children soon followed—in Okatch's words, "jumping the border" illegally into Kenya. But Harriet's mother wasn't with them. She had been detained in Uganda. Authorities pressed her for information about her husband, and when she refused to tell them anything, they sent her to prison. There, Okatch would later learn, she suffered an array of abuse.

While in Kenya, Bethuel Okatch received a job offer to teach at the University of Botswana as a physics lecturer. He reluctantly moved with his children to Gaborone. Harriet was just 11, the second oldest of six children under her father's care. Several months later, under circumstances never explained to the children, her mother was released from the Uganda prison, fled to Kenya, and joined them in Botswana.

It was 1988, and the family began to rebuild their life in Botswana as best they could. Just two years later, though, Bethuel Okatch suddenly turned ill. In three days, he was dead. No one said why. The immediate issue was fulfilling his wish to be buried in Uganda. Susan Okatch, despite the danger involved, took her husband's body back.

During this time, Harriet Okatch found letters written by a Canadian couple to her parents. In one, the Canadians wrote that they were saddened to hear that Bethuel had HIV. The revelation shocked the teenaged girl. She wondered whether her mother also was infected. She couldn't ask directly—it wouldn't have been acceptable in her family or her culture at the time.

Harriet Okatch uses the inspiration of her own mother in parenting her children.

The answer came definitively eight years later, when her mother started falling seriously ill, first with tuberculosis. That year, 1998, Harriet Okatch and her eldest sister, Achieng, graduated from the University of Botswana. Harriet Okatch's degree was in chemistry.

Now her mother could no longer work, and Harriet Okatch became the major source of financial support for the family. She found work as a quality assurance chemist at a pharmaceutical company. Her mother, who never fully recovered, returned to Kampala, the capital of Uganda. She died there several months after her arrival.

At a memorial service held in Botswana, one of her children called Susan Okatch the "eighth wonder of the world." Susan Okatch had somehow managed to support the six children by herself in a foreign country, without family support and with meager earnings. "She must have been so determined," Harriet Okatch said.

Harriet Okatch has found meaning in her AIDS research.

By the time of the service, Harriet Okatch was married and pregnant with her first child. She also had a scholarship from the University of Botswana to do doctoral work in chemistry. She started that fall and finished three and a half years later. But even with a doctorate, she couldn't find a job; employers told her she was overqualified. She heard about promising opportunities in AIDS research and started working for a Swedish aid group.

Even though the research didn't involve chemistry, she became excited about working in the AIDS field—in part because of what had happened to her parents.

"I thought this could give so much meaning to my life," she said. "I had always wanted to be a medical doctor. When I learned that my dad had died of AIDS, I thought it would be nice to find a cure. I also saw my mom suffer in the last year of her life. It was painful in that she had no drugs to help her. I thought, if only I had done something maybe she wouldn't have gone through this pain."

In 2004, Max Essex, chairman of what is now the Harvard School of Public Health AIDS Initiative, heard about Okatch and asked to meet her during a trip to Botswana. He offered her a job in his laboratory at Harvard. Okatch accepted, though she was apprehensive about the work. "It had been eight years since I had done any biology-related work," she said. "Everyone was using specialized terms, and I had no idea what they were talking about. I began taking home a biology textbook so I could immerse myself in the work. I felt I had to prove myself, coming from a chemistry background."

At Harvard, she enrolled in undergraduate biology classes as well. In Essex's laboratory, she gradually felt more comfortable and worked on a study that looked into why patients failed treatment regimens. In 2007, she moved back to Botswana, and continued along the same theme of work—looking at drug-resistance mutations.

"She's got a lot of drive," Essex said of Okatch. "She'll do well."

In mid-2008, Essex asked Okatch to speak before a group of Harvard donors who had traveled to Botswana to visit the Botswana–Harvard Partnership program. She gave three different scenarios involving people who had been affected by AIDS. She wanted to give a range of experiences.

In one of the three stories, she told about a mother raising six children on her own, how the mother had struggled, and yet how three of those children went to college and one had become an AIDS researcher.

"And that person is me," she told the group.

Essex said several in the group had tears in their eyes. "It was really moving the way she told it," he said. "She said it with a lot of sentiment for her mother, how she had worked so hard, all just before the drugs arrived in Botswana."

Okatch hopes her work will help doctors overseeing AIDS treatment. "It's so important," she said, "that we understand more about these mutations because we don't have a vaccine and we depend on these drugs."

But she has also found greater meaning in her life. "It's our responsibility to be role models for children," she said. "I'm very grateful to have had such a strong role model in my mother. But now it's time for us to take on these roles with all these other children, all the orphans."

She believes she can help—as a researcher, perhaps as a role model. "Even though AIDS is a dark cloud," she said, "it still has a silver lining, and that's hope. People like me have experienced the despair, and we went through the process of healing." ■

A worker stitches white sheets into coffins at Botswana's largest coffin-making factory.

Life After Death

John Donnelly

IT IS HARD TO COMPREHEND now all the deaths from only a few years ago. You had to be in a place like Gaborone, the capital of Botswana, during the late 1990s or the first few years of the new millennium. You had to be present over the weekend, the time for most funerals, which started at dawn and continued through the day. You had to get caught behind one of those processions or walk in one, which moved at the deliberate pace of an ox, and you had to hear the high-pitched wailing of the women that caused everyone in hearing distance to cast their eyes to the ground. Weekends then were too painful. AIDS was running wild. Deaths followed at a gallop.

And then antiretroviral drugs arrived.

The pace of deaths didn't slow the next day. It took some time. Experts built systems. Some figured out drug distribution. Some built laboratories. Some trained doctors and nurses. Doctors and nurses trained other health workers. Everyone taught those infected how to take the drugs.

Soon, the deaths began to fall off; the drugs made most people well. And slowly, over a period of several years, weekends became weekends again, a time of relaxation and joy, not interminable periods of mourning.

The life-extending drugs had tremendous impact. People found hope. Children kept their parents. Grandparents kept their children. But for those in the business of death, life changed, too. A large coffin-making factory shut down. A handful of funeral homes closed.

"The undertakers were making good business and driving luxury vehicles," said Dr. Ndwapi Ndwapi, head of the Botswana government's Masa Program, which, by mid-2008, was overseeing AIDS treatment for more than 100,000 patients across the country. Ndwapi, who began working as an AIDS doctor at Princess Marina Hospital in 2001, had taken a personal affront to the booming business in death. "I remember vowing to myself to put them out of business," he said. "By 2005 and 2006, we were seeing an avalanche of undertakers closing their doors. That was very satisfying."

The industry has emerged with fewer players. At M & N Coffin & Casket Manufacturers, Botswana's largest coffin-maker, the factory was going full-bore one winter day in 2008. They were making coffins on an assembly line: power saws ripped through pine wood, carpenters nailed pieces together, painters applied finishes, seamstresses stitched white sheets into the interiors, and strong-armed men stretched plastic over the finished products and then lifted them atop tall stacks. At the end of the line, the factory looked like a canyon of coffins of all sizes, from those that could hold babies to those large enough for hefty adults.

"The business has seen a lot of changes in the last few years," said Lesedi Molefi, M & N's administration manager, as she walked around the stacks of coffins and the more expensive caskets. "On a weekend day a few years ago, you might have ten burials and seven or eight of them were people who had died of AIDS. Today, that is no longer happening. People are not dying so much of AIDS, and so there are fewer funerals."

At Pule Funeral Services, a large funeral home in Gaborone, one attendant pointed out that you didn't need to be in the funeral business to know that fewer people were dying in Botswana now. It was only common sense, he added, something everyone noticed by the absence of funerals on the weekends.

While fewer deaths meant a drop in business, the attendant said almost all the people he knew in the industry were relieved that the death toll had dramatically slowed. The medical system had responded so strongly to the challenge, he said, adding, "We are very proud of this."

Only a few years ago, the Princess Marina Hospital morgue was almost always at capacity; it could hold two dozen bodies at a time. When the morgue was full, attendants directed ambulance workers to private undertakers. But during a winter day in 2008, the morgue was empty. Not a single body lay in its refrigerated shelves.

Senior mortuary attendant Moses Selebogo, who started working at the morgue in 1987, began opening each of the shelves' doors, pulling out empty metal beds. "See?" he said. "No bodies. Four years ago, too many people were dying. This is the way it is now. It is much quieter." Selebogo sat back in his chair. He could relax now. Fewer people were dying. He couldn't have been happier. ■

The HIV/AIDS Epidemic in BOTSWANA

a photo essay by Dominic Chavez

In 2002, physician Ndwapi Ndwapi treated the first patients to receive free antiretroviral therapy and care through Masa, Botswana's national AIDS therapy program. Within six years Ndwapi had overseen the treatment of more than 100,000 Batswana with AIDS.

Emmanuel Tawana, a police officer, has been taking antiretrovirals through the Masa Program, Botswana's national AIDS treatment initiative, since 2003. *Masa* is the Setswana word for "new dawn"; with his HIV infection under control, Tawana can look forward to many new dawns with his two young daughters.

Since 1987 Moses Selebogo has worked as an attendant in the Princess Marina Hospital morgue in Gaborone, Botswana. At the height of the country's AIDS crisis, the morgue was so overwhelmed that Selebogo had to send bodies to private mortuaries. He now measures the success of the country's AIDS treatment program by the vacancies in the morgue; on the day this photograph was taken, all the drawers were empty.

A patient waits for her name to be called at the Princess Marina Infectious Disease Care Clinic in Gaborone. The clinic—Botswana's first AIDS treatment center—serves as the major referral center for clinics across the country.

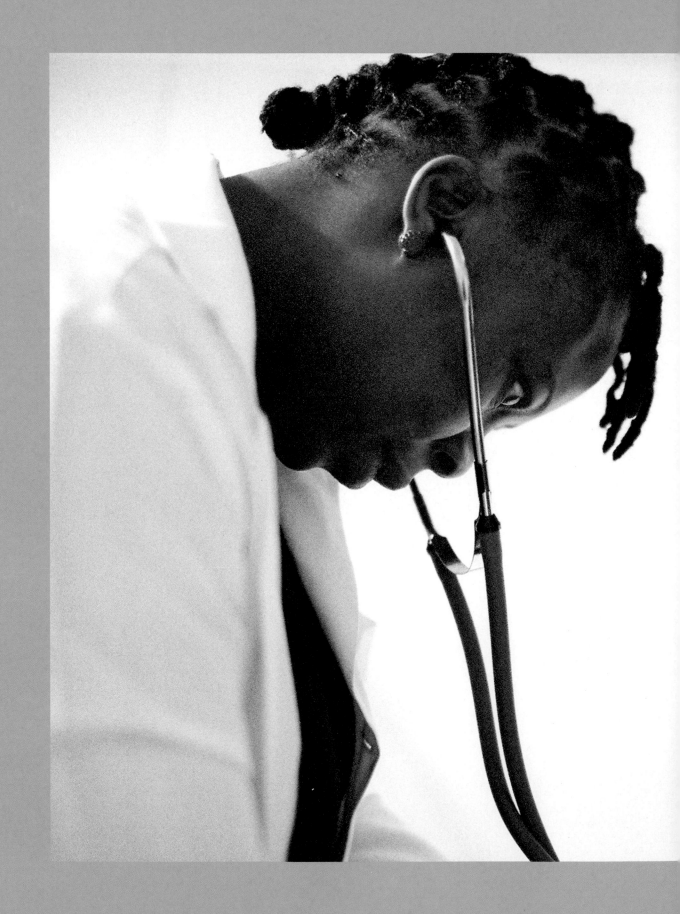

Tendani Gaolathe, an internist, examines one of her regular patients, Marea Maroku. From 2003 to 2008, this model patient took a four-hour bus ride every month to pick up her AIDS drugs. Now with the national antiretroviral treatment program de-centralized, Maroku can receive clinical care closer to home.

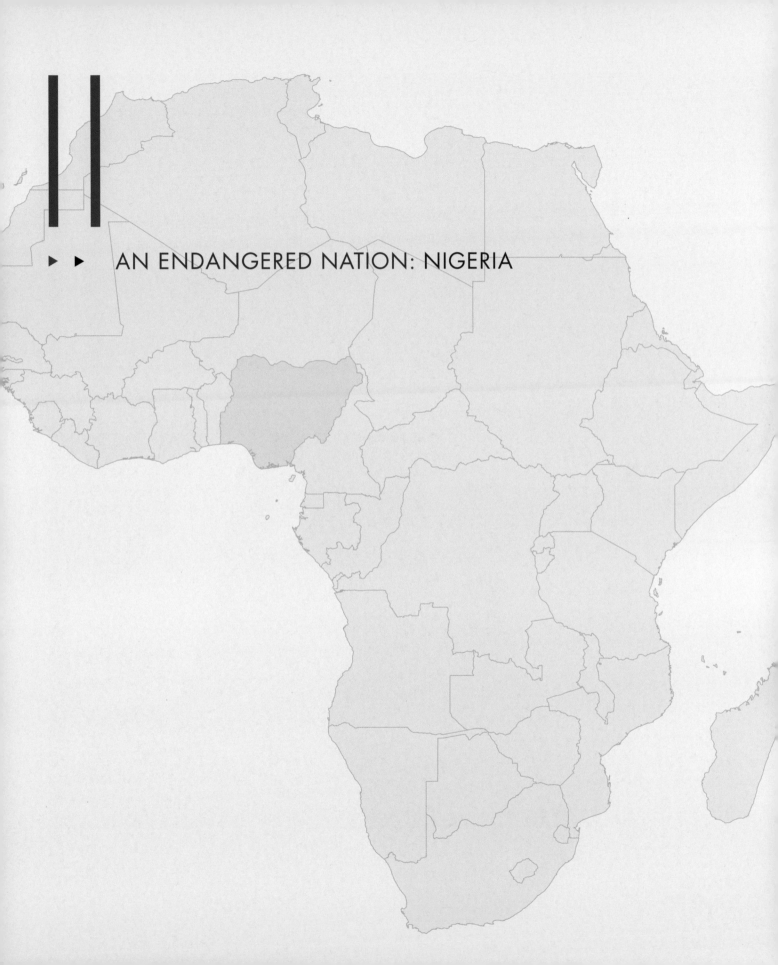

AN ENDANGERED NATION: NIGERIA

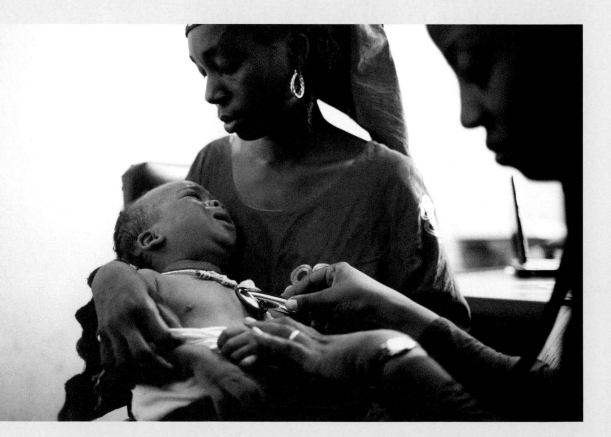

An Endangered Nation

FOR MANY YEARS, Nigeria seemed to have evaded the HIV epidemic altogether. As deaths mounted and projections grew more dire in other African nations, Nigeria remained largely unscathed. When the first several thousand blood samples tested negative for the virus, Nigerian officials felt relief. Yet those early results allowed complacency to creep in, and officials turned their attention to more pressing issues.

When the HIV wave finally began to wash over Nigeria, it resembled a tsunami. In just a few years the country found itself confronting one of the world's largest HIV epidemics.

"AIDS continues to ravage the country, and today there is hardly a community that has not been touched by the disease," Nigeria's president, Olusegun Obasanjo, told other heads of state in his remarks at the African Summit on HIV/AIDS, Tuberculosis and Other Related Infectious Diseases in 2001. Nigeria's terrible vulnerability resembled that of so many other sub-Saharan African countries. "What we have is a pandemic out of control, which is gravely threatening our nations, our children, and our future," President Obasanjo said. "We are an endangered continent!"

Nigeria mobilized on many fronts. The National Action Committee on AIDS developed the HIV/AIDS Emergency Action Plan to ensure effective responses to the epidemic, promote prevention strategies, and pursue a long-range vision for preserving the country's future. The president's open and frequent discussion of HIV helped create an environment in which AIDS-related nongovernmental organizations could flourish. And universities contributed valuable intellectual and scientific resources to combating AIDS.

Despite those efforts, people in Nigeria spoke of AIDS in hushed tones, if at all. Those who were infected hid their HIV status for fear of the stigmatization and discrimination that were sure to follow. But then the country made a bold move: it launched its own program for providing antiretroviral therapy to people living with HIV/AIDS.

Dr. Ernest Ekong, a physician in Lagos, witnessed the transformation of the national response through the transformation of individual patients. He remembers in particular a young mother of two who had struggled into his consulting room on the arms of her mother and sister. She sank into a chair and began listing to one side; her eyes were glassy. She weighed not much more than a child.

"Her case was as critical as I'd ever seen," says Ekong, who has practiced AIDS medicine since 1991. "Her immune system had been devastated."

Ekong managed to control his patient's tuberculosis, treat her other opportunistic infections, and start her on antiretrovirals. But the woman could not afford the drugs on a regular basis, and she remained gaunt and weak.

The following year, in 2004, the young woman became one of the first to enroll in a new program funded by PEPFAR, the U.S. President's Emergency Plan for AIDS Relief, which provided her with free antiretrovirals. Within a year her CD4+ cell count had risen from a precarious 39 to 310 and her viral load had become undetectable.

"My patient was like the biblical Lazarus brought back to life," Ekong says. "She regained her weight and simply blossomed, becoming beautiful again."

Ekong savors these Lazarus stories, as he calls them. And as the national clinical coordinator of the Harvard–PEPFAR program in Lagos, he has had many opportunities to witness such miracles.

By late 2008, the Harvard program had enrolled more than 85,000 people in its antiretroviral treatment and care clinics. More than 52,000 adults were receiving treatment at 16 clinics. An additional 20 clinics provided services to prevent mother-to-child transmission of the virus, while 21 clinics offered palliative care and support. Laboratories at each clinic now offer a range of tests, including HIV screening and confirmatory tests, CD4+ cell counts, viral load assessments, DNA polymerase chain reaction tests for infants, and diagnostics for tuberculosis and other opportunistic infections.

"I'm amazed at how far we've come in the past few years," Ekong says. "It hasn't been easy, but it gives me great joy to see people who were almost gone come back to life again."

The number of Nigerians receiving antiretroviral therapy through a range of coordinated programs had surpassed 269,000 by early 2008; an estimated total of 800,000 need treatment. So Ekong and his colleagues continue to expand the treatment sites, to build capacity and infrastructure, and to provide training to additional health care workers.

"We're expecting to be treating many more patients," Ekong says. "Our ultimate hope is for prevention. But in the meantime, we're grateful to be able to save lives." ■

The Challenge and Response in Nigeria

Phyllis J. Kanki

NIGERIA, THE MOST POPULOUS NATION IN SUB-SAHARAN AFRICA, IS HOME TO ONE in every five Africans. So it may come as no surprise that the story of the HIV epidemic in Nigeria can be told through numbers of great magnitude: millions of Nigerians are already infected with the virus, with many millions more at risk. Hundreds of thousands of people have died, leaving more than a million orphans. And hundreds of thousands need life-sustaining antiretroviral therapies. Perhaps most telling is the fact that the number of Nigerians infected with HIV—estimated at nearly three million—is greater than the population of some African nations.

One number has carried an especially ominous warning. Since 2001, the HIV prevalence rate in Nigeria has hovered near the 5 percent mark. That level is considered a critical threshold, at which an epidemic, if not checked, can catapult to rates as high as 40 percent.[1]

What these numbers fail to reveal, though, is the determination of a nation to ensure that the seemingly inevitable does not come to pass. Despite exorbitant costs, the Nigerian government enacted its own AIDS treatment program in advance of international aid. And countless individuals and institutions are maintaining vigilance against the further spread of the virus. Together they are seeking to paint new numbers and to create a picture of a nation surviving—and even thriving—in the face of HIV.

Economic and Social Background

The Federal Republic of Nigeria exerts considerable political, economic, and social influence on the African continent, perhaps even surpassing what might be expected based on the country's size and resources. An estimated 150 million Nigerians live in the nation's 36 states and in the Federal Capital Territory, home of the capital of Abuja. The population is diverse; more than 500 living languages are spoken in Nigeria, and more than 250 ethnic groups are disproportionately scattered across the country.

Even the country's terrain is varied, from the southern coastal plains to the desert of the extreme north; other regions include savannah, rainforest, and mountainous terrain. One-third of Nigeria's 414,091 square miles is arable land, and two-thirds of its labor force is employed in agriculture. Yet the population growth has outstripped agricultural production to the extent that Nigeria, once considered the foodbasket of Africa, is no longer a notable food exporter.

Nigeria does continue to be a major oil exporter, yet that rich resource has not been enough to raise the country's economic rank dramatically. In its *Human Development Report 2007/2008,* the United Nations Development Programme (UNDP) ranked Nigeria 158 out of 177 member states.[2] The UNDP lists Nigeria as a "low-development country"; within that group of 21 countries, Nigeria's annual per capita income falls below average. More than 71 percent of Nigerians live below the poverty line, on less than US$1 a day. Nigeria spends less than average on health and has received less external aid than other low-development countries (Table 1).

The World Bank also gives Nigeria a relatively low economic rank, based on gross national income, or GNI, which takes into account gross domestic product as well as net flows of income from abroad. In 2007 the World Bank estimated Nigeria's per-capita GNI at US$930; by contrast, the figure for the United States was $46,040.[3]

Part of the stress on Nigeria's economic health has been its rapid population growth, which soared from 88.9 million in 1991 to 140 million in 2007.[4,5] In 2008, the annual growth rate of the Nigerian population was estimated at 2.8 percent.[2] In addition, Nigeria has been undergoing a demographic transition from a high fertility and high mortality population to a low fertility and declining mortality population. The effect of this transition has brought about a population structure with a wide base of people younger than 15, representing over 56 percent of the population.

Table 1. Selected Indicators of Development, Health Expenditures, and Outcomes

Indicator	Nigeria	Senegal	Tanzania	Botswana
Human development index ranking, out of 177	158	156	159	124
Human development category	low	low	low	medium
Population (in millions)	150	12.9	38.5	1.8
Population under the age of 15 in 2005	55.9%	44.7%	28.9%	35.6%
Annual population growth (1975–2005)	2.8	2.8	2.9	2.7
Annual population growth (2005–2015)	2.2	2.3	2.4	1.2
Average life expectancy at birth (in years)	46.5	62.3	51	46.1
Under-five mortality rate per 1,000 live births	194	136	122	120
Incidence of tuberculosis per 100,000 people	536	466	496	556
Adult literacy rate	69.1%	39.3%	69.4%	81.2%
Physicians per 100,000 people	28	6	2	40
Gross national income per capita for 2007 using the Atlas method	US$930	US$820	US$400	US$5,840
Population below the income poverty line (% on US$1 a day), 1990–2005 (World Bank, 2007)	71%	17%	58%	28%
Health expenditure per capita (current US$)	US$27	US$38	US$17	US$362

Sources: Gross national income: World Bank. Gross national income per capita 2007, Atlas method and PPP. World Development Indicators Database of July 1, 2008, accessed at *http://siteresources.worldbank.org/DATASTATISTICS/Resources/GNIPC.pdf* on August 21, 2008. Health expenditure per capita (current US$): World Bank. "HNP at a Glance" database, accessed at *http://go.worldbank.org/MALQ9X8AS0* on August 21, 2008.

Note: GNI for Tanzania refers to the mainland only

Life expectancy in Nigeria had risen from 45 years in 1963 to 51 years in 1991, but by 2007, it had dropped again, to an estimated 46.5 years.[2,6] HIV/AIDS has contributed to that drop, just as it has to the increases in both the number of deaths among young adults and the number of orphans. The infant mortality rate is 99 per thousand, and the under-five mortality rate is 194 per thousand (2,7,8).

The history of Nigeria's response to the HIV epidemic has been tightly linked to the political and economic events that coincided with the country's transition to a democracy. When Nigeria's first AIDS cases were recognized in the mid-1980s, the country was under military rule. The dictatorship that held power from the mid-1960s to 1999 was associated with ethnic violence, widespread corruption, and the almost complete demise of the health sector's infrastructure. During the years of military rule, Nigeria's health systems deteriorated and international aid shrank. The resulting extreme poverty, economic vulnerability, and institutional weaknesses—coupled with sociocultural complexity and high-risk behaviors—all helped to fuel the country's HIV epidemic.

Democracy was restored in 1999 with the election of President Olusegun Obasanjo, who presided over an eight-year period of rebuilding. During his tenure, the international development community began to return to Nigeria and initiate aid programs, many of them addressing the HIV/AIDS epidemic (Figure 1). In late 2000, for example, the Bill & Melinda Gates Foundation announced a US$25 million grant to the Harvard School of Public Health to create the AIDS Prevention Initiative in Nigeria. Similarly, the World Bank initiated the Multi-Country HIV/AIDS Program, or MAP, to fund national HIV prevention, treatment, and care in a number of African countries; Nigeria received US$100 million. Nigeria also successfully applied for funds from the Global Fund to Fight AIDS, Tuberculosis and Malaria and, in 2004, received support from the President's Emergency Plan for AIDS Relief, or PEPFAR. At the same time, the government, local professionals, and civil society groups, inspired by the increased resources, have strengthened their own commitments to the prevention, treatment, and care of HIV/AIDS.

President Obasanjo's successor, President Umaru Yar'Adua, was elected in 2007. Both leaders have become associated with a proactive response to the AIDS epidemic.

History of the HIV/AIDS Epidemic in Nigeria

AIDS was first recognized as a new and distinct clinical entity in 1981 in the United States.[9,10] During the next several years, as researchers sought to identify and isolate the etiologic agent, AIDS was beginning to be recognized in other parts of the world. Central Africans residing in Europe were presenting with clinical signs and symptoms similar to those of AIDS, and early reports from Kinshasa, Zaire—now the Democratic Republic of the Congo—suggested high AIDS rates in association with a newly isolated virus, now known as human immunodeficiency virus, or HIV.[11]

Nigeria's first AIDS cases were recorded in Lagos in 1986.[12] That year, under the leadership of the late Olikoye Ransome-Kuti, then the minister of health, the Nigerian government officially acknowledged the first HIV infection in the country.

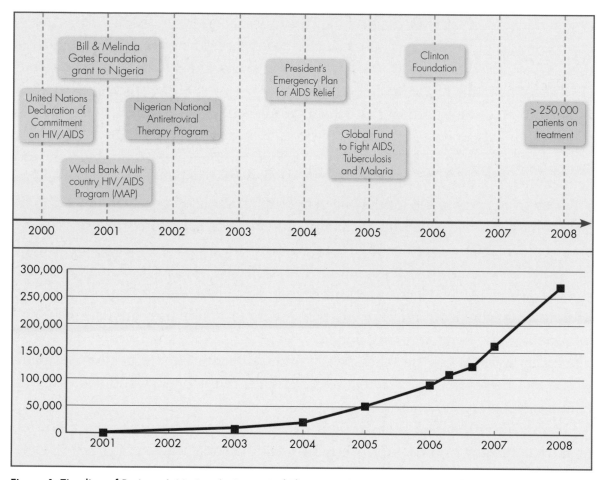

Figure 1. Timeline of Patients Initiating Antiretroviral Therapy in Nigeria as a Result of the Growing International Response

As a result of persistent advocacy by several expert virologists and physicians—including Chris Williams, Ademola Fagbami, Abdulsalami Nasidi, Tekena Harry, and Idris Mohammed—the Nigerian government formed the National Expert Advisory Committee on AIDS. HIV infections and AIDS cases continued to be identified throughout the country. The work was limited to the few Nigerian scientists who had collaborative relationships with European or U.S. HIV researchers who supplied the test kits and reagents required for HIV diagnoses.

In late 1987, the Federal Ministry of Health, with technical assistance from the Overseas Development Administration and the World Health Organization, sought to ensure transfusion safety by establishing HIV antibody testing in the blood banks and transfusions centers of 13 teaching hospitals throughout the country. The number of such HIV screening centers would later increase to cover more hospitals. The results of HIV testing in the first 2,000 blood units were negative. Unfortunately, these early data led to an optimistic view that Nigeria would be spared from the epidemic and may have lulled government officials into a false sense of complacency.

In 1988, the National AIDS and STDs Control Program (NASCP) replaced the earlier national committee. Coordinated by the Federal Ministry of Health, NASCP would continue to be responsible for the Nigerian health system's response to HIV/AIDS by developing guidelines on key interventions, supporting the monitoring and surveillance of the epidemic, and coordinating HIV treatment and care efforts across the nation.

In the 1990s and early 2000, antiretroviral therapy (ART) was being developed and tested in the United States and Europe, but most of the developing world was left without drug treatments. Efforts focused on other prevention methods, largely behavioral change and condom promotion, as researchers in the developed world sought a preventative HIV vaccine. The key to creating effective HIV prevention programs would rely, however, on a thorough understanding of the biology and epidemiology of HIV infection in those settings.

Many critical features of the HIV epidemic in Africa and other resource-poor settings were already known—and were markedly heterogeneous.[13] The heterosexual epidemic of HIV in resource-poor settings differed sharply from the epidemics among homosexual men and injection drug users in the United States and Europe. With heterosexual men and women constituting the major target population, Africa required new approaches to prevention and intervention programs. Identifying vulnerable populations based primarily on heterosexual transmission meant that such groups as sex workers were considered at high risk for acquiring and spreading HIV. Other population groups—such as military personnel, long-distance truck drivers, miners, and migrant workers—were later identified as being at increased risk for HIV infection as well.

The overwhelmingly large number of adult men and women in Africa who had been heterosexually infected with HIV also meant that significant numbers of infants and children were at risk. Even today, the world's largest burden of HIV infection in children is in Africa, with nearly 12 million orphans on the continent. Nigeria alone has 1.2 million orphans.[7,14]

HIV Surveillance Surveys

The first national HIV sentinel surveillance survey for Nigeria, conducted in 1991 among pregnant women attending antenatal clinics, revealed the country's median HIV prevalence rate to be 1.8 percent.[15] While this number was considered low, compared with rates in other African nations, the rates of infection in high-risk populations—such as sex workers, patients attending sexually transmitted infection clinics, and long-distance truck drivers—were three- to fourfold higher.[16]

The Federal Ministry of Health, supported by international donor agencies, continued to conduct the HIV sentinel surveillance surveys every two years, gradually expanding their geographic distribution across the country and increasing the number of subjects screened. Those surveys not only documented the spread of HIV infection in both urban and rural areas of the country, but they also demonstrated considerable variability in infection rates (Figure 2).

The national median HIV seroprevalence among the general population—as represented by pregnant women attending antenatal clinics in different parts of the country—increased from 1.8 percent in 1991 to 3.8 percent in 1993, 4.5 percent in 1995, 5.4 percent in 1999, and 5.8 percent (with a range of 1.0 to 13.6 percent) in 2001.[14–18] In 2000, high HIV rates were documented in patients presenting with other sexually transmitted infections (11 percent, with a range of 5.2 percent to 23.0 percent) and pulmonary tuberculosis patients (17 percent, with a range of 4.2 percent to 33.0 percent).[19] By 2000, HIV/AIDS cases had been recognized not just in every state, but in each of the country's 774 local government areas as well.[19]

In 2001, the survey was expanded nationwide.[20] Conducted over a three-month period, the survey included approximately 300 pregnant women from each of 85 sites, which represented all states and the Federal Capital Territory. More than 24,200 samples were tested for HIV. A nationwide median prevalence rate of 5.8 percent was reported, with a range among states from 0.8 percent to 16.4 percent.[20]

In 2003, the survey was repeated with a national prevalence of 5.0 percent.[21] Every state and the Federal Capital Territory reported HIV infections; in all cases the rate exceeded 1 percent. Thus, Nigeria was experiencing a generalized epidemic, in which transmission was occurring within low-risk populations and was independently fueled by transmission from higher risk populations.

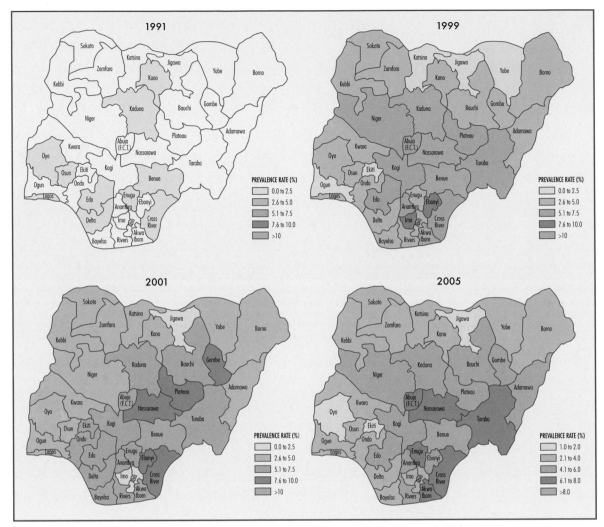

Figure 2. HIV Prevalence in Pregnant Women in Nigeria by State (1991–2005)
Sources: Federal Ministry of Health, National HIV Seroprevalence Sentinel Surveys for 1991, 1999, 2001, and 2005

A review of the prevalence figures from all the states and the Federal Capital Territory demonstrates tremendous diversity in the rates of HIV infection. Multiple determinants likely account for this considerable heterogeneity. HIV is thought to have entered the Nigerian population in the mid-1980s, just as it did in other West African nations. Yet the catalysts for its early spread in the country remain unknown. Differences among geopolitical zones, ethnic traditions, religious practices, and sexual networking habits are among the many possible factors that may have contributed to the disparities in HIV infection that would appear decades later. As HIV has continued its spread across Nigeria, it has become increasingly apparent that the epidemic does not follow the same course in different geographic locales or among various population subgroups.[13]

This variability has complicated the task of monitoring the epidemic's course, planning intervention measures, and projecting needs for the necessary care and support of infected people within the country. A thorough understanding of the nature of the multiple overlapping HIV epidemics throughout the country, especially in terms of the factors that enhance the spread of the virus among different population subgroups, is still needed.

Until 2004, the AIDS epidemic in Nigeria had been monitored primarily using cross-sectional serosurveys of HIV infection. While this method has its merits, it also has serious limitations owing to its inability to provide specific behavioral information on at-risk subpopulations or explain changes in levels of infection in mature epidemics. According to UNAIDS, such an understanding can be achieved only with more information on the subpopulations most at risk and the behaviors that increase their vulnerability.[22] Therefore, in 2004, behavioral sentinel surveillance became an important substudy in the national surveillance surveys.

The second generation of HIV surveillance provides warning signals for the spread of HIV along with some important biological markers of dispersion. It also allows the identification of relevant high-risk and bridge populations. These data then provide the basis for the development of more targeted interventions. Nigeria, which has tremendous cultural and ethnic diversity, requires continued high-quality surveillance and monitoring systems, up-to-date surveillance data with the best available methods, and expanded scientific research.

The Multisectoral National Response to the Epidemic

At the outset, the impact of the AIDS epidemic was more pronounced on Nigeria's health sector than on its other sectors, as the disease was viewed solely as a health problem. As the epidemic evolved, however, the sentinel surveys demonstrated significant HIV infection and disease in the young men and women who constituted the mainstay of agriculture, education, commerce, and industry. By 2000, Nigerian government officials recognized that the impact of the epidemic had transcended the health sector to include the socioeconomic and developmental sectors. HIV/AIDS thus became the most important health and developmental problem in Nigeria, requiring an immediate response. Despite all the preventive interventions available, the need to mount an expanded program for care and support of the millions already living with HIV/AIDS had grown urgent. The situation called for an expanded multisectoral national response to the epidemic.

In 2000, the newly elected President Olusegun Obasanjo established a Presidential Committee on AIDS and a National Action Committee on AIDS (NACA). A three-year HIV/AIDS Emergency Action Plan (HEAP) was developed in 2001 with assistance from UNAIDS and other international development groups. The partners implementing this policy included governmental institutions, nongovernmental organizations, community-based organizations, faith-based organizations, and people living with or affected by HIV/AIDS. Since the development of HEAP, activity has taken place on all fronts, including advocacy, prevention, treatment, and care. Yet these activities still had to be scaled up to improve coverage. Although HEAP provided an important strategic plan, NACA needed to coordinate the funding from multiple international donors, each with its own objectives and funding requirements. The federal government also mobilized resources for HEAP, which helped implement the Nigerian ART program through the establishment of the National ART Committee, which developed the first Nigerian Guidelines for ART.

Although AIDS case reporting through the World Health Organization had been in place in Nigeria since the late 1990s, the infrastructure and disease reporting capacity failed to capture the number of AIDS cases accurately. In early 2000, the Federal Ministry of Health adopted the UNAIDS projection methodology, which used HIV surveillance data to estimate the burden of AIDS disease. The Nigerian national HIV sentinel surveillance survey noted a small decline in median HIV seroprevalence to 5.0 percent in 2003 and another drop to 4.4 percent in 2005.[21,23] This methodology estimated that 3.3 million Nigerians between 15 and 49 years of age were infected with HIV, with 720,000 already diagnosed or living with AIDS and in need of treatment.[22]

In 2002, the National Intelligence Council illustrated the magnitude of the HIV/AIDS pandemic in five countries considered to be the major contributors to the current

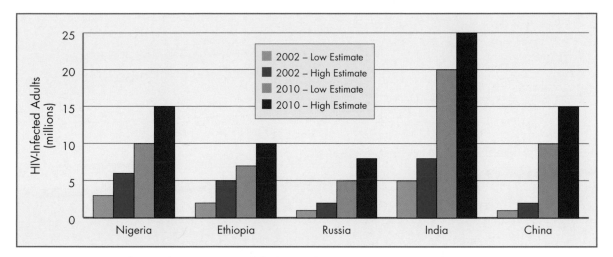

Figure 3. Estimates of HIV Infection in Top Global Contributing Nations
Source: Eberstadt N. The future of AIDS. *Foreign Affairs*, 2002;81(6).

and future HIV/AIDS global pandemic: China, Russia, India, Ethiopia, and Nigeria[24] (Figure 3). The estimates for Nigeria ranged from 3 to 6 million but were projected to increase to 10 to 15 million by 2010.[7] In 2007, the Nigerian national sentinel surveillance survey estimated a 4.4 percent HIV infection rate.[25] Based on that estimate and the most recent population census, the World Health Organization and UNAIDS provided an updated estimate of 2.8 million HIV infections in Nigeria. Although substantially lower than previous estimates, with the magnitude of the population, even a numerically small prevalence rate sets the burden of disease in the millions.

Without an effective prevention program on a large scale, Nigeria will continue to experience the devastating health, economic, and social effects of the HIV/AIDS epidemic. Although data since 2003 suggest a slight downward trend in Nigeria's nationwide prevalence, the sheer magnitude of the population, the greater than 4 percent infection rate, and the epidemiologic characteristics indicate a generalized epidemic with several million Nigerians already infected with the virus (Figure 4).

HIV Variability in Nigeria

During the twentieth century, the developed world became accustomed to significant biomedical advances in preventing and curing disease. For infectious disease agents

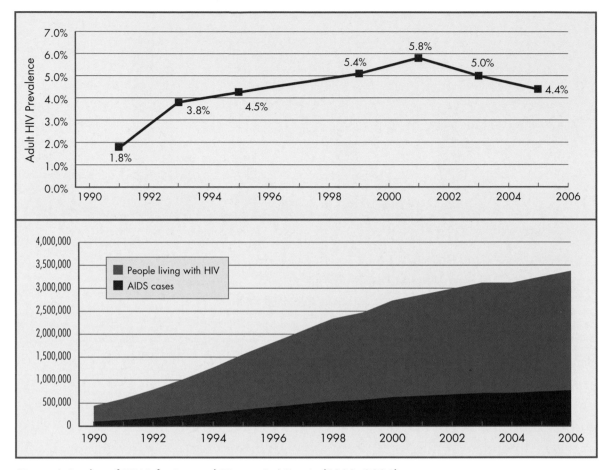

Figure 4. Burden of HIV Infection and Disease in Nigeria (1990–2006)

these advances have often taken the form of vaccines and drugs. Yet the unique characteristics of HIV have created new challenges for the biomedical research community. The virus integrates its genetic material into the infected host's DNA, rendering infection lifelong, even with currently available treatment.

When HIV was first described in the early 1980s, it became the first human virus to belong to the *Lentivirus* genus, previously known for viral infections of horses, goats, and sheep. After the discovery of HIV, related viruses in cats, cows, and monkeys would be described as well, often with associated immunodeficiency syndromes similar to human AIDS.

Perhaps the most striking feature of HIV has been its genetic diversity. In 1985, a second virus type was discovered in Senegal. Human immunodeficiency virus type 2 appeared to be closely related not only to HIV-1, but also to a number of non-human-primate–related viruses.[26] Both HIV-1 and HIV-2 have been described in Nigeria and other parts of West Africa since the late 1980s, yet other African regions appear to have had only HIV-1.[26,27]

Advances in the technology of molecular cloning and sequencing allowed for the further appreciation of the genetic diversity of HIV-1. Genetic sequence analyses have revealed multiple HIV-1 subtypes (A–D, F–H, J, and K), which are known to circulate in a distinct worldwide distribution.[28] HIV-1 subtype B, for example, accounts for an estimated 12.3 percent of cases worldwide, but infections with this subtype are primarily seen in the Americas, Western Europe, and Australia. Conversely, subtype C is estimated to have caused more than 47 percent of the worldwide infections, with the highest incidence rates in southern African countries, Ethiopia, China, and India.

Circulating recombinant forms, or CRFs, of the virus also occur in areas of the world in which multiple subtypes circulate. In 1994, David Olaleye from the University of Ibadan in Nigeria provided the first viral characterization of CRF02_AG in West Africa; since then, CRF02_AG has been considered the prototype West African HIV-1 subtype.[29] CRF02_AG, a recombinant virus made up of subtypes A and G, is responsible for a significant proportion of the new infections in Nigeria, as it is in other West African countries.[29,30]

The HIV epidemic in Nigeria, like those in other West African countries, comprises an array of HIV subtypes that are distinct from those in the developed world (Figure 5). The impact of these differences on the spread of HIV—as well as on its diagnosis, treatment, and prevention—is not yet understood. Yet the tremendous viral variability suggests that further research should accompany HIV prevention and treatment programs.

The History of HIV/AIDS Treatment and Care in Nigeria

By 2000, treatment and care of HIV/AIDS were progressing rapidly in the United States and Europe. New drugs were under development and clinical trials of multi-drug combinations were yielding significant progress in treatment of the disease. Patients

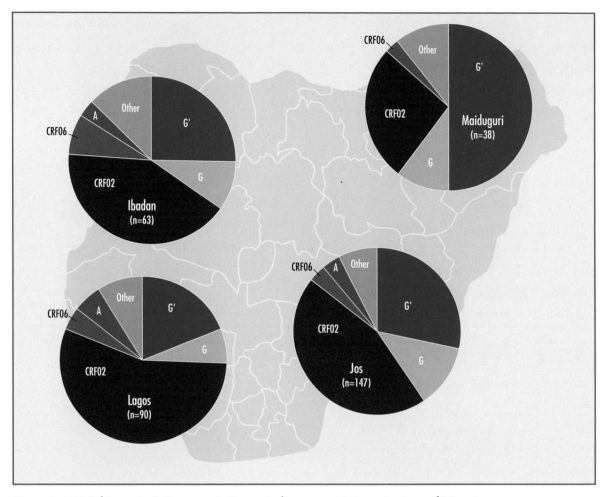

Figure 5. HIV Subtypes in Patients on Antiretroviral Treatment in Four Regions of Nigeria

in the developed world had increasing access to these drug cocktails, although the cost for such drugs with the requisite clinical monitoring was high, approximately US$1,000 to US$1,500 per month for the name-brand drugs alone.

With the cost of providing HIV treatment in developing countries seeming prohibitive, most international aid organizations focused efforts on prevention programs such as condom promotion and behavioral change campaigns. HIV researchers were optimistic that an effective HIV vaccine would soon be developed. Despite alarming increases in the number of Africans already infected with HIV, a preventative vaccine was considered the most promising approach to stopping the epidemic.

In the mid-1990s, HIV-infected Nigerians in need of ART purchased expensive antiretrovirals in Europe or the United States. Nigeria's elite teaching hospitals—such as Lagos University Teaching Hospital, Jos University Teaching Hospital, 68 Military Hospital, and the University College Hospital in Ibadan—were among the first Nigerian hospitals to monitor AIDS patients who had purchased drugs with their own money. Consequently, even before the national ART program began, some physicians were gaining experience in treating AIDS patients.

Yet those physicians were hampered in their efforts to provide optimal care because their hospitals lacked the laboratory tests needed to monitor patients on ART, especially CD4+ cell counts, which was standard care in the developed world. Even when the equipment and laboratory reagents were available to allow such monitoring, the cost of the test was borne by the patient. As a result, early ART experience heavily depended on the patient's willingness and ability to spend significant funds on both drugs and laboratory tests. In the late 1990s, the U.S. and European drug companies that produced the major antiretrovirals also began offering compassionate-use trials in Nigeria, providing physicians with the opportunity to treat small numbers of AIDS patients with donated drugs. These drugs included some of the first antiretrovirals developed, such as zidovudine and Combivir, a combination of zidovudine and lamivudine. Many of the large oil companies in Nigeria also began to provide Combivir to employees who had been diagnosed with AIDS.[31] Although clinicians have since realized that the use of such monotherapy and bitherapy is suboptimal and can lead to drug resistance, at the time the use of triple-drug regimens was neither widespread nor clinically recommended.

Following a call for action at the United Nations Millennium Summit in 2000, Kofi Annan, then the United Nations secretary-general, launched a personal campaign to form a global alliance equal to the challenge of AIDS.[32] He began by speaking to African leaders in Nigeria in April 2001 at the African Summit on HIV/AIDS, Tuberculosis, and Other Related Infectious Diseases. He then continued his advocacy around the world, urging health ministers, foundation officials, business executives, and other leaders to support his five-point call to action for better prevention, appropriate treatment and care, and accelerated research.

"There is no more time for half measures," Annan said. "In terms of lives lost, children orphaned, and the destruction of the social and economic fabric of whole societies and whole countries, AIDS is an unparalleled nightmare."[32] Annan invited member states of the United Nations General Assembly to convene for a Special Session on HIV/AIDS in New York City in June 2001.

At the conclusion of the three-day session, the General Assembly, representing 189 member states, unanimously adopted the United Nations Declaration of Commitment on HIV/AIDS. The declaration was designed as a blueprint to meet the Millennium Development Goals, endorsing equitable access to treatment and care as a fundamental component of a comprehensive and effective global HIV response.[33]

For universal access to HIV prevention, treatment, care, and support to be achieved, the declaration stated, national leadership would be required to establish policies that could sustain the momentum of treatment scale-up. These policies would support efforts to reduce HIV stigma, to build human resource capacity through training and better management, to improve supply management, to integrate HIV care with other health services, and to increase the number of people who chose to know their HIV status.[32] The General Assembly also established a Global HIV/AIDS and Health Fund to finance an urgent and expanded response to the epidemic based on an integrated approach to prevention, treatment, care, and support.

Nigeria played an important role in these efforts. In April 2001, President Obasanjo had served as host to the first African Summit on HIV/AIDS, Tuberculosis, and Other Related Infectious Diseases. At that summit he reminded participants that AIDS had killed 11.6 million Africans in the previous 15 years. "The sad reality is we are a dying continent," he said, "and it will be a challenge to prevent a monumental catastrophe."[34] President Obasanjo called on other African nations to commit additional resources to the pandemic; Nigeria had already increased its annual AIDS spending from US$100,000 to US$20 million.

In addition to his strong advocacy at that summit for continued support for HIV/AIDS programs in Africa, President Obasanjo announced the initiation of the Nigerian National Antiretroviral Therapy Program and the purchase of antiretrovirals for 10,000 adults and 5,000 children, at an annual cost of 500 million naira, or US$3.5 million. Nigeria had help: the Indian generic drug manufacturer Cipla had offered to lower the drug cocktail price from US$600 to US$350 per patient per year for any African nation that would provide the drug to eligible patients for free. Nigeria was the first to make such a large purchase of the drugs. Through its Multi-

Country HIV/AIDS Program, the World Bank provided a US$100-million grant to support this program in accordance with HEAP.[35]

The Federal Ministry of Health formed the National ART Committee, which drafted the original guidelines for providing ART.[36] This technical advisory body included a number of ART clinic directors, donor partners, and representatives from the Federal Ministry of Health, the National Food and Drug Administration and Control, UNAIDS, and the Global Fund Country Coordinating Mechanism. John Idoko from Jos University Teaching Hospital chaired the committee. The Nigerian ART guidelines largely followed World Health Organization guidelines with respect to ART eligibility, diagnosis, monitoring criteria, and first-line regimen recommendations. To help guide physicians and nurses, the Nigerian ART guidelines also included patient management recommendations and toxicity information.

At the same time, the Federal Ministry of Health issued guidelines for voluntary counseling and testing and services for prevention of mother-to-child transmission (PMTCT).[36-38] These guidelines offer critical entry points for ART programs, important opportunities for providing prevention messages, and guidance for health care providers in proper counseling and HIV testing methods.

The Nigerian PMTCT program began in 2001 with the establishment of seven federal PMTCT centers. These centers provided HIV testing to pregnant women and single-dose nevirapine to HIV-infected women and their babies. (UNICEF provided the nevirapine.) As this program identified pregnant women in need of complete ART, a particularly important patient population, it was integral to the national ART program. The PMTCT program also allowed for the follow-up of HIV-infected pregnant women after their delivery to determine whether exposed infants were infected and in need of treatment and care.

The Nigerian National ART Program, which began in February 2002, designated 25 treatment centers distributed across the country's six geopolitical zones. Treatment slots were allocated to each center with a year's supply of drugs for a total of approximately 600 eligible adult patients. In the first year, more than 6,000 adults were treated with a combination of the generic brands of two nucleoside reverse transcriptase inhibitors— lamivudine and stavudine—and one non-nucleoside reverse transcriptase inhibitor, nevirapine. Under the Nigerian national program, the monthly cost of treatment to the patient was 1,000 naira (equivalent to approximately US$7); the government highly

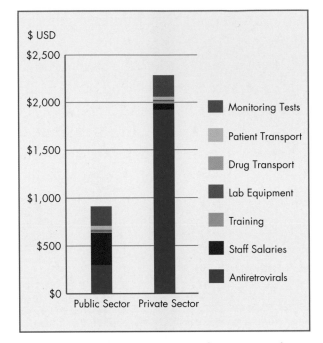

Figure 6. Annual Per-Patient Cost of Antiretroviral Treatment Provision in the Public and Private Sectors

Source: Federal Ministry of Health. *Nigeria: Rapid Assessment of HIV/AIDS Care in the Public and Private Sectors*. Abuja, Nigeria: Federal Ministry of Health, August 2004.

subsidized the remaining drug costs. The cost of laboratory tests required to qualify for the program and for continual monitoring was borne by the patient.

Most HIV/AIDS services are provided in the public sector, supported by a significant fraction of Nigeria's dedicated resources and qualified staff. Nigeria has been fortunate; despite the deterioration of the education and health sector that resulted from its long military rule, the country was able to maintain its excellence in educating health care workers. Nigeria's professional schools annually graduate thousands of physicians, nurses, laboratory technicians, and social workers. Unlike many other African nations, Nigeria's educated and skilled workforce has been able to provide an important foundation for HIV/ AIDS prevention, treatment, and care programs. In addition, Nigerian physicians, nurses, and other health care workers often represent a significant proportion of the health care workforce in the treatment and care programs of other African countries.

Nigeria is served by a variety of public and private health facilities. Private health institutions include a network of private for-profit entities, nongovernmental organizations, and faith-based organizations that provide health care to millions of Nigerians.[39] The formal linkages between private-sector and public-sector ART programs are limited, except for the referral of patients for drugs and other laboratory-related services. In 2004, per-patient costs in the public sector were estimated at US$913 (Figure 6).[39] The largest components of this cost were staff salaries (US$336), generic antiretrovirals (US$300), and laboratory monitoring tests (US$204). Smaller costs included laboratory equipment, patient and drug transportation, and staff training. An analysis of treatment costs in the private sector revealed a much higher per-patient cost of

US$2,263, with antiretrovirals accounting for 60 percent of the cost.[39]

In 2005, the AIDS Prevention Initiative in Nigeria, or APIN, provided the first evidence of the success of the Nigerian ART program, laying to rest the uncertainty about whether the requirements of ART and monitoring could be met in developing countries. APIN researchers found a 75-percent efficacy rate among the first 50 patients enrolled at the National Institute of Medical Research who had received generic antiretrovirals from the Nigerian government. This efficacy rate was comparable to those in U.S.- and European-based trial data for branded antiretrovirals.[40]

Data indicated that between baseline and week 24, the median viral load of the patients decreased by 1.23 $\log_{10}$ copies/ml, the median CD4+ cell count

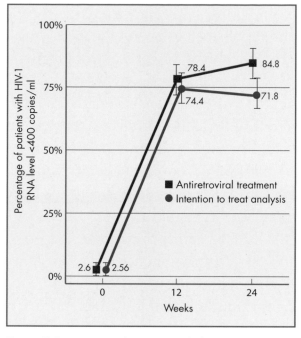

Figure 7. Response to Antiretroviral Therapy

Source: Idigbe E, Adewole T, Eisen G, et al. Management of HIV-1 infection with a combination of nevirapine + stavudine + lamivudine: a preliminary report on the Nigerian ARV program. *J AIDS*, 2005;40(1):65–69.

Note: Includes standard error bars. Points are slightly offset on the x-axis to aid visibility.

increased by 150 x 106 cells/l, the frequency of opportunistic infections fell by 48 percent, and the median body mass index increased by 1.04 kg/m². Thirty-six percent of the patients experienced minor and transient side effects.[40] The most prevalent side effect was skin rash, a common toxicity associated with nevirapine. Adherence to this triple regimen was high, at 72 to 82 percent of the patients (Figure 7). The overall results within the six-month treatment period indicated an effective suppression of viral replication and the reconstitution of the immune system of the study population. Although the global distribution of the infecting HIV-1 subtypes may differ, the clinical and biological results of this study compared favorably to those documented in cohorts treated with branded antiretrovirals in some developed countries. These early data suggested that the correct use of generic brands of antiretrovirals was a feasible option in the HIV care and support programs in resource-poor countries.

In 2003, the second year of the Nigerian National ART Program, the government ran out of stock of one of the three drugs in the ART regimen, a result of the length of time required for government procurement and the inability of drug companies to respond quickly to new drug orders.[39] HIV prevention programs in Nigeria that were funded by international aid organizations were reluctant to provide funding for antiretrovirals to assist during the stock-out, and many patients had to purchase the drug with their own funds or go without.

In late 2003, President George W. Bush launched the U.S. President's Emergency Plan for AIDS Relief, or PEPFAR, to provide prevention, treatment, and care to 15 focus countries.[41] The legislation authorized US$15 billion to a comprehensive program to combat HIV/AIDS in partner countries in southern Africa, East Africa, West Africa, the Caribbean, and Asia. Nigeria was one of two West African countries selected.

The following year, the Harvard School of Public Health and the AIDS Relief Consortium initiated PEPFAR-funded HIV treatment and care programs in Nigeria. The program provided funding for all aspects of treatment and care following the Nigerian ART guidelines for eligibility, drug regimens, and monitoring. In collaboration with the Nigerian National ART Program, which had initiated treatment for 13,000 patients by mid-2004, PEPFAR-funded clinics provided free treatment and care to an additional 8,000 patients during the first year of the program.

The Nigeria PEPFAR grew substantially over the next four years. AIDS Relief, Family Health International, the University of Maryland, and Columbia University's Mailman School of Public Health initiated treatment and care programs at various sites across the country. Annual funding increases enabled a rise in the number of patients on ART, the addition of new sites, the training of personnel, and the development of infrastructure and capacity building critical to meeting programmatic goals.

In January 2005, President Obasanjo announced that the Nigerian National ART Program would no longer require patients to pay a 1,000-naira fee. Moreover, hospitals and clinics stopped charging for HIV-infected children and pregnant women. PEPFAR has provided free laboratory monitoring for patients enrolled in the national program; both programs have worked together to provide an integrated treatment and care program that supplies free antiretrovirals and monitoring to all eligible patients. Although nearly 50,000 Nigerians with HIV/AIDS were receiving free antiretrovirals by the end of 2005, this number was still less than 10 percent of the Nigerians estimated to need ART (Figure 1).

The types of drugs and regimens for optimal ART were also changing worldwide. The patents for many of the early antiretrovirals were expiring, and many generic versions were being manufactured in India, Thailand, Brazil, and elsewhere. In addition to less expensive versions of these antiretrovirals, fixed-dose combinations were made available to reduce the pill burden and improve adherence. The PEPFAR program provided important assistance in expediting the U.S. Food and Drug Administration review and approval of these drugs.[41] As a result, by 2008, the cost of drugs for both adult and pediatric patients had dropped to levels well below US$300 per year.

Despite these advances, however, the newer and more efficacious drugs being developed in the United States and Europe remain prohibitively expensive and are not included in ART programs in Africa. Consequently, while antiretrovirals are currently available in many African countries, cost constraints have resulted in a relatively small pharmacy whose choices are limited compared with the array available in the developed world.

In 2004, Nigeria received more than US$28 million in the first round of funding by the Global Fund to Fight AIDS, Tuberculosis and Malaria.[42] These funds, largely granted to NACA, provided substantial support for HIV prevention efforts. In 2007, the Nigerian government received a fifth-round award of more than US$46 million to help provide direct support for antiretroviral treatment and care.

The Clinton Foundation, which has been active in supporting HIV/AIDS treatment programs in Africa, has provided funding for the Nigerian ART program since 2006.[43] Through an established collaboration with the government of Nigeria, the Clinton HIV/AIDS Initiative organized for the donation and distribution of antiretrovirals for pediatric patients and certain second-line drugs for adults to ART sites across the country. The initiative also worked with the government and PEPFAR to strengthen the implementation of prevention-of-mother-to-child-transmission programs in the donation of HIV DNA kit assays, which are critical to the diagnosis of HIV infection in exposed babies. The donation of these drugs and laboratory test reagents has allowed the estimated per-patient costs of ART provision for both adults and pediatric patients to drop by 20 percent.

By the end of 2006, the Nigerian ART program had provided drugs to 90,000 patients through an expansion of the government program in conjunction with the substantial scale-up of the PEPFAR-funded sites. The increase of support from multiple sources created the need for more frequent and complex reporting at the level of individual clinical sites. Many of the original 25 federal ART sites also received support from the PEPFAR program, and they continued to participate in the Nigeria ART program with a percentage of patient slots, in which patients received government-provided drugs with monitoring tests provided by PEPFAR. In addition, other patients seen at the same sites received PEPFAR-funded drugs and services.

To achieve the most effective and efficient use of resources, all efforts were made to ensure that the coordinated response followed the principle of Three Ones: one HIV/AIDS action framework that provides the basis for coordinating the work of all partners, one national AIDS coordinating authority that has a broad-based multisectoral mandate, and one national monitoring and evaluation system. The Nigerian ART program fully integrated and implemented treatment to ensure that any distinctions in the source of material or financial support were seamless at the level of the patient and the health care worker.[41]

The United Nations Millennium Development Goals envision universal access to ART for all eligible patients by 2015. Until recently, only 5 percent of the six million people who required antiretrovirals in resource-poor countries could access these drugs.[14] Access to ART rose threefold from 2006 to 2008, however, as a result of major contributions from the massive scaling-up programs supported by PEPFAR; the Global Fund for Tuberculosis, AIDS and Malaria; the World Bank; the Clinton Foundation; and many others.

Nigeria has nearly three million people living with HIV/AIDS, an estimated 800,000 of whom urgently need antiretroviral therapy.[14,25] Clearly, much remains to be done if the country is to achieve its millennium development goals by 2015. The progress thus far suggests, however, that these ambitious goals are feasible.

During the first six years of its existence, the Nigerian National ART Program rapidly increased provision of antiretrovirals to patients in need. The PEPFAR program has also contributed significantly to the nearly exponential increase in patients initiated on antiretrovirals between 2004 and 2008. In early 2008, the number of patients on ART in Nigeria exceeded 269,000 (Figure 1). Assuming that the rate of new HIV infections continues to stabilize or even decreases, at the current rate of ART provision scale-up, the country could well reach its goal of treating 800,000 Nigerians by 2010.

Future Challenges

The review of the history of the AIDS epidemic in Nigeria and the initiation of the treatment and care program demonstrates a compressed timeline during which the government, international donor agencies, and the Nigerian health sector rose to the occasion of an unprecedented health crisis. Despite the significant achievements in monitoring the epidemic and implementing AIDS treatment on a large scale throughout the country, enormous challenges remain. Patients accessing Nigeria's treatment and care programs tend to reside in urban centers, for example; other patients must travel long distances to receive the antiretrovirals and services available at large tertiary-care hospitals.

The health structure of Nigeria is multitiered, with the lower tiers distributed primarily among poor, rural areas. Secondary and primary health centers have more limited infrastructures and staffing and will require significant strengthening and support in order to implement ART programs. Many of these lower-tiered clinics and health centers lack physicians, laboratory technicians, and pharmacists, yet providing such trained personnel on a large scale is unsustainable. Globally, treatment programs throughout resource-poor countries are developing models of task shifting. These new models allow the provision of treatment and care to be streamlined by shifting as necessary the conventional functions of physicians, pharmacists, and nurses.

In 2006 and 2007, the PEPFAR program in Nigeria sought to expand ART services to all local government areas within its target states. Plateau State in the central belt of the country was the Harvard–PEPFAR program's designated "saturation state." The plan was to build upon the significant treatment and care program developed at Jos University Teaching Hospital (JUTH), a federal tertiary-level hospital in the state's capital, and develop secondary hospitals and primary health centers throughout the state, within the 17 representative local government areas. The initiation of the network of satellite sites was preceded by a needs assessment at each of the secondary and primary clinic sites slated to participate. In late 2006, JUTH began training and infrastructure building at six secondary hospitals in Plateau State; each in turn was responsible for developing the capacity of two or three primary health centers in its immediate vicinity (Figure 8).

In 2007, JUTH developed the capacity of another eight secondary hospitals in the state, with an extension to the hospital's two dozen primary satellite health care clinics slated to take place in 2008 and 2009. This effort, spearheaded by John Idoko, a professor at Jos University, has not only resulted in patients from more rural areas gaining access to HIV treatment and care but has also allowed patients to receive care at clinics closer to their homes rather than traveling long distances to Jos. Unlike the typical hub-and-spoke model, this networked approach has allowed one tertiary care hospital to expand access to these programs to 56 hospitals or clinics throughout the state. Although patient numbers at each of the lower-tiered centers are substantially lower than the 10,000 patients provided with ART services at JUTH, the networked model should better serve the patient population. In addition, the model has substantially strengthened the level of health services provided throughout the state.

The need for HIV/AIDS testing and monitoring has created new challenges for physicians, other health care providers, and laboratory investigators. Voluntary counseling and testing, for example, is still based in urban centers and is therefore inaccessible to many Nigerians. New diagnostic tools are needed as well. While the simple rapid test and the new enzyme-linked immunosorbent assay, or ELISA, formats for HIV antibody diagnosis have improved, they remain expensive for Nigerian patients.

Clinical management of HIV infection and therapy requires the regular measurement of CD4+ lymphocytes in the blood. These techniques are costly, however, and require a significant infrastructure to perform. In addition, tests for viral load—an important clinical parameter by which to evaluate the severity of disease and to monitor the efficacy of therapy—not only are expensive but also require complex technologies that have not been previously used in much of the developing world. Fortunately, new methodologies under development are expected to be as sensitive as current ones but much less costly to perform.

Training, capacity building, and infrastructure requirements for HIV diagnosis, intervention, and treatment are also constant needs in Nigeria. These needs promise to become even more dramatic as the country continues its scale-up and rollout of AIDS treatment and care.

Treatment of HIV/AIDS is complex and lifelong. Although triple-drug regimens effectively decrease morbidity and mortality, the drugs' long-term efficacy depends on patient adherence as well as the minimization of drug toxicity. We are still early

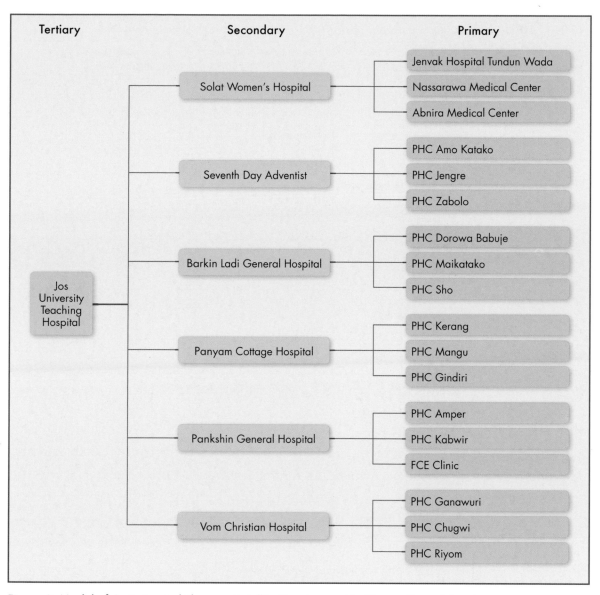

Figure 8. Model of Antiretroviral Therapy Satellite Development in Plateau State, Nigeria

Abbreviations: PHC: primary health center; FCE: Federal College of Education

in our experience with ART in resource-poor countries, although early data suggest that the efficacy of these drugs is high and consistent with clinical trial data from the United States and Europe. Nonetheless, even with best efforts to optimize adherence and minimize drug toxicity, patients will fail their first-line regimens and require

Table 2. Differences in Clinical and Laboratory Requirements Based on Health System Level

Steps in HIV Treatment and Care	Developed World Standard of Care	Tertiary Care Institutions in Africa	Secondary and Primary Clinics in Africa
HIV diagnosis	ELISA test Western blot confirmation	Rapid test ELISA confirmation	Multiple rapid test algorithm
AIDS diagnosis	HIV diagnosis CD4+ cell count Clinical signs	HIV diagnosis CD4+ cell count Clinical signs	HIV diagnosis Clinical signs
Diagnosis of related infections, such as tuberculosis, hepatitis, and PCP	Screen for all agents at baseline	Screen for TB with x-ray and sputum Serology diagnosis for hepatitis viruses	Screen for tuberculosis with clinical exam Monitor with clinical exams
Monitor for drug efficacy	Clinical exam, CD4+ cell count, viral load	Clinical exam, CD4+ cell count, viral load	Clinical exam, CD4+ cell count or hematology
Monitor for drug toxicity	Clinical exam, hematology, clinical chemistry	Clinical exam, hematology, clinical chemistry	Clinical exam, hematology
Evaluate treatment failure	HIV drug resistance	Clinical improvement based on drug regimen switch	Clinical improvement based on drug regimen switch

Abbreviations: ELISA: enzyme-linked immunosorbent assay; PCP: *Pneumocystis carinii* pneumonia

alternative or second-line drugs. The development of drug resistance in patients is the major reason ART regimens fail to provide clinical improvement. In an early assessment of drug resistance in patients failing their first-line regimens, we found that the combination of specific drug-resistance mutations would require 85 percent of such patients to take second-line regimens with the more expensive protease inhibitors. They would also be limited in other drug choices that would allow for an optimal second-line regimen.[44]

In addition, it remains to be seen whether the fact that the HIV circulating in Nigeria is not HIV-1 subtype B will alter the efficacy of these drugs or the rate at which drug resistance develops varies by subtype.[45,46] Early data suggest a 10-to-17-percent baseline resistance to major classes of antiretrovirals in viruses from Nigerian patients who were not taking the drugs.[46] These data also suggest that transmission of drug-resistant virus is already occurring in Nigeria. It is not yet clear, however, whether differences in the viral subtypes in Nigeria have affected the rate of drug resistance development or the transmission of drug-resistant viruses.

Conclusion

Treatment is available to HIV-infected populations in most of the developed world. Effective HIV care and treatment programs are complex, however, and require substantial resources, training, capacity building, and infrastructure development.

The successful implementation of the Nigerian ART program has demonstrated that a rapid scale-up of such programs can be concurrent with efforts to bolster existing health care systems. International agencies have significantly supported the rapid scale-up of the Nigerian program. Yet the long-term sustainability and independence of the program will require increased financial commitments from within Nigeria. The further development of the monitoring and evaluation of the existing national ART program—with ongoing, evidence-based assessments of treatment efficacy—will ensure that the early success of the program will be sustained. The implementation of large-scale intervention programs has also necessitated novel and innovative public health approaches to optimize care and delivery. New, cost-effective techniques for HIV diagnosis, clinical monitoring, and drug resistance testing need to be developed and evaluated.

The early involvement and support of the Nigerian government in the HIV/AIDS campaign laid the groundwork and reflected the strong leadership necessary for the continuation and sustainability of the Nigerian National ART Program. As Nigeria and much of Africa awaits more effective and affordable antiretrovirals, additional scientific research will be necessary to monitor the epidemic, to consider unique aspects of the viruses required for therapeutic intervention, and to develop novel models for scaling up ART services.

By the close of 2008, Nigeria's ART program had succeeded in providing lifesaving drugs and care to more than a quarter of a million Nigerians with AIDS. This remarkable achievement speaks largely to the dedication and resolve of the many thousands of health care providers, the engagement and leadership of the Nigerian government, and the commitment of the international development community. Nigeria has responded to the ominous spread of HIV infection with an approach that couples prevention with antiretroviral treatment and care. Despite the formidable obstacles ahead, progress to date should provide optimism that Nigeria will soon achieve the goal of AIDS treatment to all those in need.

REFERENCES

1. Adeyi O, Kanki PJ, Odutolu O, Idoko JA, eds. *AIDS in Nigeria*. Cambridge, Massachusetts: Harvard Center for Population and Development Studies, 2006.

2. United Nations Development Programme. *Human Development Report 2007/2008*. New York: United Nations Development Programme, 2008:231.

3. World Bank. Gross National Income 2007, Atlas Methods and PPP. World Development Indicators Database of July 1, 2008. Washington, DC: World Bank, 2008. http://siteresources.worldbank.org/ DATASTATISTICS/Resources/GNIPC.pdf; accessed October 28, 2008.

4. National Population Commission of Nigeria. *Population Census of the Federal Republic of Nigeria: Analytic Report at the National Level, 1991*. Abuja: National Population Commission of Nigeria, 1998.

5. National Population Commission of Nigeria. *Population Census of the Federal Republic of Nigeria: Analytic Report at the National Level, 2007*. Abuja: National Population Commission of Nigeria, 2007.

6. Index Mundi. Nigeria life expectancy at birth. http://indexmundi.com/nigeria/life_expectancy_at_birth. html; accessed October 28, 2008.

7. UNAIDS. Epidemiological Fact Sheet on HIV and AIDS: Core Data on Epidemiology and Response. Nigeria, 2008. Geneva: UNAIDS, 2008.

8. UNICEF. At a glance: Nigeria. www.unicef.org/ infobycountry/nigeria.html; accessed October 28, 2008.

9. Gottlieb MS, Schroff R, Schanker HM, Weisman JD, Fan PT, Wolf RA. *Pneumocystis carinii* pneumonia and mucosal candidiasis in previously healthy homosexual men: evidence of a new acquired cellular immunodeficiency. *N Engl J Med,* 1981;305: 1425–1431.

10. Siegal FP, Lopez C, Hammer GS, et al. Severe acquired immunodeficiency in male homosexuals, manifested by chronic perianal ulcerative herpes simplex lesions. *N Engl J Med*, 1981;305:1439–1444.

11. Clumeck N, Mascart-Lemone F, de Maubeuge J, Brenez D, Marcelis L. Acquired immune deficiency syndrome in Black Africans. [Letter] *Lancet*, 1983; 1:642.

12. Nasidi A, Harry TO, Ajose-Coker OO, et al. Evidence of LAV/HTLV III infection and AIDS related complex in Lagos, Nigeria. *II International Conference on AIDS*, Paris, France, June 23–25, 1986 (abstract FR86–3).

13. Kanki PJ. Viral determinants of the HIV/AIDS epidemic in West Africa. *BMJ West Africa Ed*, 2004;7(2): 69–71.

14. UNAIDS. *Report on the Global AIDS Epidemic*. Geneva: UNAIDS, 2008:7.

15. Federal Ministry of Health, Nigeria. *HIV/Syphilis Sero-Prevalence and STD Syndromes Sentinel Survey among PTB and STD Patients in Nigeria, 1991*. Abuja: Federal Ministry of Health, 1991.

16. Federal Ministry of Health, Nigeria. *HIV/Syphilis Sero-Prevalence and STD Syndromes Sentinel Survey among PTB and STD Patients in Nigeria, 1993*. Abuja: Federal Ministry of Health, 1993.

17. Federal Ministry of Health, Nigeria. *HIV/Syphilis Sero-Prevalence and STD Syndromes Sentinel Survey among PTB and STD Patients in Nigeria, 1995*. Abuja: Federal Ministry of Health, 1995.

18. Federal Ministry of Health, Nigeria. *HIV/Syphilis Sero-Prevalence and STD Syndromes Sentinel Survey among PTB and STD Patients in Nigeria, 1999*. Abuja: Federal Ministry of Health, 1999.

19. Federal Ministry of Health, Nigeria. *HIV/Syphilis Sero-Prevalence and STD Syndromes Sentinel Survey among PTB and STD Patients in Nigeria, 2000*. Abuja: Federal Ministry of Health, 2000.

20. Federal Ministry of Health, Nigeria. *HIV/Syphilis Sero-Prevalence and STD Syndromes Sentinel Survey among PTB and STD Patients in Nigeria, 2001*. Abuja: Federal Ministry of Health, 2001.

21. Federal Ministry of Health, Nigeria. *HIV/Syphilis Sero-Prevalence and STD Syndromes Sentinel Survey among PTB and STD Patients in Nigeria, 2003*. Abuja: Federal Ministry of Health, 2003.

22. UNAIDS. *Report on the Global AIDS Epidemic*. Geneva: UNAIDS, 2004:190–191.

23. Federal Ministry of Health, Nigeria. *HIV/Syphilis Sero-Prevalence and STD Syndromes Sentinel Survey among PTB and STD Patients in Nigeria, 2005*. Abuja: Federal Ministry of Health, 2005.

24. Eberstadt N. The future of AIDS. *Foreign Affairs,* 2002;81(6).

25. Federal Ministry of Health, Nigeria. *HIV/Syphilis Sero-Prevalence and STD Syndromes Sentinel Survey among PTB and STD Patients in Nigeria, 2007.* Abuja: Federal Ministry of Health, 2007.

26. Barin F, M'Boup S, Denis F, et al. Serological evidence for virus related to simian T-lymphotropic retrovirus III in residents of West Africa. *Lancet,* 1985;ii: 1387–1390.

27. Kanki P, Mboup S, Ricard D, et al. Human T-lymphotropic virus type 4 and the human immunodeficiency virus in West Africa. *Science,* 1987;236: 827–831.

28. McCutchan FE. Understanding the genetic diversity of HIV-1. *AIDS,* 2000;14:S31–S44.

29. Howard TM, Olaleye DO, Rasheed S. Sequence analysis of the glycoprotein 120 coding region of a new HIV type 1 subtype A strain (HIV-1IbNg) from Nigeria. *AIDS Res Hum Retroviruses,* 1994;10: 1755–1757.

30. Abimiku AG, Stern TL, Zwandor A, et al. Subtype G HIV type 1 isolates from Nigeria. *AIDS Res Hum Retroviruses,* 1994;10:1581–1583.

31. Macilwain C. AIDS: on the brink. *Nature,* 2007; 445:140–143.

32. United Nations. Secretary-General Urges United States Business Leaders to Take Concerted Action Against "Unparalleled Nightmare" of AIDS. Press release, June 1, 2001.

33. United Nations. *Declaration of Commitment on HIV/AIDS.* http://www.un.org/ga/aids/coverage/Final DeclarationHIVAIDS.html; accessed November 9, 2008.

34. Donnelly J. UN chief seeks billions for AIDS. *The Boston Globe,* April 27, 2001:A1.

35. World Bank. Multi-Country HIV/AIDS Program (MAP). http://go.worldbank.org/I3A0B15ZN0; accessed October 28, 2008.

36. Federal Ministry of Health, Nigeria. *National Guidelines for the Use of Antiretroviral Drugs in Nigeria.* Project Document, July 2001.

37. Federal Ministry of Health, Nigeria. *National Guidelines for Voluntary Counseling and Testing (VCT) Services in Nigeria.* Abuja: Federal Ministry of Health, May 2002.

38. Federal Ministry of Health, Nigeria. *National Guidelines on the Implementation of Prevention of Mother to Child Transmission of HIV Programme in Nigeria.* Abuja: Federal Ministry of Health, August 2001.

39. Federal Ministry of Health, Nigeria. *Nigeria: Rapid Assessment of HIV/AIDS Care in the Public and Private Sector.* Abuja: Federal Ministry of Health, August 2004.

40. Idigbe E, Adewole T, Eisen G, et al. Management of HIV-1 infection with a combination of nevirapine + stavudine + lamivudine: a preliminary report on the Nigerian ARV program. *J AIDS,* 2005;40(1):65–69.

41. Office of the Global AIDS Coordinator. *The President's Emergency Plan for AIDS Relief. U.S. Five-Year Global HIV/AIDS Strategy, 2004.* www.pepfar.gov; accessed October 28, 2008.

42. The Global Fund to Fight AIDS, Tuberculosis and Malaria. www.theglobalfund.org; accessed October 28, 2008.

43. Clinton HIV/AIDS Initiative. http://www.clinton foundation.org/what-we-do/clinton-hiv-aids-initiative; accessed October 28, 2008.

44. Chaplin B, Ekong E, Idoko J, et al. HIV drug resistance in patients failing first line ART in Nigeria. *Submitted.*

45. Sankalé J-L, Langevin S, Odaibo G, et al. The complexity of circulating HIV-1 strains in Oyo State, Nigeria. *AIDS Res Hum Retroviruses,* 2007; 23(8):1020–1025.

46. Ojesina AI, Sankalé J-L, Odaibo G, et al. Subtype-specific patterns in HIV-1 reverse transcriptase and protease in Oyo State, Nigeria: implications for drug resistance and host response. *AIDS Res Hum Retroviruses,* 2006:22(8):770–779.

John Idoko, a clinician and a scientist, is principally motivated by his compassion for people who are suffering.

The Chance of a Lifetime

John Donnelly

Professor John Idoko was pleased with the news. The Seventh-Day Adventist Hospital had enrolled 300 of his AIDS patients in just under a year. Of those, 192 were receiving antiretroviral therapy. For Idoko, the news meant his plan was working: small hospitals like this one, as well as health centers, could begin to absorb the growing numbers of AIDS patients, taking pressure off his clinic at Jos University Teaching Hospital in Nigeria's central plateau.

But Idoko, a medical doctor and the principal investigator for a U.S. government–funded Harvard AIDS treatment program in Jos, wanted to know more. Did the hospital have enough laboratory supplies? Were they seeing high numbers of women attending the antenatal clinic? What about their success in preventing HIV transmission during birth?

His hosts said all was well—but they paused on the last question. They said because the hospital charged 2,000 naira, or US$17, per delivery, many women were giving birth in their homes to save money. Traditional birth attendants charged as little as 50 naira, or 40 cents.

"It would be a shame, with all the good work you do here, to allow them to deliver at home—probably with an elderly woman with no schooling doing the delivery," said Idoko, standing amid a half-dozen hospital officials.

Idoko is not a tall man, but his physical presence is felt in a room. The first impression he gives is that he is a serious person. The second, when he smiles, is that he isn't serious all the time. But Idoko wasn't smiling as he stood before the hospital workers. He was focused on the issue of money as a barrier to good health care. "You have the option of charging less to bring in more," he told his rapt audience. "Maybe you could make money that way."

For several moments no one said anything. A hospital doctor finally spoke up, saying the facility needed to cover their costs.

Idoko left in a grumpy mood. It would have been easy for him to focus on the numbers of AIDS patients on treatment—those were the numbers everyone, especially donors, asked about first. But that's not Idoko. He speaks his mind, and if something isn't right, he isn't afraid to say so.

"It's really an eye-opener," Idoko said as he drove away from the hospital, referring to the HIV-positive women who didn't deliver at the hospital. "Many women here are thinking, 'Why should I use the money to deliver my baby, when I can use the money for other things?'"

The issue troubled him for good reason: Nigeria has some of the highest maternal mortality rates in the world—the lifetime risk for women is one in 18—and the country is second only to South Africa in the number of people infected with HIV. For hours, Idoko kept thinking about those women who might pass the deadly virus to their babies for the lack of a few dollars. Those who know him well say he has such preoccupations often.

"He is doing this work from his heart, not just his head," said Professor Adetokunbo Lucas, a Nigerian medical doctor and one of the world's sages on global health. "His head is very good, but his heart provides the support for the head. He is a very bright scientist and clinician, but behind all of that is a compassion for the sick, especially

John Idoko pauses in front of the maternity clinic at the primary health center in Jengre, Nigeria.

the poor who are sick and who do not normally catch the attention of a distinguished person like John Idoko."

Early Defiance

John Alechenu Idoko rose from humble beginnings. He was born in a village called Aigaji in the north-central part of Nigeria in 1950—a time when the country's population was estimated at 32 million people, just one-fifth of what it is today. He was the second of eight children born to his mother, Agnes; the first-born, a boy, died at age two, elevating John Idoko as the oldest child in what would become a long line of children. His father, Francis Idoko Adole, a policeman, would end up with three wives and 28 children.

"I came out of a traditional African culture," Idoko recalled from his home in Jos. "It was a rural setting, and people had to till the farmland. That meant you needed more people to till the land, and that meant you needed more wives, who had more children."

He can now laugh when he explains his father's way of life. But when he was in secondary school, he didn't find it a laughing matter. He disagreed with the polygamous culture—in part because he believed then, as he would many years later, that Nigeria needed to reduce its birth rate in order to prosper and preserve the environment. In the late 1960s, when he was still a teenager, he confronted his father.

"I was very hard on my dad," Idoko said. "I called him and his wives together and told him, 'You don't need all these wives and all these children.' They drove me from the house."

Father and son did not speak for several years, and the son's upbraiding apparently did not change the ways of the elder Idoko, whose last child was born in 1989. (His legacy, though, was not just in the number of children, but in the education of the children; as many as 21 of them either have a university education or are in line to get one.)

Looking back on the confrontation, John Idoko regretted how it affected his relationship with his father, who died in 1995. But he also saw it as a turning point in which he defined himself: he would be an independent thinker who would freely express his thoughts.

"I wanted to send the message to my father that I am a major supporter of family planning," Idoko said. "What we need here in Nigeria is quality, not quantity. When I hear Nigeria has 150 million people, I don't get excited because I know that means 150 million problems."

Idoko left his home of Benue State for Ahmadu Bello University Medical School in Zaria, located in Nigeria's Muslim-dominated north. A serious student, he chose to become a doctor because he believed it to be a noble profession—and because he had witnessed one doctor's life. In Otukpo, a town ten kilometers from his village, the local doctor would drive his "long car" through town. As the boys and girls called out to him, the doctor would beep his horn back. "He was so popular," Idoko recalled.

In his third year in medical school, in 1975, a colleague lent Idoko's books to a first-year student named Lucy Ogenyi. She was just one of eight women in a class of

60 pre-med students. The two met one day when Idoko retrieved his books; three years later they married. Even some 30 years later, she remembered him clearly in their first meetings. He was in his mid-20s and she called him a talker. "He talked a lot about books and medicine," she said. "He could talk for hours on end."

Overhearing this, Idoko tried to defend himself, feigning hurt: "Books can be really interesting."

Lucy continued: "I knew right then he was going into immunology or infectious diseases because all he would do was talk, talk, talk about it."

Idoko graduated and indeed did start work as an infectious disease doctor at the university hospital. Soon after, Lucy had their first of four children. She considered an internship in pediatrics, but an incident one night helped change her mind.

"John was on call that night," she said. "We had ten people living with us in the flat. Our baby was crying, and someone came to our door. They had a six-month-old baby, and that baby passed on. It was hard for me to take it in."

After feeling such remorse from one death, she wanted to choose a path that would not include many, many more deaths. She decided to go into public health, instead of medicine, as her husband delved even deeper into immunology and took a fellowship at the London School of Hygiene & Tropical Medicine in 1986. But just a few months after he left, religious tension between the Muslims and Christians erupted into riots. Many people were killed, and Lucy took their children to Jos.

Several months later, Idoko joined his family. He became an associate professor and physician at Jos University Teaching Hospital. He and Lucy liked Jos almost immediately. The higher altitude, at nearly 4,000 feet, meant the city was more temperate than most of Nigeria. Life was calm then in Jos as well; tension fueled by religious strife would come only years later.

They were just settling into their lives until one night when a virus, HIV, unsettled them.

Tackling the Epidemic

That night came in 1990, when a police officer knocked on their door. "He said the hospital had admitted a patient with HIV," Idoko recalled. "The police had seized the patient's passport, and then they had locked him up."

John Idoko talks with AIDS clinicians near the Seventh Day Adventist Hospital in Jengre.

Idoko grew angry. "I asked the officer, what is his crime? The officer had no answer. They eventually released him, but that's how much fear and ignorance about the virus was around in those days."

The first three HIV cases in Jos were all miners from Mali and Côte d'Ivoire. But in the next years, Idoko began seeing more and more patients infected with HIV. Finally, in 1995, he approached hospital administrators to ask for space to start an AIDS clinic. The administrators had no place to offer, so Idoko made his office the clinic.

That year, he also decided to form a nongovernmental organization called HaltAIDS, which began spreading HIV prevention messages in hole-in-the-wall bars on Saturday nights and in the back alleys of Jos where street vendors hawked all kinds of meat. "I realized you can affect many more people by getting out into the community," Idoko said. "You can really galvanize people by using volunteers and by organizing support groups with people from the community."

It also was a very public sign that Idoko, even as his job at the hospital was getting busier, would embrace more responsibility outside the hospital. He seemed to have an ability to take on more work at a time when others would shrink from it, gathering more energy as the stakes grew higher.

And the stakes were rising for Idoko and the others doctors, nurses, and health workers around him. By the turn of the century, HIV was spreading at a frightening rate in Nigeria and in much of sub-Saharan Africa. Idoko managed to sign onto four drug trials, which supplied antiretrovirals to several hundred patients.

But it was a few hundred among many thousands, and the price—several hundred U.S. dollars a month—was still too expensive for most. Adult wards at his hospital were overflowing with patients with full-blown AIDS. Untold numbers of people under his care—and under the care of other doctors—were dying because they didn't have the money to buy antiretrovirals.

But help was coming. In 2003, the AIDS Prevention Initiative in Nigeria, a Bill & Melinda Gates Foundation–funded project run by the Harvard School of Public Health, helped develop a laboratory and treatment center. The following year, the U.S. President's Emergency Plan for AIDS Relief, or PEPFAR, began spending tens of millions of dollars on antiretroviral treatments throughout Nigeria, including Jos. That funding allowed the Nigerian government to reduce the price of the drugs to just a handful of dollars per month; by 2005, the government made the treatment free for everyone.

Idoko was no longer spending most of his time seeing AIDS patients. He was now managing the program, which was growing with dozens of new patients every week. He no longer had to worry much about the supply of drugs to patients, but he instead faced many other headaches. Waiting times had grown terribly, and patients were arriving at the clinic as early as five in the morning in hopes that they wouldn't have to spend the whole day waiting to see a doctor or a nurse.

And so Idoko and Professor Phyllis Kanki—principal investigator for the Harvard–PEPFAR programs in Nigeria, Tanzania, and Botswana—scrambled to expand their space and staff in an attempt to stay ahead of the demand. Since 2003, they have added space to the operation almost every year. In 2008, they oversaw the biggest expansion: the construction of a two-story building next door to the current clinic that nearly doubled the size of their space. They needed every square foot, Idoko said. After starting with just a few dozen patients in 2003, the clinic, with well over a hundred staff members, was treating more than 10,000 patients just five years later.

Design for Life

Idoko's most revolutionary initiative, though, may have had nothing to do with blueprints for new buildings. Instead, it may have started with a sketch on a legal pad for a new model of care. Idoko's plan was to decentralize the treatment of patients, sending hundreds from his tertiary hospital to district hospitals such as the Seventh-Day Adventist Hospital in Jengre.

Idoko drew his tiered network system on a pad of paper, giving names to the categories of care. "Here, we have our hospital—I call that the Cadillac," Idoko said, chuckling. "That's the hub. The general or district hospitals are Volkswagens. The primary health care clinics are the bicycles."

Below that, he explained, still drawing, were the community health care centers, which he called the "donkeys." At the bottom of his rung were home and family, or, in his words, "the foot."

"What we want to do," he said, "is to take the services to where people live." Asked whether he believed health workers at some centers would appreciate their workplaces being called a "donkey," Idoko laughed. "Well, they have donkeys in the villages," he said, holding his palms upward as if this were an obvious name for the tiny health outposts. "All of these parts to the system are very important—and the donkeys are small centers, sometimes one room."

Donkeys they would stay. The system was just one of several that he and Kanki had implemented over the last several years.

The other changes—decentralizing the prevention-of-mother-to-child-transmission-of-HIV services, changing to an electronic record system, and allowing patients who were doing well to see a doctor every three to six months, instead of monthly—had become models for others around the continent to emulate. African clinicians and hospital administrators had traveled to Jos to learn from a program that could trace its roots to that night in 1990 in which Idoko liberated a man with HIV from jail.

Dr. Patricia Agaba, who trained under Idoko as a medical student and later became site coordinator of the PEPFAR site in Jos, said that Idoko has kept an open mind about the program from the start. It means, she said, that the ideas of many people have influenced the course of the initiative.

"He's very approachable," she said of Idoko. "He's ready to listen to an idea no matter its source, whether you're a cleaner, a professor, or a senior nurse. He pays a lot of attention to detail; he's quite academic. But his style of leadership is that he gives you a free hand. He asks you to do a task, and then he lets you do it."

One of his most endearing traits, she said, is that he's not always serious. "He cracks jokes all the time—even with patients," she said.

But running not so deep under Idoko's playfulness is that serious side—the side that Lucy Ogenyi grasped at once several decades ago. Over the years, he had developed a keen sense of purpose married to a growing set of tasks.

Nurturing the Future

One day in the middle of 2008, Idoko was juggling his usual heavy number of demands—looking for ways to cut his budget as he was running a deficit; getting ready for the international AIDS conference in Mexico City; overseeing the construction of his new headquarters; and thinking about how the hospital in Jengre could lower the price of deliveries of babies in order to attract more women.

But he also was thinking about something completely unrelated to treating AIDS patients—his hobby, as he called it. Back in his home village of Aigaji, Idoko had planted 15,000 stands of palm trees. He was in the midst of turning the nursery into a business and employing a few dozen people.

"I needed a challenge outside medicine," he said. The nursery provided him with an excuse to return to his home village every month or two—and a way to give back to his community. He had already helped fund the building of a school there, and he had taken a young man from the village to Jos, where he was attending university and living with the Idoko family.

"Do you know what that means to the boy? A little difference in his life really helps," Idoko said, smiling broadly. "It gives him a chance."

A chance—that's what he had received, that's what he could give to the young man staying with his family, that's what he wanted for his AIDS patients. It drove Idoko, this idea of a chance in life. Nothing could be more important. ∎

The most difficult part of Asabe Sati Andrew's work is having to tell people they are infected with HIV.

The Burden of Proof

JOHN DONNELLY

ASABE SATI ANDREW spotted the girl in the crowded waiting room of the AIDS treatment clinic for mothers and children at Jos University Teaching Hospital. She motioned her to enter a tiny office. The girl and her father followed.

Sati, who counsels children at the hospital's program through the AIDS Prevention Initiative in Nigeria, or APIN, greeted them and soon got right to the point.

"Do you know why your daddy brought you here?" Sati asked ten-year-old Loveth Samuel.

Loveth said no.

"No?" Sati said, her voice rising in surprise. She turned to Samuel Mutring, the father. "You didn't tell her?"

The father said he hadn't.

"We always tell parents that even if we think the children don't know what's going on, they know," Sati said. "They look at the Internet, they talk to each other. Don't deny her of her right to know."

The father agreed, and Sati began to tell the girl that she was about to have an HIV test. "Your daddy loves you so much," Sati said, taking the girl's hands and leaning closer to her. "He shows that by wanting you to know all about your health status. Here is where we do HIV tests. Do you know what HIV is?"

And so it went—direct information, delivered with eye contact, while holding the child's hand. It is something she has done hundreds of times—telling children from the age of ten and older about the basics of HIV, about the HIV test, and about the two possible results—you're either positive or negative.

"It's hard talking to children about this," Sati said one morning during a rare quiet moment. "God usually helps me. My experience does as well."

She meant her experience with HIV. In 2004, she learned she was positive and soon after started treatment administered by APIN staff. The antiretroviral therapy has kept her healthy, pushing her CD4+ count to nearly 500 and depressing her viral load to undetectable levels. But Sati didn't simply progress from depression to joy. She has had lots of turbulence in her life, mirroring her work at the AIDS center with children and their families.

Sati, the mother of three daughters and expecting a fourth baby, grew up as the middle child in a family of four boys and three girls. Both her parents worked in relatively low-level jobs in the state government in Jos, on the country's high central plateau—her father a steward, her mother a cleaner. But her father died when she was just six years old, creating great financial difficulties for the family—and greatly influencing Sati's life. After finishing secondary school, she wanted to continue her education, but had no money. Then a man arrived with an offer: become his second wife, he said, and he would pay for future schooling.

She agreed, but he didn't keep his word. Instead, he moved Sati to East Africa, where he had taken a job. There, she had two children and lost touch with her family in Nigeria. She felt imprisoned, so she plotted an escape. She persuaded a friend's husband, a pilot, to take her and her children back to Nigeria on a cargo flight.

Back in Nigeria, she started rebuilding her life. She enrolled in Plateau State Polytechnic, studying public administration. She took another class in computer

training. She found a church she loved—
EYN Church of the Brethren. And in the
church band, she also found a man to
love—Andrew Mwada Mshelia.

They made plans to get married, but
one issue troubled Sati. She didn't know
her HIV status. She felt fine. But she also
hadn't tested herself in several years.

In April 2004, her test came back
positive—only she wouldn't believe it. "I
thought this was not possible," she said.
Three months later, she went for a second
test. The result was the same. Now she
believed, and now she had to tell Mshelia.

"I stopped hiding it," she said, remem-
bering that moment. "I told him that day
that he should do the test." Mshelia went,
and he learned he was infected as well.
Both started treatment together.

In 2004, Sati learned she was infected with HIV.

"One thing we had was faith," Sati said.
"We comforted ourselves. We don't look at ourselves as sick. Some people may give
up when they hear the news. They may look at HIV as the end of the world. But we
did not. There is still life with HIV."

"For us," said Mshelia, "the news was hard, but at the end of the day, we needed
to know."

They married, and they began taking antiretroviral drugs twice a day. APIN
hired Sati as a counselor in its mother-and-child clinic in Jos. In 2004, the program
received a huge boost when the U.S. President's Emergency Plan for AIDS Relief, or
PEPFAR, provided a multi-million dollar commitment. By May 2008, that funding
had enabled the Jos University Teaching Hospital site to administer AIDS treatment
to more than 10,800 adults and children.

At the clinic, it was hard to miss Sati. It was mid-2008, before APIN expanded
into larger quarters, and the tiny waiting room and hallway outside Sati's office was

Sati finds strength through her faith and her family.

packed each morning with women and children. Babies wailed. Nurses called out names. Mothers whispered together as they listened for their names.

Sati, who often wears traditional dresses in vibrant colors, moved around the room with purpose. She was nonstop movement, in fact—from doctors' offices, to the laboratory, to her cramped office, ushering mothers and children one by one into the counseling quarters. Her eight-hour day took on a certain rhythm. She called out patients who had been referred to her by a doctor, or were coming to test their children. She also saw older children to make sure they were taking their drugs every day on schedule.

"Some children are so fed up with taking drugs," said Sati, who earns about US$215 a month. "So I ask them, 'What do you want to be when you grow up?' They tell me they want to be a footballer, or a doctor, or a teacher. I tell them, 'If you want to be that footballer, you have to take your drugs.' I ask them if they want to die and leave their mommy and daddy."

"That's when they say, 'No!'" she said, shouting out the word and laughing. "So I tell them, 'Take your drugs or else you could die.'"

She had one boy, Theophilus Stephen, 15, waiting to see her. She began by asking him closely about taking his antiretrovirals.

"How do you take your drugs?" she asked.

"I take them morning and night—seven and seven," he said.

"Have you missed any days?"

"No."

"Are you sure?"

"Yes."

She looked at him for several seconds to test his answer.

"Who reminds you to take the drugs?"

"My uncle and grandmother."

Theophilus, she learned, had lost his mother when he was just seven years old. His father had remarried and didn't want him in his house. The boy had been so sick in the previous year that he spent nearly six months at Plateau Hospital. His body had become skeletal. Even now, while he seemed healthy, he still wasn't fully himself. He remained thin; his weight was 37 kilograms, or 81 pounds. His CD4+ count, once a dangerously low 14 in 2007, had climbed, less than a year later, to 75.

Sati reverted to her favorite question. "What do you want to be when you grow up?" she asked.

"A doctor," Theophilus said.

"If you don't take your drugs, no way you can be a doctor," she said. "You can die on the road if you don't take your drugs."

The boy's eyes widened just a touch; she had his attention.

In the counseling sessions with mothers, she was less dramatic—but intense nonetheless. She talked to each mother for about ten minutes, always stressing that they should be prepared for either result of the test. The news, she told them, would be ready at 1:30 that afternoon.

At the appointed time, they were sitting outside her door.

Now, no one was talking. Everyone was worrying about what was to come.

With blood-test results in hand from the laboratory, Sati walked into her office, and began calling in women and children.

A mother and child entered alone. Sati closed the door behind them.

"Are you ready?" Sati asked Salome Odeh, 33, who was awaiting results on her 18-month-old son, David. The boy was asleep on her back, held tightly in place by a cloth wrapped around her body. Odeh had been through the prevention-of-mother-to-child-transmission program, which aims to halt the transmission of HIV during birth and through breastfeeding. Four earlier tests had shown that David was negative, but a fifth one was required, at 18 months, just to be sure.

"Do you remember what I said earlier—that there could be only two results?" Sati said.

The woman nodded.

"David is negative," Sati said.

"Thank God! Thank God! God is great!" Odeh said, clenching her fists and closing her eyes. Tears flowed as she continued to praise God. She thanked Sati quietly, tried to collect herself, stole a look at her boy over her shoulder, and was gone.

Another mother and child entered. The result was the same—negative—and the woman leapt out of her chair she was so happy.

Asimawu Sadiq, 32, and her fifth born, 18-month-old Safiyanu, entered. But now Sati didn't ask a question right away. Instead, she shuffled through her papers, again and again.

"This is the final test, isn't it, Madam?" Sati said, looking at Sadiq, pausing again. "It shows that he is positive."

The mother looked blankly at Sati for several seconds. Then her lip quivered, her head dropped, and she started to weep.

Sati waited a few moments.

"Madam, what are you going to do next?"

Sadiq said she didn't know.

"Tomorrow, you are going to come back here and we will open a file for the child and start taking care of him," Sati said. "We will take a blood test to see if he needs to go on treatment. Madam, we will now help you take care of him. What about your other children, and your husband? Can you discuss taking an HIV test with them?"

The woman said she wasn't sure—especially about her husband.

"It is better to know your status," Sati said.

"I know," said the woman.

"Okay," Sati said. "Please come tomorrow. You will have calmed down, settled down, and we can start looking after the boy."

The woman nodded and left. Sati seemed deflated.

"That's what I face every day," she said. "When I first started my job, when they cried, I cried with them. Now when they cry, I just wait. Then we can talk. When they come in for the results, some have tears of joy, others have tears of pain."

She walked out to the waiting room.

"Loveth Samuel!"

She was looking for the ten-year-old girl who had come with her father.

Both appeared at her office door. They entered, and the father swung the door shut.

Sati looked straight at Loveth.

"When I told you about the results, I said it would be either negative or positive, didn't I?" Sati said. "There are only two possible results, right?"

The girl nodded.

"The result is negative," Sati said.

The girl's face revealed nothing. Her father bowed his head, and put his hand on his face.

"It means you do not have the virus," Sati told Loveth. "Do you understand? Are you happy?"

"Yes," the girl said.

Sati warned her against sharing razor blades with anyone else, and she told Loveth's father that he should test his other two children.

"I will," he said. "Thank you. I am very happy." But Samuel Mutring seemed subdued—and perhaps for good reason. He was still awaiting the results of his own HIV test.

They left, and Sati continued her roll call, bringing in people, shutting the door, and preparing them for the news. She reminded each that it could be just one of two answers. Pretty simple. Either positive or negative. Then she gave the verdict. ∎

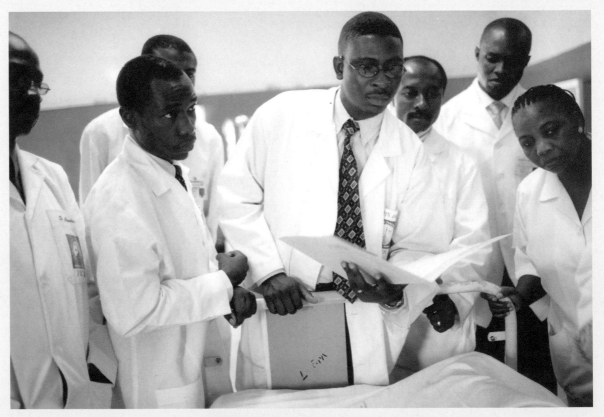

Physicians at Jos University Teaching Hospital consult with a patient on rounds.

A Gift of Time

John Donnelly

W E ALL HAVE SOMEONE. Someone with AIDS who touched us deeply and stayed with us, perhaps becoming a motivation, consciously or unconsciously, to do something. My someone is Hajara Abubakar.

I met Hajara in April 2001 at Jos University Teaching Hospital as I followed Dr. John Idoko on his rounds. In Ward 3, Idoko had stood by her bedside and gazed down at her. She weighed 61 pounds. Hajara waved a bone-thin finger at the doctor, motioning him to move close. She started to whisper, and Idoko put his ear near her mouth.

"I'm trying to find money for the drugs," she said. "I don't have enough."

Only a few days earlier, at an AIDS summit in the Nigerian capital of Abuja, Kofi Annan, then the United Nations secretary-general, had announced plans to start a multibillion-dollar fund to fight AIDS, tuberculosis, and malaria. He told African leaders that the commitment primarily meant working toward the goal of giving every person with AIDS access to life-extending antiretroviral drugs.

I was a reporter with *The Boston Globe,* and I was just starting to write about AIDS in Africa. Annan's visionary speech was fresh in my mind as I looked at Hajara.

It was painful to look. I knew neither Annan nor any world leader could save her or anyone else with full-blown AIDS in hospitals around the continent that day. His help would come in a few years. She needed help in a few days. All I could do was listen to her, as Idoko went to see his other patients. And so I bent close, as Idoko had, and she told her story with great difficulty.

She said her husband had died, presumably from an AIDS-related illness, though he had never tested for the virus. She said she would sometimes look at herself in a mirror and not recognize the image. "I think it's not me," she said. "I think it's a dying person."

Her family had rallied around her, pooling their savings—US$147—so she could buy drugs. But it wasn't enough to buy even that month's supply.

Two weeks later, my story from Jos appeared on the front page of the newspaper, with a picture of Hajara. She was sitting up in bed. Her mouth was open and at first glance it looked like she was smiling. But she wasn't. Her eyes gave her away. They were staring blankly at a point in the distance. Her mouth was open in pain. She could barely sit up. At the end of the story, I wrote that her family hadn't come up with enough money to buy drugs for a month.

She was US$139 short.

In the following days, readers sent cards and checks to an AIDS treatment fund for patients in Jos that had been set up by the AIDS Prevention Initiative in Nigeria at the Harvard School of Public Health. More than US$10,000 arrived, mostly in small donations. Some readers sent in as little as US$10. One person mailed US$139. People wanted to save Hajara.

Just days after the article appeared, Idoko, after hearing that money was being donated to the AIDS fund, tried to find her. She had left the hospital. He learned she had died in her village.

Months later, the Harvard and Jos project leaders held a small ceremony at the hospital to acknowledge and give praise to the readers' donations for treatment of patients. They put the money in a fund to buy drugs. The gift was a gesture of extraordinary kindness to a situation that inspired outrage.

The money had a big impact on those in Jos. "The way we looked at it was if all those people from the outside were so inspired and so helpful to us, it was a real inspiration to move ahead," Idoko said years afterward. "That really moved the project forward."

Since that time, I have returned three times to Jos and each time I've gone to see Idoko and his AIDS treatment program. With each visit, something new amazes me. At first it was that people had come to his program in droves, after treatment became affordable. Then I saw that all the surrounding hospitals and clinics were offering services to prevent mother-to-child transmission of HIV during birth. And in 2008, during my most recent visit, his clinic was being run with an efficiency that would make any U.S. hospital proud—and it was filled with healthy-looking people.

AIDS clinics had become wellness clinics. AIDS had become a chronic disease like cancer and diabetes. Satellite clinics, not just central hospitals, were now treating patients. Patients were coming in every three to six months to see a doctor, not every month.

AIDS was about managing an illness. Hajara's misfortune, along with that of millions of others, was that the revolution of treatment had come too late for her.

On my last visit, I met a man who had started treatment in April 1999—two years before my visit with Hajara. The man, a health worker who didn't want his name revealed, and his family had somehow come up with enough money to buy drugs intermittently from 1999 to 2002, when the price dropped dramatically. Since 2002, he had taken antiretrovirals daily.

Without the drugs, he said, "I would have been gone long ago. I wouldn't be alive today. With the help of God and drugs, I've been able to have a few more years."

He then corrected himself: "*Many* more years."

I've been thinking about his words. In 1999, those who could buy antiretrovirals lived, and those who couldn't died. The inequity couldn't have been clearer. Now, treatment is free; inequity of wealth no longer plays the defining role in whether someone lives. That progress has been starkly drawn for me and for many others. Just seven years earlier Hajara Abubakar had whispered for help, all the way to her grave. I hear her still. ■

The HIV/AIDS Epidemic in NIGERIA

a photo essay by Dominic Chavez

Access to treatment has
lifted the death sentence
for hundreds of thousands
of Nigerians living with
HIV/AIDS. Even so, the
stigma of the disease continues to permeate society,
and patients receiving
lifesaving treatment
are not always willing
to be identified.

Nigeria's national antiretroviral therapy program began in 2002 at 25 federal medical centers. Two years later, PEPFAR, the U.S. President's Emergency Plan for AIDS Relief, supplemented the Nigerian government's efforts to provide free antiretrovirals and clinical monitoring to people living with HIV/AIDS. Jos University Teaching Hospital has already provided antiretrovirals to more than 10,000 patients.

Prevention of mother-to-child transmission of HIV is a cornerstone of efforts to combat the AIDS epidemic in Africa. In Nigeria, millions of pregnant women need HIV testing as part of their prenatal care. Antiretrovirals taken during pregnancy and at birth can dramatically reduce the risk of transmission to infants.

Dedicated doctors, nurses, counselors, and laboratory workers are critical to the success of antiretroviral therapy. Zuweira Hassan, a physician at Jos University Teaching Hospital, is beloved by her patients for both her skill and her devotion.

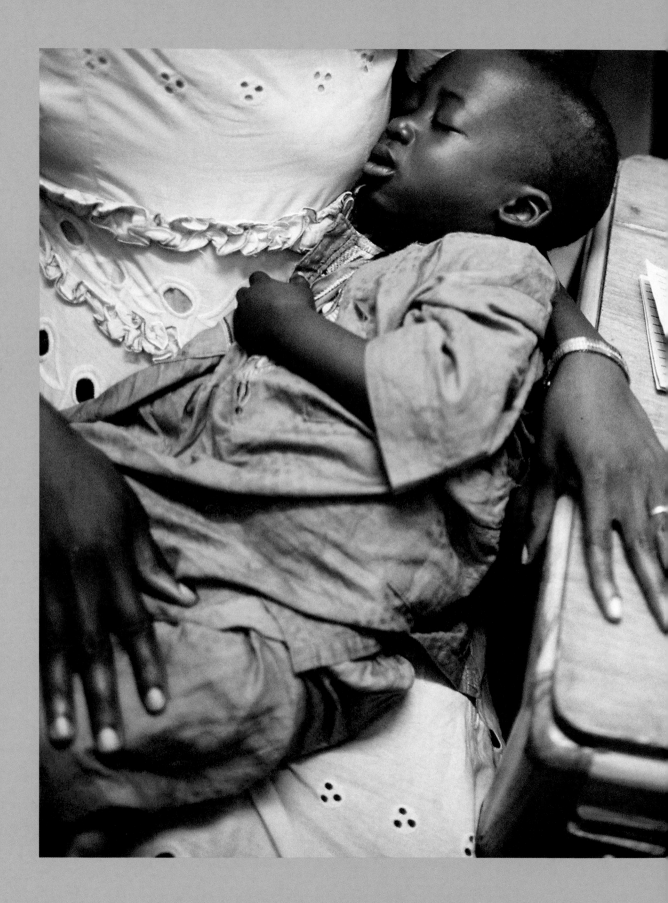

Identifying HIV infection in children is complex. The infants of HIV-infected women require a special diagnostic test, as the babies may still carry maternal antibodies to the virus, and older children often have coinfections that may make it difficult for physicians to tease out symptoms.

Nearly three million Nigerians are infected with HIV, and as many as 800,000 need treatment. Six years after the Nigerian National Antiretroviral Therapy Program began—and four years after support from the U.S. President's Emergency Plan for AIDS Relief arrived—Jos University Teaching Hospital continues to serve AIDS patients in desperate need of antiretrovirals.

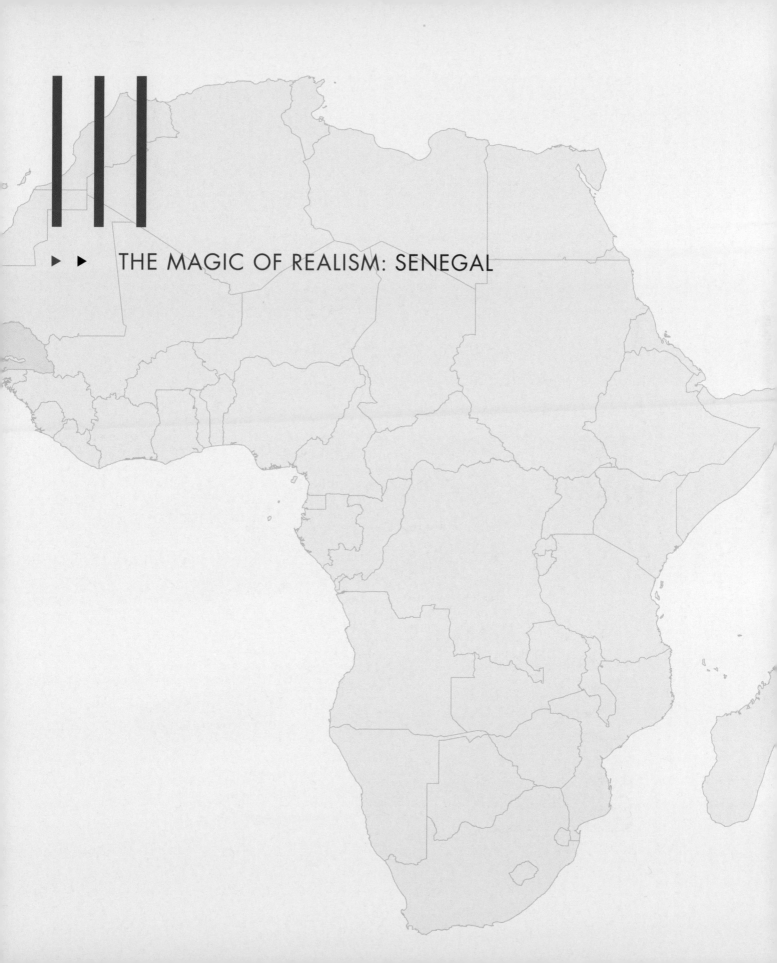

▶ ▶ THE MAGIC OF REALISM: SENEGAL

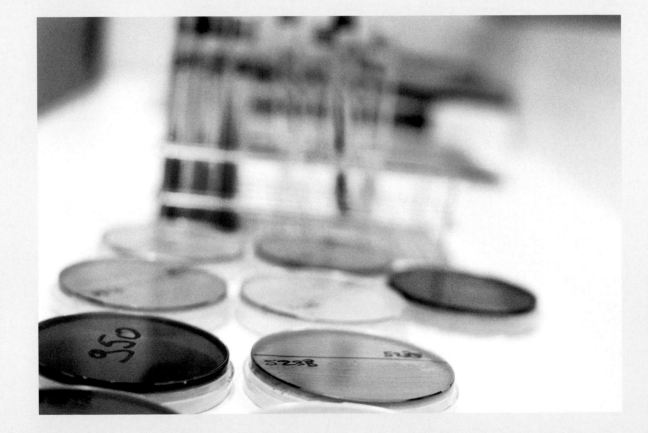

The Magic of Realism

B AOBABS, SOME HUNDREDS of years old, are venerable features of
the Senegalese landscape. With gnarled branches that stretch
skyward and yet resemble roots, the trees look upside-down, as if
planted in the stars. To the people of Senegal, the baobab symbolizes
both life and death.

When AIDS cast the long shadow of death across Africa, Senegal
remained rooted in the magic of realism, confronting the epidemic
with the strength and durability of the baobab. And the country's
pragmatism has paid off: for more than two decades, despite its status
as one of the world's poorest countries, Senegal has maintained one of
the lowest HIV infection rates in sub-Saharan Africa.

The country's success derives from many critical ingredients.
Among them has been a clear-eyed vision of the epidemic instead of

the denial and delay that left so many other African nations vulnerable to viral devastation.

"We started early," says Professor Awa Marie Coll-Seck, the country's former health minister. "Our government never asked us to hide the figures. At the same time, we had friends working in other countries who were almost going to jail because they said, 'I have a case in my clinic.'"

Senegal became one of the first African nations to benefit from the early involvement of political leaders. Then-President Abdou Diouf launched an anti-AIDS campaign in 1986, before the virus had a chance to become dangerously entrenched in the population. He encouraged civic organizations and Muslim and Christian religious leaders to raise awareness of AIDS, and he used the media and schools to promote safe-sex messages.

The country has also benefited from strong leadership within the scientific community. When Professor Souleymane Mboup, then a researcher at the University of Dakar, launched an international AIDS research collaboration in 1985, his single-room laboratory held a battered microscope, a collection of mouth pipettes, and a lone Bunsen burner. The electricity often failed. Laboratory workers prepared microscope slides on a makeshift, foil-covered countertop, and they used ice shavings to protect fragile cells.

Today, the laboratory, fully stocked with state-of-the-art equipment, has grown into the largest and most advanced AIDS biomedical facility in West Africa. And the collaboration—the Inter-University Convention, comprising scientists from Université Cheikh Anta Diop in Senegal, the Harvard School of Public Health in the United States, and the universities of Tours and Limoges in France—conducts Africa's longest-running AIDS research study. Together the scientists examine the biological and epidemiological characteristics of both HIV-1, the human immunodeficiency virus that has caused a worldwide epidemic, and HIV-2, the second AIDS virus, whose spread has been largely limited to West Africa.

Another factor in the country's success has been the practice of allowing sex workers to remain semi-legal as long as they are registered and receiving health care. For more than two decades, scientists and clinicians in the Inter-University Convention have worked closely with cohorts of registered sex workers in several cities. This unusual collaboration has helped the women stay healthy and allowed the researchers to track both the course of the epidemic within the country and the course of the viruses within individuals.

Senegal has since approached its AIDS treatment programs with the same kind of pragmatism it used in designing its HIV prevention initiatives. In 1998, far in advance of international donor support, the country's national AIDS program, Programme National de Lutte Contre le SIDA, launched the Initiative Senegalese for Access to Antiretrovirals, or ISAARV. The Senegalese government contributed US$600,000 to the effort, enough to support treatment of fewer than a hundred patients for one year.

The pilot program consumed a significant portion of the country's health budget. Yet the vision was long range; the program's strategic goals were to develop an infrastructure for providing antiretroviral therapy and its eventual integration into the existing health care system. The government had made an investment not just in the future of those patients, but in the future of all its infected citizens.

That investment has paid off. The program demonstrated the feasibility of delivering antiretroviral therapy in an African setting. And two years later, when UNAIDS granted Senegal accelerated access to antiretrovirals, the country was poised to expand the program. The number of Senegalese receiving therapy has since climbed from 980 in 2002 to 8,500 in 2008. Senegal has overcome the restrictions of poverty to pass the major milestone of providing antiretroviral therapy to more than half its citizens in need. ■

▶ OVERVIEW

The Challenge and Response in Senegal

Phyllis J. Kanki

EARLY IN THE AIDS CRISIS IT BECAME CLEAR THAT SENEGAL CARRIED AN UNUSUAL double burden—not one but two AIDS epidemics, from two distinct types of human immunodeficiency viruses. Yet that double burden has yielded a double blessing as well: early devotion to laboratory research helped buttress early efforts at prevention. Senegal's strong government and exceptional scientific leadership joined forces to keep either epidemic from flourishing.

Senegal is now viewed as a model country for its response to the AIDS crisis. Not only has its scientifically based, pragmatic approach helped it maintain one of the lowest HIV infection rates in Africa, but its bold measures have ensured that poverty would not limit the treatment options of its infected citizens. And the contributions of Senegal's research community have helped shape our understanding of the AIDS epidemic in Africa and bolstered efforts to provide effective HIV prevention and treatment.

Economic and Social Background

Nearly 13 million people live in the Republic of Senegal. Although over 70 percent of the population resides in rural areas, more than 2 million Senegalese are concentrated

135 ◄

in the coastal capital city of Dakar, on the westernmost point of the continent. The country spans some 76,000 square miles, from the coastline along the Atlantic Ocean to the western Sahel.

More than 20 ethnic groups inhabit the country. The Wolof are the largest group, at 43 percent; the Peul and Toucouleur compose the second largest at 24 percent. Ninety-five percent of Senegalese are Muslim, with approximately 4 percent Christian and 1 percent practicing other religions. French is the official language, though 94 percent of the population speak Wolof. The major industry is food processing.[1]

This former French colony became independent in 1960 with the election of the first president, Leopold Senghor. When he retired two decades later, his designated successor, Abdou Diouf, assumed the presidency and served for four consecutive terms, from 1981 to 2000. Abdoulaye Wade was elected president in 2000 and re-elected for a second term in 2007. The marabouts, religious leaders of the various Senegalese Muslim brotherhoods, also carry considerable political clout in the country.

With one of the more democratic, stable, and peaceful post-colonial transitions in Africa, Senegal has enjoyed significant international donor support. Both its history of peace and stability and its strong international stewardship have ensured that, despite its relatively small population, Senegal exerts considerable political influence on the continent.

In 1994, with the support of the international donor community, Senegal initiated a bold economic reform. This reform began with a 50 percent devaluation of Senegal's currency, the CFA franc, which had a fixed rate based on the former French franc and more recently on the Euro. From 1995 to 2001, as a result of the reform, government price controls and subsidies were progressively diminished and growth in the gross domestic product steadily increased by nearly 5 percent annually. Under the International Monetary Fund's Highly Indebted Poor Countries debt relief program, Senegal has benefited from the eradication of two-thirds of its bilateral, multilateral, and private-sector debt. The economic foreign aid to Senegal in 2007 was an estimated US$477 million.[1]

Senegal is considered a low-development country (Table 1). In its *2007/2008 Human Development Report,* the United Nations Development Programme (UNDP) ranked Senegal 156 out of 177 member states.[2] In 2007, the World Bank estimated Senegal's per-capita gross national income—which takes into account gross domestic

Table 1. Selected Indicators of Development, Health Expenditures, and Outcomes

Indicator	Senegal	Nigeria	Tanzania	Botswana
Human development index ranking, out of 177	156	158	159	124
Human development category	low	low	low	medium
Population (in millions)	12.9	150	38.5	1.8
Population under the age of 15 in 2005	44.7%	55.9%	28.9%	35.6%
Annual population growth (1975–2005)	2.8	2.8	2.9	2.7
Annual population growth (2005–2015)	2.3	2.2	2.4	1.2
Average life expectancy at birth (in years)	62.3	46.5	51	46.1
Under-five mortality rate per 1,000 live births	136	194	122	120
Incidence of tuberculosis per 100,000 people	466	536	496	556
Adult literacy rate	39.3%	69.1%	69.4%	81.2%
Physicians per 100,000 people	6	28	2	40
Gross national income per capita for 2007 using the Atlas method	US$820	US$930	US$400	US$5,840
Population below the income poverty line (% on US$1 a day), 1990–2005 (World Bank, 2007)	17%	71%	58%	28%
Health expenditure per capita (current US$)	US$38	US$27	US$17	US$362

Sources: Gross national income: World Bank. Gross national income per capita 2007, Atlas method and PPP. World Development Indicators Database of July 1, 2008, accessed at *http://siteresources.worldbank.org/DATASTATISTICS/Resources/GNIPC.pdf* on August 21, 2008. Health expenditure per capita (current US$): World Bank. "HNP at a Glance" database, accessed at *http://go.worldbank.org/MALQ9X8AS0* on August 21, 2008.

Note: GNI for Tanzania refers to the mainland only

product as well as net flows of income from abroad—at US$820.[3] Despite its low gross domestic product and gross annual income, only 17 percent of Senegalese live below the poverty line of US$1 per day.[2] Compared with other low-development countries, Senegal spends a significant amount on health, at US$38 per capita.[2]

As in other African nations, a significant proportion of Senegal's population is young, with 45 percent under the age of 15. The average life expectancy is 62 years, which is relatively high for a low-development country and may reflect the significant health expenditures invested by the government and the socialist-based health care system.[2,4]

Although Senegal has one of the lowest HIV infection rates on the continent, other infectious diseases—such as bacterial and protozoal diarrhea, meningococcal meningitis, hepatitis, schistosomiasis, malaria, and other insect-borne illnesses—are still prevalent and adversely affect life expectancy. Senegal's infant mortality rate of 59 per thousand and the under-five mortality rate of 136 per 1,000 are both lower than average for countries in the low-development group.[2]

A History of the AIDS Epidemic in Senegal

The first AIDS case in Senegal was recognized in 1986, a relatively early discovery compared with those in many other African nations and certainly early for West Africa. This recognition followed the discovery of HIV-2, a human immunodeficiency virus related to the prototypical HIV-1.

In 1984, Harvard researchers had described a virus closely related to HIV-1 in monkeys—first in captive immunodeficient Asian macaques and then in wild African monkeys. This simian immunodeficiency virus, or SIV, was found to be approximately 50 percent related to HIV-1 at the genomic level.[5,6]

Based on the close relationship of SIV to the human virus, it seemed logical that viruses more highly related to SIV might also exist in human populations. In late 1984, serum samples from registered sex workers in Dakar demonstrated unusual reactivity to HIV-1 antigens. Surprisingly, though, these samples were more highly reactive with SIV than with the HIV-1 antigens (Figure 1).[7,8] Immunoblot and radioimmunoprecipitation methods showed that the virus infecting these women was more closely related to SIV. Additional virologic and molecular sequence analyses identified this new virus as a unique human immunodeficiency virus, eventually termed HIV-2.[8]

HIV-2 was discovered through a unique collaboration among Souleymane Mboup and his team at what is now Université Cheikh Anta Diop, Francis Barin at the University of Tours in France, François Denis at the University of Limoges, and our team at the Harvard School of Public Health in Boston, Massachusetts, which included Richard Marlink, Jean-Loup Romet-Lemonne, Max Essex, and me. Since 1985 this Inter-University Convention has worked together to gain an understanding of the biological and clinical significance of HIV-2 (Figure 2).

One striking finding of the initial studies was that this new virus appeared in 8 percent of healthy sex workers but not in people with symptomatic disease. The HIV-1 prevalence rate, in contrast, was less than 1 percent and found in women originating outside of Senegal.[9,10]

Abdourahmane Sow and his colleagues in the infectious disease department at Fann Hospital in Dakar had identified Senegal's first AIDS cases in 1986. These patients were infected with HIV-1 and often were either from Central Africa or had a history of travel there.[11] This finding led to more questions about the pathogenic potential of HIV-2, which had yet to cause an AIDS epidemic despite its higher prevalence rate.

Even before the cases were discovered, Senegal's Ministry of Health had established the Programme National de Lutte Contre le SIDA (National Program for the Fight Against AIDS), or PNLS. In 1986, the program was transferred to the Office of the Prime Minister, and in 2002, it became the Conseil National de Lutte Contre le SIDA

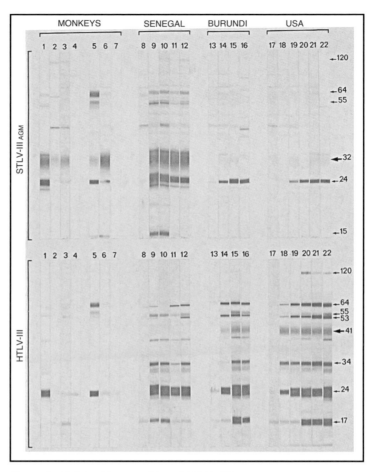

Figure 1. Original Immunoblot of HIV-2 Discovery
This immunoblot with STLV-III (SIV, or simian immunodeficiency virus) and HTLV-III (HIV-1) antigens showed seroreactivity of Senegalese registered sex workers to SIV antigens, comparable to primates. The immunoblot allowed the serologic discovery of the SIV-related virus in people, later named HIV-2.

Source: Barin F, MBoup S, Denis F, et al. Serological evidence for virus related to simian T-lymphotropic retrovirus III in residents of West Africa. *Lancet*, 1985; 2:1387–1389.

Abbreviations: STLV: simian T-lymphotropic virus; HTLV: human T-lymphotropic virus

(National Council for the Fight Against AIDS). These national programs made early and significant commitments to HIV prevention through such steps as establishing a national sentinel surveillance program for HIV, promoting condoms, and educating sex workers and other high-risk populations (Figure 3).

Figure 2. An Early AIDS Poster Produced by the Inter-University Convention

One notable step was the establishment in the mid-1980s of a blood supply safety program. Although Senegal had achieved its independence from France several decades earlier, it had maintained strong ties to a number of universities, research and public health institutes, and national agencies in France. These institutions provided the necessary HIV serology tests to the national transfusion centers and major hospitals in Senegal, as well as in other Francophone West African countries.

In 1986, after initiating studies to determine the biological properties of HIV-2, the Inter-University Convention met in Senegal to hold the first of many national AIDS conferences. Careful investments in training and the research capacity development of Mboup's laboratory at Dantec Hospital facilitated these initial research projects.

In 1987, studies to determine the geographic distribution of HIV-2 also documented the presence of HIV-1 infection in other West African countries such as Côte d'Ivoire, Guinea-Bissau, Guinea, and Mauritania.[12] The screening of more than 2,000 high-risk people from Central Africa, including many with AIDS and a range of sexually

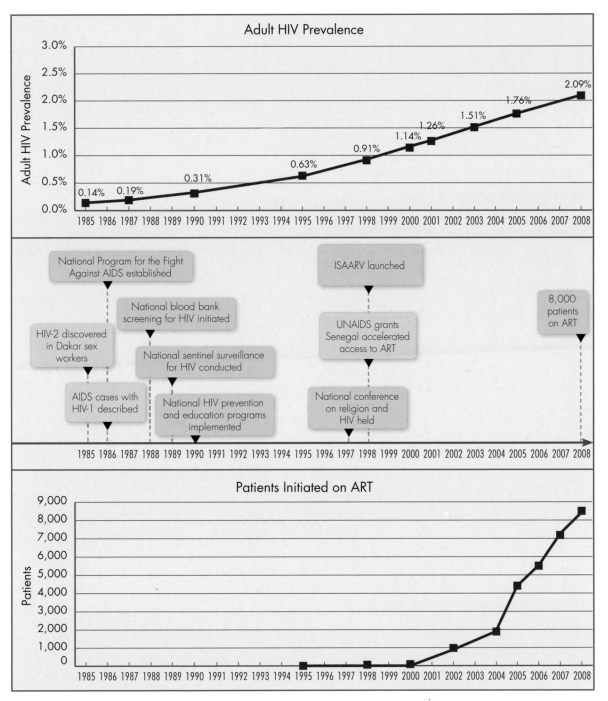

Figure 3. Timeline of Response to HIV/AIDS Epidemic in Senegal Plotted over National Prevalence and Number of Patients on ART

Abbreviations: ART: antiretroviral therapy; ISAARV: Initiative Senegalese for Access to Antiretrovirals

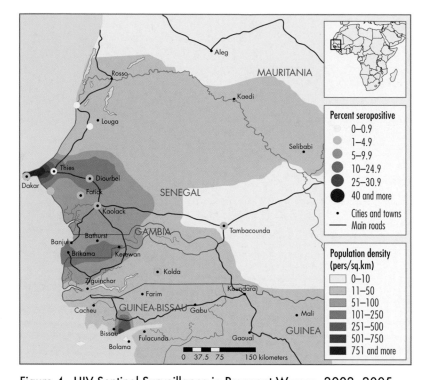

Figure 4. HIV Sentinel Surveillance in Pregnant Women, 2002–2005

Source: World Health Organization. *Epidemiological Fact Sheets on HIV/AIDS and Sexually Transmitted Infections.* Geneva: World Health Organization, December 2006.

transmitted infections (STIs), revealed no evidence that HIV-2 was present in the same regions in which HIV-1 was prevalent.[13] Other pockets of infection with HIV-2 were detected in Mozambique and Angola. Although distant from West Africa, these nations were often on the same Portuguese trade routes as Guinea-Bissau and Cape Verde, two West African nations with some of the highest infection rates.[14] Even in Senegal, HIV-2 prevalence rates were substantially higher in the southern region of Casamance, which borders Guinea-Bissau, than in the northern region.[15]

In 1989, the PNLS initiated a national sentinel surveillance program for HIV, funded first by the World Health Organization (WHO), then by USAID. As a result of the ongoing research studies, Mboup's laboratory developed the capability of performing HIV-1 and HIV-2 serologic diagnosis with the most current assays available. His laboratory was well qualified to receive funding support for the national sentinel surveillance program surveys in Senegal, a surveillance system that has continued now for more than two decades. Like other sentinel surveillance surveys, this program uses infection rates among women attending antenatal clinics around the country to estimate national prevalence rates (Figure 3). Few African countries have so clearly documented their national prevalence rates over such a long time as has Senegal.

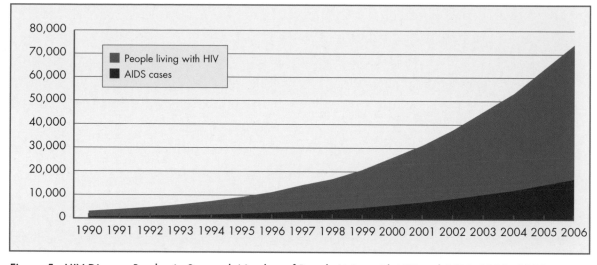

Figure 5. HIV Disease Burden in Senegal: Number of People Living with HIV and AIDS, 1990–2006
Source: UNAIDS. *2008 Report on the Global AIDS Epidemic.* Geneva: UNAIDS, 2008.

In Dakar, HIV-1 prevalence among antenatal clinic women was 1 percent or lower from 1986 to 1998 (Figures 3 and 4). The median countrywide HIV prevalence rate rose gradually from 0.9 percent in 1998, to 1.1 percent in 2000, to 1.5 percent in 2003. Between 2004 and 2007, the HIV prevalence ranged between 1.6 percent and 2.0 percent. HIV prevalence did not vary significantly across the country despite differences between such urban sites as Dakar and the more rural sites included in the survey (Figure 4).

High-risk populations frequently have higher prevalence rates than the general population, with the differential often based on risk determinants that may include partner exchange rates, other STIs, and myriad other sociocultural factors. Although HIV-1 prevalence has remained low among antenatal clinic women in Dakar, HIV-1 prevalence among sex workers has increased gradually from less than 1 percent in 1986 to 14 percent in 2002, while HIV-2 infection has decreased from 8 percent to 5 percent over the same time period (Figure 5).[16] HIV-1 prevalence among sex workers outside of Dakar—in Kaolack and Ziguinchor—continued to rise, from 0 percent in 1986 to over 20 percent in 2002; HIV-2 infection rates were variable.[15]

HIV-1 prevalence among male patients in STI clinics in Dakar increased from 1 percent in 1989 to nearly 5 percent in 1993. In 2002, 4 percent of male STI clinic patients tested positive for HIV-1 or HIV-2. Prevalence rates among high-risk groups ranged from 1 percent to 20 percent and were 10-fold to 20-fold higher than those in the general population.

The HIV prevalence rates among high-risk groups in Senegal were significantly lower, though, than prevalence rates reported in high-risk groups of other African countries.[15] Rates among Nairobi-based sex workers in Kenya, for instance, ranged from 74 percent to 90 percent during the same time period.

STIs are significant cofactors for HIV transmission, and population groups at high risk for HIV are similarly at risk for other STIs.[17] As a result, programs that prevent STIs through education, early diagnosis, and treatment are considered critical components of HIV prevention and intervention efforts. At the same time, improvements in the efficacy of HIV prevention programs may help lower STI rates. Senegal enhanced its efforts in STI diagnosis and control within a health system that had already been established but poorly resourced. Ibrahima Ndoye, an STI expert, has been a key leader in ensuring that the national AIDS control program addressed STI prevention and control in these important risk populations.

According to UNAIDS, Senegal's decision to make major investments in HIV prevention and awareness programs early in the epidemic was critical to maintaining its low rates of HIV infection.[18] In 1988, Senegal launched a national campaign aimed at preventing HIV in women and students. Curricula on HIV and other STIs were developed and became integrated into school curricula. International support for counseling and testing programs and AIDS education initiatives helped increase awareness and decrease stigma. Nongovernmental organizations were formed to promote HIV prevention and to provide support for people with HIV/AIDS. The dialogue between key health experts and government officials at the highest level helped to facilitate the national AIDS control program's progress with resources and political backing.

Health experts in the country also recognized the importance of religious leaders in the promotion of HIV/AIDS programs.[18] In 1997, Religion and AIDS, a national conference on HIV prevention, convened Muslim and Christian religious leaders. During that conference, Muslim leaders agreed to incorporate AIDS education into religious teaching programs. Although they did not participate in condom promotion efforts, they did support fidelity and abstinence as the best means of preventing HIV infection.[19] Similarly, a Christian nongovernmental organization, SIDA Service, provided free and anonymous testing for HIV. The organization also promoted abstinence and fidelity rather than condom use.

The participation of religious leaders and faith-based organizations reinforced traditional sexual norms, which may have served to protect Senegal from a more widespread sexually transmitted epidemic. This approach allowed outreach to high-risk populations through programs that promoted AIDS awareness and provided information about modes of transmission, the need for behavioral change, and the importance of condom use.

Prevention efforts have often focused on populations considered to be at high risk because of their elevated levels of sexual activity with multiple partners. As a result, sex workers have been viewed as a major high-risk population in most parts of the globe. In the 1970s, the Senegalese government mandated the registration of sex workers. This registration, limited to women above the age of 18, required monthly health checkups at public health clinics in order to maintain their semi-legal status.

The Institut d'Hygiène Sociale clinic in Dakar was one of the designated clinics at which self-identified sex workers could register and receive medical care on a monthly basis. Before the discoveries of HIV-1 and HIV-2, these women were provided STI diagnosis and treatment with screening for diseases such as syphilis, chancroid, and gonorrhea. After we discovered HIV-2 infection in these women in 1985, we initiated a prospective study of all women visiting this clinic. The study tracked the levels of HIV-1 and HIV-2 infection in these women over the years and provided important new information on the biology of these viral infections in African women.[20]

When the national antiretroviral therapy (ART) program began in the late 1990s, sex workers became eligible for free drugs and treatment. But of equal importance was how the research study had helped strengthen the health care system. Senegalese physicians had consulted with women at these clinics since 1986, providing free medical care, referral, and treatment. Regular education and counseling on HIV, STIs, and condom use had also been provided since that time. Although the rates of HIV infection were higher in these high-risk women than among the general population, these rates were considerably lower than those seen in other sex worker populations in Africa and Asia.

Military personnel are often considered at high risk for HIV because of their age group, high mobility, and migration levels. Fortunately for outreach efforts to this group,

Mboup was not only a professor of virology and microbiology at the University but also a colonel in the Senegalese Army. He had served as the army's specialist on HIV since the mid-1980s and had helped develop the HIV education and prevention program for the Senegalese Armed Forces. In addition to regular education, Senegalese troops involved in peace-keeping missions were given additional counseling and prevention sessions and screened for HIV and STIs at regular intervals.[19] The U.S. Department of Defense, which funded the research collaboration between Harvard and Université Cheikh Anta Diop, encouraged military-to-military collaborations for prevention programs as well as research on molecular epidemiology and HIV vaccines.

At the end of 2001, with 24,000 adults (and 2,900 children) living with the virus in Senegal, UNAIDS estimated the rate of infection among adults to be 0.5 percent—the lowest national HIV prevalence rate in sub-Saharan Africa.[16] The significant involvement of the Senegalese government with health officials involved in HIV prevention resulted in early discussion revolving around the provision of ART to patients in need. While the issue was still being debated in the international health and donor community, Senegal became one of the first African countries to pilot a national ART program for its HIV-infected population.

In 2002–2006, the government of Senegal and the PNLS embarked on a new strategic plan, which continued their multisectoral response to the epidemic. Government ministries, the private sector, religious and civil society organizations, and people living with HIV/AIDS were all included in these programs.[20]

Sentinel surveillance continues to document HIV infection rates below 2 percent in Senegal. UNAIDS and WHO have classified HIV epidemics into three broad categories: low-level, concentrated, and generalized.[21] In low-level epidemics the infection has never spread to significant levels in any sub-population and infections are largely confined to high-risk populations such as sex workers, injection drug users, and men who have sex with men. In a concentrated epidemic state, HIV has spread substantially in one or more sub-populations but is not well established in the general population; a 5 percent level has been the usual threshold for concentrated epidemics. Senegal's epidemic is therefore considered a concentrated one because high-risk populations have infection rates above 5 percent. It is notable, though, that the country has succeeded in maintaining this status for more than two decades.[21,22]

Viral Variability in Senegal

HIV-1, HIV-2, and SIV are all complex retroviruses belonging to the *Lentivirus* subfamily. HIV, the first human lentivirus within the retrovirus family, was first described in the early 1980s coincident with the description of AIDS in the developed world. These RNA viruses are characterized by their ability to integrate their genetic material into host cells and their long course of virus infection and disease.

HIV-1 isolates have been broadly classified into group M, for major, consisting of at least eight to ten subtypes; group O for outlier; and group N, for not M and not O.[23] Group O, first described in Cameroon, is believed to be more closely related to HIV-1 viruses from wild gorilla populations than to HIV-2; to emphasize its distinction from both HIV-1 groups M and N and from HIV-2, it was designated as the outlier virus.[24,25]

HIV-1 and HIV-2 are 40 to 50 percent related at a primary nucleotide level and demonstrate significant genetic variability within each virus type.[26] Although all HIVs are considered capable of inducing AIDS, the disease course and rate of development appear to differ among the groups. Group N and O infections in humans, for example, are rare in humans.[27,28]

Since the discovery of HIV-2 in Senegal in 1985, research studies conducted both in the laboratory and among HIV-2–infected people have highlighted distinct biological differences between these related viruses.[29] The global distribution of HIV-2 appears to be independent of HIV-1. HIV-2 seems to be primarily limited to West Africa; other pockets of infection appear to follow the former Portuguese trade routes from West Africa to Brazil and India.[14] The rates of HIV-2 transmission from mother to child and through heterosexual sex are 10-fold to 30-fold lower than those of HIV-1.[30]

Our prospective studies conducted in a registered female sex worker cohort in Dakar have provided us with unique opportunities to measure the infection and progression rates of both HIV-1 and HIV-2.[28] Through comparisons of disease progression in people with known time of infection, these studies have demonstrated slower rates of progression to AIDS among people with HIV-2 and even a potential protective effect of HIV-2 from subsequent HIV-1 infection.[29,31] The Senegalese sex worker cohort represents one of the longest HIV natural history studies in the world.[32]

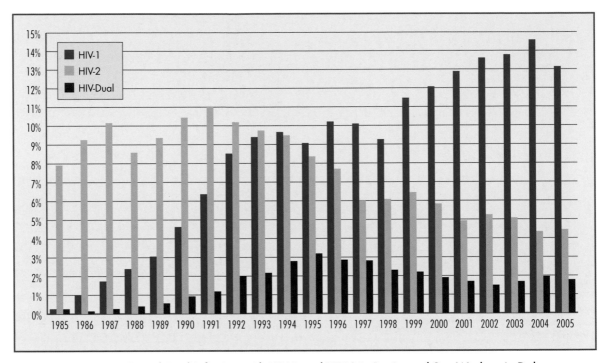

Figure 6. HIV-1, HIV-2, and Dual Infection with HIV-1 and HIV-2 in Registered Sex Workers in Dakar (1985–2005)

Source: Hamel DJ, Sankalé J-L, Eisen G, et al. Twenty years of prospective molecular epidemiology in Senegal: changes in HIV diversity. *AIDS Res Hum Retroviruses*, 2007;23(10):1189–1196.

All HIVs are thought to spread through the same routes: blood contamination, sexual intercourse, and mother-to-child transmission. HIV integrates its genetic material into the infected host's DNA; therefore, infection is lifelong, even with currently available treatment. Although mortality is high without treatment, the incubation time from HIV-1 infection to AIDS is long and can range from eight to ten years in the developed world.

Perhaps the most striking feature of HIV is its genetic diversity. Multiple HIV-1 subtypes (A–D, F–H, J, and K) exist worldwide. In areas of the world where multiple viral subtypes coexist, circulating recombinant forms (CRFs) also occur.[33] The CRF02_AG virus, for example, originally described by David Olaleye from the University of Ibadan in Nigeria, has been considered the prototype West African HIV-1 subtype.[34] CRF02_AG is responsible for a significant proportion of HIV-1 infections in Senegal as it is in other West African countries.[32,35]

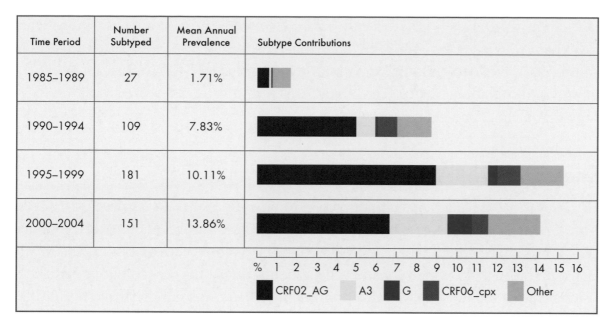

Figure 7. HIV-1 Subtypes in Registered Sex Workers in Dakar (1985–2004)

Source: Hamel DJ, Sankalé J-L, Eisen G, et al. Twenty years of prospective molecular epidemiology in Senegal: changes in HIV diversity. *AIDS Res Hum Retroviruses,* 2007;23(10):1189–1196.

We have documented the 20-year molecular epidemiology of HIV-1 subtypes and HIV-2 in the registered sex worker cohort in Dakar.[32] The molecular epidemiology of HIV-1 and HIV-2 subtypes described in this population demonstrates the dynamics of diverse HIV-1 and HIV-2 subtypes over time, with an eventual decrease in HIV-2 and an increase in the diversity of HIV-1 subtypes seen since the late 1990s (Figures 6 and 7). Temporal shifts also demonstrate the increasing contribution of novel variants, including CRFs and the newly described sub-subtype A3, discovered in Senegal.[32,36]

Antiretrovirals were designed, tested, and validated with European and North American subtype B viruses. Non-B subtypes predominate worldwide, however, especially in Africa. It is therefore not unexpected that ART efficacy might be influenced by viral subtype. HIV-2 and HIV-1 group O viruses are genetically distant enough from HIV-1 that they are naturally resistant to non-nucleoside reverse transcriptase inhibitors (NNRTIs) such as nevirapine and efavirenz and possibly some nucleoside reverse transcriptase inhibitors (NRTIs) and protease inhibitors.[37–39] Subtype G viruses have decreased in-vitro susceptibility to protease inhibitors.[40] In Uganda, it is thought that women infected with subtype D were more likely than those with subtype A to develop resistance to nevirapine when they received a single dose of it to prevent mother-to-child transmission.[41] Non-subtype B HIV-1 viruses have many amino acid mutations that confer minor resistance to protease inhibitors; their biologic significance remains unknown.[42]

The History of Antiretroviral Therapies in Senegal

In 1998, the PNLS launched a pilot project to provide ART to Senegalese with AIDS. The Senegalese government contributed US$600,000 to the initiation of the program, which was called the Initiative Senegalese for Access to Antiretrovirals, or ISAARV.[43] Based on the high costs of drugs and patient monitoring at the time, program designers estimated that the funding would support the treatment of a hundred patients for one year. The strategic goals of this program were to develop the local infrastructure necessary for ART provision and to integrate ART into the existing health care system.

ISAARV established four committees to support the program. The Eligibility Committee was charged with overall responsibility for patient recruitment. The physicians, biologists, pharmacists, people living with HIV/AIDS, and administrators who composed this 15-member committee developed the original guidelines for patient eligibility and the allocation of subsidy to eligible patients. In later years, committee members would help modify those guidelines to accommodate scale-up efforts.

The Medical Committee defined and reviewed all clinical aspects of the program. Committee members met monthly to review possible candidates for treatment, to approve the ART regimens proposed by clinicians, and to discuss patient management and outcomes. The Welfare Committee took responsibility for the psychosocial aspects of the program, such as promoting adherence and coordinating social support for patients through pharmacists, psychiatrists, and social workers. The Drugs and Reagents Management and Supply Committee took responsibility for managing drugs, organizing the pharmacy dispensing, and interacting with private ART wholesalers.

The 1998 pilot project was designed to determine the feasibility, acceptability, and efficacy of ART. The project initially treated 58 AIDS patients at two major hospitals in Dakar—Fann and Principal hospitals—with the objectives of implementing the treatment within a designated budget, monitoring patients through related research projects, and using appropriate drug regimens and patient monitoring protocols.[43] Awa-Marie Coll-Seck, then head of infectious disease at Fann Hospital, played a major role in the inception of ISAARV. When Coll-Seck left to assume a leadership position at UNAIDS in Geneva, Papa Salif Sow continued her legacy. The French National Agency for AIDS Research and the European Union funded the research projects that enabled the patient monitoring.[44]

The medical criteria for enrollment in the program were based on a WHO consensus report on ART in Africa, which gave priority to diagnosed AIDS patients, excluding those in the terminal stage of disease, and to patients with CD4+ cell counts below 350 cells/mm^3 and viral loads of greater than 100,000 copies/ml of plasma.[45] Patients with major opportunistic infections at baseline received treatment for those infections before being placed on ART. Psychosocial requirements included the patient's capacity to adhere to the drug regimen.

At the time, the cost of AIDS treatment in the United States was approximately US$550 a month. Senegalese patients were asked to contribute US$34 per month when possible, with the Senegalese government providing the remainder.

The ART regimens included two NRTIs and one protease inhibitor. The four NRTIs available were stavudine, didanosine, zidovudine, and lamivudine. The protease inhibitor provided was indinavir. Most patients received a combination of stavudine, didanosine, and indinavir. Clinical trials later revealed that the regimen, considered appropriate at the time, led to high rates of neurotoxicity. It is no longer a recommended regimen.[44,46]

During the first 18 months of treatment, the self-reported adherence monitored at monthly intervals was high, at 87.9 percent, although it decreased after one year of treatment.[44] The median viral load dropped by 2.5 logs; the percentage of patients with undetectable viral loads—fewer than 500 copies—was 79.6 percent at 1 month, 71.2 percent at 6 months, 51.4 percent at 12 months, and 59.3 percent at 18 months. The CD4+ cell count rose by a median of 82, 147, and 180 x 10^6 cells/l at months 6, 12, and 18, respectively. Seven patients died during the study period and seven clinical AIDS-defining events occurred, including four cases of esophageal candidiasis, two of tuberculosis, and one of *Mycobacterium avium* complex. The cumulative probability of remaining alive or free of new AIDS-defining events was 94.8 percent after 6 months, 85.0 percent after 12 months, and 82.3 percent after 18 months.

A total of 47 adverse events were reported in 30 patients; 51.5 percent were related to the gastrointestinal toxicity of indinavir and 25.5 percent were diarrhea caused by didanosine.[44] Most of the adverse events were mild (22 of 47, or 46.8 percent) or moderate (16 of 47, or 34 percent). Sequence analyses of viruses from patients undergoing treatment found that two of the patients were infected with group O viruses. The rest were infected with group M viruses, predominantly CRF 02_AG. Two patients developed drug resistance during the follow-up period.

Although the pilot study was conducted on a small number of patients, it demonstrated the feasibility of ART delivery in an African setting. Notably, the adherence rates for patients taking antiretrovirals were considered high and comparable to rates seen in industrialized countries.[44] The virologic suppression was also comparable to that seen in cohort studies conducted in Europe and the United States, despite the fact that patients were infected with non-subtype–B viruses. Although mortality was significant—7 patients of 58 died, at a rate of 12 percent—this was attributed to the advanced stage of disease of patients at the time of enrollment and possible limitations in opportunistic infection management.

In 1999, at the end of the pilot trial, the government of Senegal assumed all costs of the ART program.[43] Although only 85 patients were being treated, the exorbitant costs consumed a significant portion of the country's health budget. It appeared that inadequate support would be available to expand the program from the relatively small number of patients who had been supported through the partially funded pilot.

In 2000, Senegal joined Uganda and Côte d'Ivoire in becoming one of three countries granted accelerated access to antiretrovirals by UNAIDS. Responding to a call from Kofi Annan, then the United Nations secretary-general—five major pharmaceutical companies—Boehringer Ingelheim, Bristol-Myers Squibb, Glaxo Wellcome, Merck, and F. Hoffmann-La Roche—agreed to work with UNAIDS to expand the global response to HIV/AIDS and to help lower drug costs. The World Bank, UNICEF, and the United Nations Population Fund also supported this public–private partnership.[43] UNAIDS negotiated with the major antiretroviral manufacturers to provide discounted pricing of their drugs for use in developing countries. The health ministry of Senegal signed individual agreements with each participating pharmaceutical company. Although prices were reduced by as much as 97 percent, the program had strict guidelines for access, with significant restrictions that many interpreted as patent protection for the pharmaceutical companies and an effort to limit competition from the generic ART companies that were now springing up in India.

The reduced cost of antiretrovirals provided through the accelerated access program allowed ISAARV to continue to enroll eligible patients. By 2002, the program had increased its patient numbers more than ten-fold, with 980 patients receiving antiretrovirals. Patients in the ISAARV program were now asked to contribute US$4 per month for treatment rather than US$34.[47]

As the UNAIDS Accelerated Access Initiative was being established, major pharmaceutical companies were also developing their own programs to address the need for ART in developing countries. The Merck Company Foundation launched the Enhancing Care Initiative (ECI) with a grant to the Harvard AIDS Institute, now known as the Harvard School of Public Health AIDS Initiative. This US$5 million grant supported a multisectoral collaboration to identify practical country-led approaches to providing effective HIV/AIDS care that was tailored to local needs and resources. AIDS care teams were established in Senegal, Brazil, South Africa, and Thailand.[48]

In Senegal, the ECI team had performed a situation analysis that had identified gaps in the medical infrastructure that were restricting access to HIV/AIDS testing and care outside of Dakar. The analysis resulted in a focus on disparities in the quality and extent of care between rural and urban populations. Following a survey of doctors treating HIV/AIDS patients and the patients themselves, the Senegalese team found that training was a major obstacle to the decentralization of the treatment and care program. The ECI team also developed and standardized guidelines for the management of opportunistic infections for use in health facilities. Team members created educational posters to publicize guidelines for opportunistic infection management, and they distributed posters on postexposure prophylaxis to health facilities. Working with policy makers in Senegal, the team recommended improved training of health personnel in the management of opportunistic infections and palliative care.[48] The government supported this effort, which had already prioritized HIV/AIDS care training for physicians with the goal of swiftly improving the health care infrastructure.

ISAARV embarked on a *parrainage*, or mentoring program, to decentralize ART to Senegal's 14 regions. The goal was to train physicians working in areas outside of Dakar and the national hospital to manage all aspects of the ART program. The mentor was a Dakar-based physician at a major academic clinical center with significant expertise in ART. The mentor's responsibilities included overseeing all treatment aspects in the assigned region, helping the region establish a medical committee, and serving as a point person to address all system issues related to treatment and care, such as drug logistics, reagents, patient management monitoring forms, and data collection. Each region had a designated mentor who initially spent four days in the outside regions. Mentors provided information on inclusion criteria and monitoring procedures for patients on ART. Mentors visited the trainees at the regional clinics every three months and maintained ongoing contact through telephone calls and emails to address specific problems as they arose.

By 2000, the optimal ART regimens had been changed to drug cocktails of two NRTIs and one NNRTI. Protease inhibitors were reserved for HIV-2 treatment and second-line treatment for AIDS patients with HIV-1. The expanded number of drugs now available for treatment meant an increased need for continuous, updated training for physicians, pharmacists, and counselors. As the ISAARV program expanded treatment, it restructured its program to minimize the delay in initiating ART with two remaining committees, the Medical Committee and the Drugs and Reagents Management and Supply Committee.

Senegalese scientists had experience in providing training. Many West African scientists regularly trained in laboratory methods for HIV and STIs in Mboup's laboratory, which had been designated as a WHO reference laboratory for HIV. A WHO working group on HIV-2, which held many training workshops in Senegal on HIV-2 diagnosis, ultimately developed the standard requirements for HIV-2 diagnosis.[26] Similarly, clinicians from Francophone Africa participated in residency programs at Fann Hospital in Dakar. This association not only facilitated HIV prevention and treatment programs in partner countries but also built their research capacities.

The United Nations Development Programme supported the formation of the Network of HIV Research in Africa. The Harvard School of Public Health provided complimentary training and research capacity-building efforts through an international AIDS research training grant provided by the John E. Fogarty International Center of the U.S. National Institutes of Health. Since 1987, this program has funded training programs in HIV virology and immunology for Senegalese microbiologists at Harvard as well as a range of training programs in Senegal.

A patient education program has also been developed in local languages under the supervision of social workers at each health facility.[49] The goal was to give patients an understanding of the basic ART principles, with an emphasis on drug adherence. Co-trimoxazole prophylaxis was provided to all patients with CD4+ cell counts below 350, as studies in both the developed and developing world had showed the benefits of this important opportunistic infection prophylaxis for immunosuppressed people even if they were not taking antiretrovirals.

During this time, a number of other initiatives were launched to support the ART program. To protect health care workers exposed to HIV through needle-stick exposure or contaminated fluids, for example, a postexposure prophylaxis program was established at all clinics and hospitals. This program allowed access to the necessary drugs for a limited course of treatment after the presumed exposure.[50] A national program to prevent mother-to-child transmission was also developed in Senegal to identify HIV-infected women and to provide them with antiretroviral prophylaxis in an effort to reduce transmission of the virus to their babies.

In 2000, the French National Agency for AIDS Research and Institut de Médecine et d'Epidémiologie Appliquée, or IMEA, collaborated with ISAARV to evaluate a once-daily, triple-drug regimen for AIDS treatment; this included didanosine, lamivudine, and efavirenz.[51] This was a prospective, open-label study of 50 treatment-naive HIV-1–infected patients. The intent-to-treat analysis at six months showed 95 percent (83 to 99 percent, with a 95 percent confidence interval) of patients had suppressed viral loads below detection of 400 copies per milliliter. The CD4+ cell count at baseline was 164 and increased by a mean of 199 at 15 months of treatment. No serious adverse events occurred, and adherence was excellent, as determined by patient self-report and plasma drug concentrations. This study showed that a once-daily ART regimen was acceptable and efficacious in patients treated in an African setting with advanced-stage disease.[49]

By 2002, more than 400 patients had been enrolled in the ISAARV program or associated clinical trials supported by the French. To monitor the efficacy of the program and to follow-up on what appeared to be high mortality in the first Senegalese patients treated, Jean-François Etard and colleagues in France and Senegal described the mortality and cause of death in a seven-year retrospective cohort analysis. The overall incidence of death was 6.3 per 100 person years (5.2 to 7.7, with a 95 percent confidence interval).[52] The death rates were highest during the first year after ART initiation, with one-third of the patients dying within the first six months. The death rate decreased over time, yielding a cumulative probability of dying of 17.4 percent (13.9 to 21.5 percent, with a 95 percent confidence interval) at two years and 24.6 percent (20.4 to 29.4) at five years. Mycobacterial and central nervous system infections caused by cryptococcosis or toxoplasmosis were the most frequent causes of death. The analysis of responses to ART from 18 developing countries described the risk of dying in the first year as 5.8 percent, which was significantly higher than what was observed in developed countries.[53] The study confirmed the observation that mortality was linked to more severe disease at entry. It did not fully explain, however, the slightly higher mortality found in Senegalese patients on ART, as compared with other observational cohort studies in Africa or Europe.

The Senegalese and French researchers continued to monitor and evaluate the early ART programs in Senegal. These were some of the first published studies of ART provision in an African setting. The concurrent research studies on HIV-2 and the subtypes of HIV-1 allowed Senegalese researchers to evaluate the impact of viral type and subtype on treatment responses and the emergence of drug resistance. Laurence Vergne and colleagues described the drug-resistance mutations in a select cohort of 80 patients.[54] The emergence of drug-resistance mutations was 16.3 percent (13/80) in patients followed for a median of 24 months; rates of drug resistance were lower (11.8 percent) in treatment-naive patients than in ART-experienced patients (41.7 percent). Early reports from Côte d'Ivoire and Gabon that had just introduced ART to their populations had reported a drug resistance among patients at more than 50 percent, presumed to be largely linked to bitherapy usage. Therefore the preliminary drug-resistance studies in Senegal confirmed relatively low rates of drug resistance associated with a well-organized and monitored ART program consisting of three drugs. It should be noted, however, that as ART regimens have changed over the years, continual drug resistance monitoring should be considered in both treated and untreated HIV-infected populations.

Most ART regimens used in Africa today consist of drugs that were developed in the 1980s and are now off patent from the original pharmaceutical developers. These drugs, such as zidovudine and stavudine, are rarely used in ART in the developed world because of their toxicity profiles, reduced efficacy, and low threshold for the development of drug-resistance mutations.[46] In addition, with limited drug choices available for ART in Africa, alternative and second-line drugs may not be available when drug resistance causes patients to fail their therapy. Surveillance of drug resistance with the rollout of ART should be developed to help guide regimen and monitoring policies.

In 2002, Senegal had four hospitals or clinics providing ART. During the next five years, though, this number increased to 55 clinical sites, and the national mentoring system succeeded in training more than 110 new physicians in ART provision. By early 2007, ART was available not only in 16 clinical sites in Dakar, but also in 39 other hospitals and clinics spanning all 14 regions of the country. The number of Senegalese receiving ART grew from 980 in 2002, to 5,915 in early 2007, to 8,500 in 2008. Senegal has now passed the major milestone of providing ART to more than half the patients in need. At the current rate of patient enrollment, Senegal will likely meet the millennium goals of universal access by 2015.[55]

Conclusion

In the late 1990s, international development and HIV experts debated the seemingly insurmountable obstacles to providing lifesaving ART to the millions of Africans living with HIV/AIDS. Many countries, despite the constraints of poverty, took courageous steps to reverse this death toll. Senegal was one of those countries. Since the beginning of the epidemic, Senegalese scientists, physicians, and health experts have conducted research on HIV-1 and HIV-2 that was instrumental in the early development of a national prevention program, one that appears to have been among the most successful in the world. More than two decades later, Senegal continues to have one of the lowest HIV infection rates on the continent.

The experience and research capacity of Senegal's AIDS experts have served them well. They have provided continuous molecular surveillance of their HIV epidemic, initiated treatment programs with evidence-based outcome evaluations, and participated in research and trials of vaccines for infectious disease threats, including HIV.

Senegal has been blessed with both a strong government response and an exceptionally high quality of scientific leadership. The track record of the latter is apparent; often in collaboration with researchers from France, the United States, and elsewhere, the Senegalese research team has published hundreds of articles in peer-reviewed scientific journals. These studies have helped shape our understanding of HIV in Africa and contributed to our efforts to provide effective HIV prevention and treatment.

Few countries have had HIV/AIDS experts emerge so early in the epidemic and then maintain such consistently high levels of work in HIV prevention and care across a span of decades. Senegal has Souleymane Mboup, Papa Salif Sow, Tidiane Siby, Ibrahima Ndoye, Jean-Louis Sankalé, Abdoulaye Dieng-Sarr, Ibrahima Traoré, Mamadou Ciré Dia, Aissatou Guèye-Ndiaye, Ibou Thior, Aissatou Gaye, Ndèye Coumba Touré, Mame Awa Touré, Birahim Pierre Ndiaye, Aziz Hane, and many, many others.

These scientists and clinicians have stood the test of time, building their country's capacity to sustain a long-term prevention and treatment program that has clearly worked and protecting their nation from an epidemic that has killed millions of Africans. They deserve credit for the many lives they have saved and the example they have set for others.

REFERENCES

1. Central Intelligence Agency. The World Factbook. https://www.cia.gov/library/publications/the-world-factbook; accessed September 23, 2008.

2. United Nations Development Programme. *Human Development Report.* New York: United Nations Development Programme, 2008:231.

3. World Bank. Gross National Income 2007, Atlas Methods and PPP. World Development Indicators Database of July 1, 2008. Washington, DC: World Bank, 2008. http://siteresources.worldbank.org/DATASTATISTICS/Resources/GNIPC.pdf; accessed October 28, 2008.

4. World Bank. HNP at a Glance database. http://go.worldbank.org/MALQ9X8AS0; accessed August 21, 2008.

5. Kanki PJ, McLane MF, King NW, Jr., et al. Serologic identification and characterization of a macaque T-lymphotropic retrovirus closely related to HTLV-III. *Science*, 1985;228:1199–1201.

6. Kanki PJ, Kurth R, Becker W, et al. Antibodies to simian T-lymphotropic retrovirus type III in African green monkeys and recognition of STLV-III viral proteins by AIDS and related sera. *Lancet*, 1985;i:1330–1332.

7. Barin F, Mboup S, Denis F, et al. Serological evidence for virus related to simian T-lymphotropic retrovirus III in residents of West Africa. *Lancet,* 1985;ii:1387–1390.

8. Kanki PJ. Simian retroviruses in Africa. In: Essex M, Mboup S, Kanki PJ, Kalengayi MR, eds. *AIDS in Africa.* New York: Raven Press, 1994;97–108.

9. Barin F, Denis F, Baillou A, et al. A STLV-III related human retrovirus HTLV-IV: analysis of cross-reactivity with the human immunodeficiency virus (HIV). *J Virol Methods*, 1987;17:55–61.

10. Kanki P. Clinical significance of HIV-2 infection in West Africa. In: Volberding P, Jacobson MA, eds. *AIDS Clinical Reviews 1989.* New York: Marcel Dekker, Inc., 1989;95–108.

11. Kane F, Alary M, Ndoye I, et al. Temporary expatriation is related to HIV-1 infection in rural Senegal. *AIDS*, 1993;7:1261–1265.

12. Kanki P, Mboup S, Ricard D, et al. Human T-lymphotropic virus type 4 and the human immunodeficiency virus in West Africa. *Science,* 1987;236:827–831.

13. Kanki P, Allan J, Barin F, et al. Absence of antibodies to HIV-2/HTLV-4 in six Central African nations. *AIDS Res Hum Retroviruses,* 1987;3(3):317–322.

14. Smallman-Raynor M, Cliff A. The spread of human immunodeficiency virus type 2 into Europe: a geographical analysis. *Int J Epidemiol,* 1991;20:480.

15. Mboup S, Kanki P, Barin F, et al. Epidémiologie d'un nouveau retrovirus humain apparenté au virus STLV-IIIagm: virus HTLV IV. In: Williams O, ed. *Viral Diseases of Man in Africa.* Lagos: OAU/STRC Scientific Publication, 1988;37–64.

16. UNAIDS. *2008 Report on the Global AIDS Epidemic.* Geneva: UNAIDS, 2008.

17. Plummer FA, Simonsen JN, Cameron DW. Cofactors in male–female sexual transmission of human immunodeficiency virus type 1. *J Infect Dis,* 1991;163:233–239.

18. UNAIDS. Acting early to prevent AIDS: the case of Senegal. Best Practices Collection. June 1999. http://data.unaids.org/Publications/IRC-pub04/una99-34_en.pdf; accessed September 23, 2008.

19. Lorn MM. Senegal's recipe for success. *Africa Recovery,* 2001;15(1–2):24–29.

20. Kanki P, Mboup S, Marlink R, et al. Prevalence and risk determinants of human immunodeficiency virus type 2 (HIV-2) and human immunodeficiency virus type 1 (HIV-1) in West African female prostitutes. *Amer J Epidemiol,* 1992;136:895–907.

21. Schwartlander B, Ghys PD, Pisani E, et al. HIV surveillance in hard-to-reach populations. *AIDS,* 2001;15(Suppl 3):S1–S3.

22. Ghys PD, Stanecki K. *Epidemiological Patterns and Trends and Their Implications for HIV Prevention.* Geneva: UNAIDS, 2008.

23. Myers G, Korber B, Hahn BH, et al., eds. *Human Retroviruses and AIDS 1995: A Compilation and Analysis of Nucleic Acid and Amino Acid Sequences.* Los Alamos, New Mexico: Theoretical Biology and Biophysics Group, Los Alamos National Laboratory, 1995.

24. Gurtler LG, Hauser PH, Eberle J, et al. A new subtype of human immunodeficiency virus type 1 (MVP-5180) from Cameroon. *J Virol,* 1994;68:1581.

25. Van Heuverswyn F, Li Y, Neel C, et al. Human immunodeficiency viruses: SIV infection in wild gorillas. *Nature,* 1994;444(7116):164.

26. Biberfeld G, Brown F, Esparza J, et al. WHO working group on characterization of HIV-related retroviruses: criteria for characterization and proposal for a nomenclature system. *AIDS,* 1987;1:189–190.

27. Marlink RG, Ricard D, Mboup S, et al. Clinical, hematologic, and immunologic cross-sectional evaluation of individuals exposed to human immunodeficiency virus type 2 (HIV-2). *AIDS Res Hum Retroviruses,* 1988,4:137–148.

28. Marlink RG, Kanki PJ, Thior I, et al. Reduced rate of disease development with HIV-2 compared to HIV-1. *Science,* 1994;265:1587–1590.

29. Kanki PJ, Sankalé J-L, Mboup S. Biology of human immunodeficiency virus type 2 (HIV-2). In: Essex M, Mboup S, Kanki P, Marlink RG, Tlou S, eds. *AIDS in Africa.* 2nd ed. New York: Kluwer Academic/Plenum Publishers, 2002;171–182.

30. Kanki P, Mboup S, Travers K, et al. Slower heterosexual spread of HIV-2 compared with HIV-1. *Lancet,* 1994;343:943–946.

31. Travers K, Mboup S, Marlink R, et al. Natural protection against HIV-1 infection provided by HIV-2. *Science,* 1995;268:1612–1615.

32. Hamel DJ, Sankalé JL, Eisen G, et al. Twenty years of prospective molecular epidemiology in Senegal: changes in HIV diversity. *AIDS Res Hum Retroviruses,* 2007;23(10):1189–1196.

33. McCutchan FE, Salminen MO, Carr JK, et al. HIV-1 genetic diversity. *AIDS,* 1996;10(Suppl 3):S13–S20.

34. Olaleye OD, Bernstein L, Ekweozor CC, et al. Prevalence of human immunodeficiency virus types 1 and 2 infections in Nigeria. *J Infect Dis,* 1993;167:710.

35. Touré-Kane C, Montavon C, Faye MA, et al. Identification of all HIV type 1 group M subtypes in Senegal, a country with low and stable seroprevalence. *AIDS Res Hum Retroviruses,* 2000;16(6): 603–609.

36. Meloni ST, Sankalé JL, Hamel DJ, et al. Molecular epidemiology of human immunodeficiency virus type 1 sub-subtype A3 in Senegal from 1988 to 2001. *J Virol,* 2004;78(22):12455–12461.

37. De Clercq E, Baba M, Tanaka H, et al. Potent and selective inhibition of human immunodeficiency virus (HIV)-1 and HIV-2 replication by a class of bicyclams interacting with a viral uncoating event. *Proc Natl Acad Sci USA,* 1992;89(12):5286–5290.

38. Descamps D, Collin G, Letourneur F, et al. Susceptibility of human immunodeficiency virus type 1 group O isolates to antiretroviral agents: in vitro phenotypic and genotypic analyses. *J Virol,* 1997;71:8893–8898.

39. Masse S, Lu X, Dekhtyar T, et al. In vitro selection and characterization of human immunodeficiency virus type 2 with decreased susceptibility to lopinavir. *J Antimicrob Agents Chemother,* 2007;51(9): 75–80.

40. Reid P, MacInnes H, Cong ME, et al. Natural resistance of human immunodeficiency virus type 2 to zidovudine. *Virology,* 2005;336(2):251–264.

41. Eshleman S, Becker-Pergola G, Deseyve M, et al. Impact of human immunodeficiency virus type 1 (HIV-1) subtype on women receiving single-dose nevirapine prophylaxis to prevent HIV-1 vertical transmission (HIV network for prevention trials 012 study). *J Infect Dis,* 2001;185:914–917.

42. Ojesina AI, Sankalé J, Odaibo G, et al. Subtype-specific patterns in HIV type 1 reverse transcriptase and protease in Oyo State, Nigeria: implications for drug resistance and host response. *AIDS Res Hum Retroviruses,* 2006;22(8):770–779.

43. Desclaux A, Lanièce I, Ndoye I, et al., eds. L'initiative Sénégalaise d'accès aux médicaments antirétroiraux. Paris: Agence nationale de recerches sur le SIDA, 2002.

44. Laurent C, Diakhate N, Gueye NF, et al. The Senegalese government's highly active antiretroviral therapy initiative: an 18-month follow-up study. *AIDS,* 2002;16(10):1363–1370.

45. World Health Organization. *Antiretroviral Therapy for HIV Infection in Adults and Adolescents: Recommendations for a Public Health Approach.* Geneva: World Health Organization, 1996.

46. Redfield R, Amoroso A, Davis CE. Antiretroviral therapy in resource-limited settings. In: Essex M, Mboup S, Kanki P, Marlink RG, Tlou S, eds. *AIDS in Africa.* 2nd ed. New York: Kluwer Academic/Plenum Publishers, 2002:322–344.

47. Desclaux A, Ciss M, Taverne B, et al. Access to antiretroviral drugs and AIDS management in Senegal. *AIDS,* 2003;17(Suppl 3):S95–S101.

48. AIDS Care Team Senegal, Enhancing Care Initiative. Future plans: analysis of the costs and cost-effectiveness of scaling up HIV care in five sites in Senegal. http://www.eci.harvard.edu/teams/senegal/index. html; accessed September 23, 2008.

49. Landman R, Schiemann R, Thiam S, et al. Once-a-day highly active antiretroviral therapy in treatment-naive HIV-1-infected adults in Senegal. *AIDS,* 2003; 17(7):1017–1022.

50. Tarantola A, Koumare A, Rachline A, et al. A descriptive, retrospective study of 567 accidental blood exposures in healthcare workers in three West African countries. *J Hosp Infect,* 2005;60(3):276–282.

51. de Beaudrap P, Etard JF, Gueye FN, et al. Long-term efficacy and tolerance of efavirenz- and nevirapine-containing regimens in adult HIV type 1 Senegalese patients. *AIDS Res Hum Retroviruses,* 2008;24(6): 753–760.

52. Etard JF, Ndiaye I, Thierry-Mieg M, et al. Mortality and causes of death in adults receiving highly active antiretroviral therapy in Senegal: a 7-year cohort study. *AIDS,* 2006;20(8):1181–1189.

53. Braitstein P, Brinkhof M, Dabis F, et al. Mortality of HIV-1 infected patients in the first year of antiretroviral therapy: comparison between low-income and high-income countries. *Lancet,* 2006;267:817–824.

54. Vergne L, Kane CT, Laurent C, et al. Low rate of genotypic HIV-1 drug-resistant strains in the Senegalese government initiative of access to antiretroviral therapy. *AIDS,* 2003;17(Suppl 3):S31–S38.

55. Conseil National de Lutte Contre le SIDA. *Rapport de situation sur la riposte nationale a l'épidémie de VIH/ SIDA, Sénégal: 2006–2007.* Dakar: Conseil National de Lutte Contre le SIDA, 2008.

His role in an early, unexpected discovery in the AIDS field transformed Souleymane Mboup's life.

A Bearer of Gifts

John Donnelly

IN 1977, WHEN SOULEYMANE MBOUP, a young laboratory scientist in the Senegalese army, asked Marie Louise Lopez to marry him, he knew he faced a formidable obstacle—Lopez's parents. Mboup was a Muslim, Lopez a Catholic, and her parents didn't want their daughter to marry outside her faith. That didn't deter Mboup, who pressed ahead, and the two married.

Years passed, feelings softened. Mboup and his father-in-law drew close. "At the end, before he died," Mboup said, "he was saying that I was his own son."

Such is Mboup's persuasive power: he possesses a charm and grace to win over even the toughest adversaries. He goes out of his way, in fact, to do it. "One thing about my father," said Marieme Mboup, the second of his four children, "is he doesn't want people to get mad at him. He does his best to make everybody happy."

That helps explain the innate kindness of Mboup, a man who smiles and laughs easily and who treats office cleaners and world-renowned AIDS experts alike with the same courtesy and respect.

But it only partly explains how Mboup rose from a family of 20 children (his father had five wives) to become one of the leading AIDS researchers in the world; to direct one of Africa's top medical laboratories; to contribute to more than 300 articles in peer-reviewed publications; and, most recently, to preside over the 15th International Conference on AIDS and STIs in Africa, held in his hometown of Dakar in December 2008.

There's also his ambition, which is not small; his love for work, which knows few boundaries; and his strong desire to solve riddles for some of the most pressing problems in infectious diseases today. He has never shied away from the biggest problems.

"His dream," said his daughter Marieme, "is to stop AIDS."

A Rebel with a Cause

Mboup was born in the outskirts of Dakar in 1951, nine years before Senegal won its independence from France. His father, Ibrahima Mboup, was a peanuts trader who moved from the central part of Senegal to the capital of Dakar to become a white-collar worker in a government statistics office. Most critically for his son, the elder Mboup believed his children should be well educated, ensuring that Souleymane, his nine immediate siblings, and his ten half-siblings would get as much schooling as they desired. Among Souleymane's immediate siblings, seven would attend universities—a rare accomplishment at a time in which few Senegalese families sent their children through secondary school.

Souleymane's father and mother, Yacine, made another decision that would largely shape his life: They sent him to live with one of his grandmothers, as a kind of "gift" to her, he explained. His grandmother had lost a son, and Ibahima and Yacine Mboup believed Souleymane would help ease that loss. The grandmother, Fatou Ndiaye Mbaye, believed she should prepare Mboup for many tasks ahead in his life—if in a rather unorthodox fashion.

"She raised me," Mboup remembered, "not exactly as people raised boys at the time." Cleaning the house and washing the dishes were among his duties.

She also taught him humility. But she apparently didn't break a rebellious, independent streak in the young man. That showed when he finished high school in 1971. At the urging of a friend, he took an exam to go to medical school through the Senegalese army. He passed. But then he refused to enlist.

"The army sent someone to my house every day," he said. "The first time they came, I said I was the brother of Souleymane, and Souleymane had gone away."

Still, the persistent army representatives kept coming. After a month of visits, on the final day of the enlistment period, Mboup went to the army office. When he showed up, an army representative looked at him and said, "Where is your brother? We're looking for Souleymane." After some minutes, he persuaded them that he was the person they wanted. That moment led to a career in the military still going strong decades later.

Mboup started as a student at the Dakar Military School of Health and chose a career in the laboratory that focused on microbiology, virology, and immunology.

By 1981, at age 30, he held a master's degree in chemistry–biochemistry from the University of Dakar and one in immunology from Institut Pasteur in Paris.

Two years later, he had earned a doctorate in bacteriology–virology from the University of Tours in France and a doctorate in pharmacy from the University of Dakar, which was later renamed Université Cheikh Anta Diop. He would soon become a full professor in microbiology at the university.

But something much bigger was about to happen to Mboup—the discovery in Senegal in 1985 of a new AIDS virus. That virus would become known as HIV-2.

In Full Flight

Of the many factors that led to the discovery of HIV-2 in Senegal, one key building block was a French government program that called for the registration of all sex workers in the country. The genesis was to protect French citizens from sexually transmitted infections; in the early 1970s, syphilis predominated. In return for registering with health authorities—and getting regular health checkups—the sex workers were allowed to continue working. These regular checkups also created a readily accessible population group that happened to be at high risk for contracting HIV, making them a sought-after group for researchers intent on understanding the AIDS epidemic in Africa. In short, the researchers could with little difficulty begin testing the progression of HIV in these high-risk women, who were already visiting a health clinic every month.

In Dakar, Mboup had previously worked with a French scientist, Dr. Francis Barin, who had ties to a laboratory run by Dr. Max Essex, chairman of what was then the Department of Cancer Biology at the Harvard School of Public Health. Barin and the Harvard group were looking at blood samples from Senegal of both humans and monkeys, and a researcher in Essex's laboratory, Dr. Phyllis Kanki, had found evidence of a virus type that matched neither the monkey virus nor the previously known type found in humans.

Barin called Mboup. "He said, 'Do you remember the samples you sent to Harvard? Can you find the person? Are you ready to go to the States?'" Mboup recalled. "I asked why, and he said they had discovered something very important and they needed me to take fresh samples to Boston immediately."

The samples came from a group of sex workers in Senegal—some in Dakar, but some as far as 82 kilometers away. Mboup needed to get samples from 30 of the women, and he had to do it on the same day of his flight. So Mboup, who had just one technician working with him, started driving all over the city's suburbs to find the sex workers and collect their blood samples. In the last-minute rush before the flight, he wrapped the vials of blood in wrapping paper—in order to disguise them. When he arrived in New York the next day, a customs agent asked him what was inside the wrappings.

"Gifts," he said.

In a sense, he was telling the truth. A few hours later, in the Harvard laboratory, Kanki examined the hand-delivered samples and confirmed her earlier findings: The virus in Senegal was unlike the one found before. The researchers had made a historic discovery that would alter the understanding and the arc of AIDS research.

"After that," Mboup said, "everything changed in my life—at great speed."

In November 1985, Kanki, Essex, Mboup, and Barin presented their findings on the new HIV type at the 1st International Conference on AIDS and STIs in Africa, held in Brussels, Belgium. Their continued research would later show that the new virus was genetically located between one found in healthy green African monkeys and the previously known virus found in humans, which would later be identified as HIV-1.

Over the coming years, the group—working out of Senegal, Harvard, and the universities of Tours and Limoges in France—would amass a series of studies that described the virology, immune response, and natural history of HIV-2. Their central finding so far has been that HIV-2, confined mostly to West Africa, is less virulent than HIV-1 and takes a far longer time to progress to full-blown AIDS. Some sex workers who contracted HIV-2 in the mid-1980s, or before, have continued to have high CD4+ counts and virtually undetectable viral loads; they have remained healthy. The scientists' work has greatly added to the body of knowledge about AIDS, and they hope their research will someday assist in the formulation of an AIDS vaccine.

The French Connection

The fast track for Mboup wasn't without its difficulties, though. One of the greatest issues for him was breaking out of the Francophone sphere of influence and casting

his star with U.S. researchers. In the mid-1980s, such a move was not done in scientific circles in French-speaking West Africa, but Mboup forged ahead with his new alliances. French scientists fumed and argued with him. "For a while, they considered me as someone who didn't work with them," he said. "But it got better. They finally realized they couldn't do anything without me."

Mboup can laugh at the memory now, but it wasn't easy at the time. He had all the hard-won contacts inside Senegal; his laboratory provided the necessary tests for the sex workers, including HIV; and he had the backing of the military medical institutions and the leaders in the country's health ministry. One reason to choose the Harvard group was the prestige of the institution. But for Mboup there was an even more compelling reason: The Americans wanted the Senegalese to develop the capacity to do the work themselves. It would be a far less complicated relationship than with the French overseers of the project, even if his relationships with the French scientists had always been strong; the Americans carried no baggage from colonial times. Even after his arrangement with Harvard, Mboup's team and French scientists have continued working closely together, forming strong collaborative ties.

"In the mid-1980s," Mboup said, "the most important thing for me was to show that it was possible to do important work by ourselves. We wanted to gain the trust of international researchers so we could gain credibility. When you are trying to work at the same level as the others, whatever that level is, it means that others must trust you. You must make them know they should have an interest in working with you."

In that key respect, Mboup's ambition was not for his own advancement. It was an ambition for those who followed him.

"I don't really think in general of myself and my own interests," he said one morning in 2008, looking back at the span of his career and particularly those moments when he began his partnership with the Americans. "I think about what is it I can bring to my country, to my partners, to Senegalese researchers. If I do this, I help everyone out."

Taking Precautions

Mboup's helping hand has been felt down the ranks—both in the military, where he has been pharmacist colonel since 1996, and in the university. "So many of us have learned from Souleymane," said Dr. Papa Salif Sow, head of the Department of Infectious Diseases at Université Cheikh Anta Diop. "I learned from him that to lead a team it is important to be open and to demonstrate to everyone that you are a hard worker. All the young people learn about behavior from Souleymane. He is totally different from the other department heads at the hospital. No one has the same vision."

Dr. Tidiane Siby, who worked under Mboup for seven years on the sex worker study before starting a private laboratory company, called Mboup "atypical" for a laboratory director or researcher because of his "sweet nature—and the fact that he has always been able to see the bigger picture beyond the work that he himself was doing."

At the Laboratory of Bacteriology and Virology at Le Dantec Hospital in Dakar, the results of Mboup's vision are in plain view. In 1985, his laboratory consisted just of himself and a technician. By 2008, Mboup was overseeing a staff of more than a hundred people, including nearly 60 scientists. The laboratory keeps expanding, almost annually, moving into new quarters as more people are hired; it has also expanded its training capabilities, bringing in 30 lab technicians from around Francophone West Africa every year for six weeks. The work itself also continues to grow; several researchers, for example, are now looking at the interactions between HIV and malaria.

The laboratory, run by Africans, is perhaps the most sophisticated one in West Africa. But it's not just the high-tech equipment that makes the operation work. Mboup, for instance, decided to put in a cafeteria, which increased productivity as well as created more social interaction among staff. "It's good way to link people," he said. "But it also keeps them here the whole day, instead of leaving from noon to two in the afternoon for a lunch break."

The hub of the operations is Mboup's office. People are in and out through the padded doors almost every few minutes, arriving with questions or simply greetings. Mboup never seems to mind the interruptions—he greets everyone the same way, happy, ready with a quip or a question about how a family member is doing. And just as he has surrounded himself with people he cares about, he has also stuffed his office with the memorabilia of his work life. If anyone ever wanted to start a museum about the history of AIDS in Senegal, Mboup's office would be a good place to start. His walls are lined with awards, framed pictures, and gifts that carry deep meaning.

On one wall, in an out-of-the-way spot, is a yellowed copy of Kanki's Western blot test results that first revealed the existence of a new virus. Across the room is the first AIDS poster ever in Senegal, showing a soldier firing a gun at a target. "*Prenez vos précautions*," the poster declares. *Take precautions.* The soldier isn't firing a bullet, but rather a condom at an image of the virus. "I like that poster," Mboup said, smiling at the old image. "Fighting AIDS is as serious as fighting a war."

And then on one ledge rests a carved replica of a dhow, a Senegalese fishing boat. It was a gift to Mboup from an AIDS patient by the name of Mbengue, a fisherman who lived in a village outside Dakar.

Mboup held the dhow for a moment. "He died," Mboup said. "He died before antiretroviral drugs arrived."

He grew quiet, a rare moment of showing sadness.

That night, in his house just outside Dakar, there were few such quiet moments. Three of the Mboups' four children were there for dinner, and two of their grandchildren were running around the house, from the first floor to the rooftop, where Mboup had just started a vegetable garden. In wooden beds on stilts, he was growing turnips, mint, lettuce, beans, eggplants, cucumbers, peppers, and carrots.

Standing around the vegetables, his children told stories about their father.

"He works too much," Marieme said. "If you want him to take holidays, you have to beg him. I tell him he will be tired when he retires. I don't think he can stay in one place."

Mboup smiled and offered a half-hearted defense. "On Sundays, I do take time off," he said. "I walk for three hours."

His wife, Marie, overheard him. "We've been together for more than 30 years, and I still can't slow him down. We've gotten used to it."

Mboup had a lot on his mind in the months leading up to the international conference on AIDS in Africa. The meeting, which drew more than 5,000 people to Dakar, had been nearly all consuming. Yet slowing down didn't seem to be an option for Mboup. He still had to run his laboratory, and he still had to plan new projects.

"I say I am going to stop someday," he said late that night after dinner. "People tell me I will never stop. Maybe that's a gift from God, I don't know, that allows me to work with different people, different characters."

He smiled at the word *characters*. He was in a reflective mood, thinking about the span of years behind him and where he stood today.

"We have been here since the beginning and we are still here," he said. "This is one of the few countries still maintaining the fight against AIDS for 20 years. In other countries, people changed, people moved on. Not here. The same people who started here are still here."

His smile was gone. His knees bounced up and down as he sat; he was restless, ready to move on. He wasn't done with his work—not even close. ∎

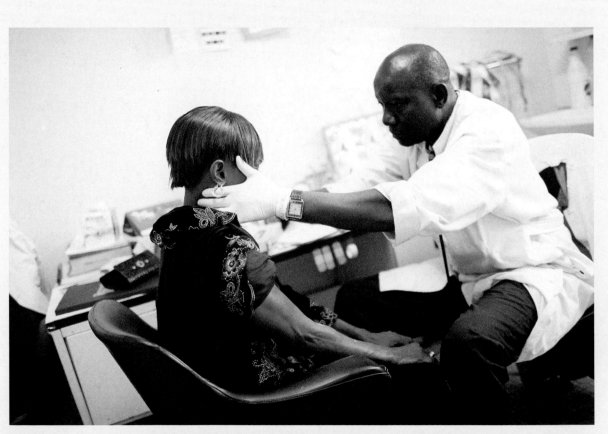

Ibrahima Traoré follows a cohort of sex workers who have proven to be key collaborators in HIV prevention.

A Mine of Information

JOHN DONNELLY

T HESE ARE NOT ordinary doctor–patient relationships. The patients are sex workers—women working in a profession that puts them at a high risk of contracting sexual infections, including HIV. The doctors are specialists in sex workers—they treat them and, for more than two decades, have been drawing blood samples from them, for a study on the progression of the second AIDS virus, HIV-2, which was discovered among sex workers in Senegal in 1985. But what most defines these relationships is not the virus. It's their longevity, and the warmth that has developed between the doctors and their patients over the years.

"We can discuss things easily with them because we've spent a lot of time together," said Dr. Ibrahima Traoré, an infectious disease specialist who has worked with the sex workers since 1990. "If you didn't know them, they would be a difficult population. But they're not difficult for us."

"We know what has happened to them during their lives," said Dr. Mamadou Dia, the sex workers' other main physician at the Institut d'Hygiène Sociale clinic in Dakar. The two doctors, who conduct research as part of the Dakar–Harvard University sex worker project, have been treating the sex workers since 1987. "We'd better know them—because they don't talk about their sex work activities with anyone else," said Dia. "They talk to us. Most of their families don't know."

A confluence of factors created what has become the longest studied cohort of African sex workers in the AIDS era. Since 1985, the studies have given researchers a rich source of data about the characteristics of HIV, including how the virus changes over a prolonged period.

The first factor that contributed to the start of the study is a Senegalese law that has allowed the profession to exist in a quasi-legal state since the 1970s: as long as the women register with authorities and receive regular checkups to help curb the spread of sexually transmitted infections, police leave them alone. The law has also given doctors and researchers an easily accessible group of people engaged in work that exposes them to a host of viruses.

The second factor is Senegal's relatively strong health care system, including a robust laboratory capacity, which has allowed doctors to monitor the women every month. And the third was the advent of the AIDS epidemic—and notably the discovery of HIV-2 by Harvard and Senegalese researchers—which created an immediate demand to study the sex workers and to ensure they stayed healthy.

The discovery of HIV-2 in 1985 raised a host of questions, including some that persist today. But the overarching one was to learn about the natural history of HIV-2, including whether it would mimic the history of HIV-1, which is by far the most common type of the virus. (HIV-2 is concentrated in Senegal and Guinea-Bissau, and even in these two countries, HIV-1 has grown to be the dominant type in the population.)

"The services provided by the government of Senegal naturally evolved into the study—and the study then evolved into access to treatment," said Dr. Phyllis Kanki, a Harvard professor and one of the discoverers of HIV-2. "The study also provided doctors in a clinic that had never had doctors, and they did tests for other infections beside HIV."

The program, though, wasn't without challenges. Sometimes sex workers didn't show up for appointments, which meant social workers and researchers had to go

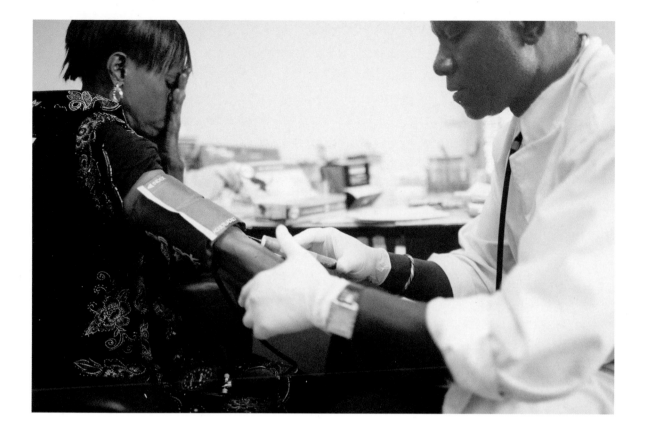

looking for them. They found some in bars or hotel lobbies. But researchers often had to follow several leads before tracking them down.

Dr. Tidiane Siby, who worked on the sex workers project from 1987 to 1994, remembers tracking one woman to her home. "We found many well-dressed people there," Siby recalled. "We were embarrassed, but we were also in a hurry. She took us outside, where we could talk privately."

"We asked her, 'What's going on?'"

"She said, 'I got married one week ago.'"

"I said, 'What, are you crazy? Do you know what you're doing?'"

"She said, 'I assume he knows—he found me in a bar.'"

Most encounters are far less dramatic, and they usually take place in the privacy of the doctor's office. The annual cohort for the study has averaged around 700 sex workers; since 1985, the study has examined—and doctors have treated—more than 3,600 sex workers. While the HIV rates among the sex workers have remained low in Senegal by African standards, there has been some shifting of the proportions of HIV-1 and HIV-2 in the decades since the second virus was discovered. At the same time that the HIV-2 rate among sex workers has dropped from around 10 percent to about 5 percent, the HIV-1 rate has increased from less than 1 percent to approximately 14 percent. The number of sex workers infected with both viruses has remained stable, at near 2 percent.

One morning in the summer of 2008, Traoré was looking for a patient who was late for her appointment. He called her cell phone and she answered. He introduced himself, and a few seconds later, the doctor was laughing.

"She recognized my voice," he said, after hanging up. "That's how well we know each other."

The patient, Debo Sow, 41, appeared about ten minutes later. Sow, the mother of eight children, said that the government program to treat sex workers has saved her life.

"I don't just think that," she said. "I *know* it. I would be dead. I couldn't even walk when I was first treated."

Now, thanks to antiretroviral therapy, she said, she feels healthy. Her CD4+ count, which once was well below 200, has soared to 674.

Sow started a support group called Karleen, which has 49 HIV-infected members who are connected in some way to the sex trade. It includes not only some of the women who are treated at the clinic, but also undocumented sex workers, barkeepers, and partners of the sex workers. "When we were on our own, we all hid our status," Sow said. "Now we discover that others are positive, and not only that, but they are willing to help each other."

Traoré listened to her closely. When Sow finished, he spoke up. "We counsel them as sisters," he said. "If they have other problems, even things that have nothing to do with health, they come to see us."

Just that morning, Traoré said, a sex worker, a longtime patient, came to his office with her daughter, who was substantially overweight. "She told me that her daughter wasn't listening to her advice about trying to lose weight, and she asked me to help," he said. "So I talked to the daughter about the right foods to eat, how important it was to do some physical exercise. Sometimes it helps to have an outsider say those things. I think she listened to me well."

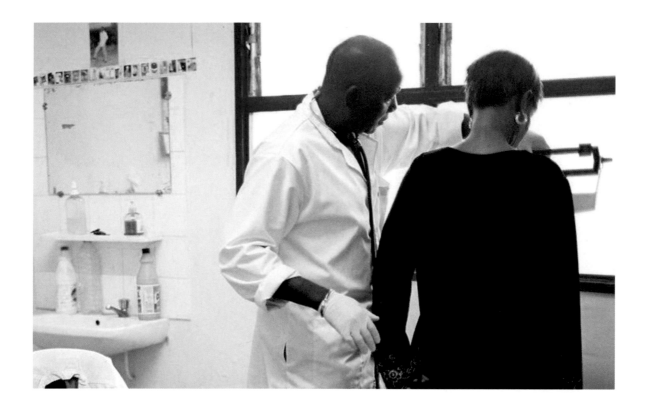

The daughter listened, Traoré believed, because he was a doctor, and because her mother trusted him. That trust was never easily won, Traoré said. "With the sex workers, we are dealing with a clandestine population. They are a very important population for us if we are going to stop the transmission of HIV. We have to know them well—and we do." ∎

Papa Salif Sow tends to his patients' nutritional needs as well as their medical ones.

Strong Medicine

JOHN DONNELLY

PAPA SALIF SOW, an AIDS doctor and Senegal's national AIDS treatment program director, was making his regular rounds one day in late 2003 when he stopped at a bed to check on a patient who was recovering from meningitis.

Sow asked the patient how he was doing. "Fine," the man told the doctor. "But I need to talk with you. In two days, I haven't eaten."

The doctor was shocked—Fann Hospital, where he worked, did not provide free food to most patients, but still almost everyone came with a family member or friend who made meals for them.

Then, only a few days later, Sow saw a television ad promoting micro-gardens, or small backyard gardens. Sow put the two events together in his mind, arranged to meet with the garden entrepreneur, and then devised a plan to start a garden in the back of the hospital's Infectious Disease Unit.

At first the hospital's doctors and nurses thought it was a bad idea. "They told me their job was to treat patients, not feed them," Sow said.

But Sow persisted, arguing that AIDS patients needed nutrition as well as their life-extending antiretroviral medicines. Weeks later, the hospital directors and his peers relented, and soon, Sow, with the help of the gardeners he hired, was growing a riot of herbs and vegetables on hospital grounds.

Five years later, Sow's idea, sparked by a patient's hunger, has grown into a mainstay at the hospital. The garden now produces more than a hundred pounds of vegetables each month, providing sustenance for 45 patients every day. Kitchen cooks prepare hot meals for breakfast and lunch.

And that's only a small part of the impact: Steve Bolinger, an expert in agriculture who helped expand and refine Sow's project during its first years, has started a nongovernmental organization called Development in Gardening, or DIG. He has exported the idea to Uganda and soon hopes to start projects in South Africa and Lesotho. Former U.S. First Lady Laura Bush, in a visit to the garden in June 2007, called the project "a great role model . . . for other hospitals or other communities across Africa to improve gardens as part of their [AIDS] treatment."

After she harvested carrots and herbs for use in that day's lunch at the hospital, Bush said, "I think it's often overlooked, that one essential thing in the treatment of AIDS, or HIV, is good nutrition. And the gardens that we've seen here at the Fann Hospital give patients who are HIV positive a chance to have good vegetables and protein in their diet, and so have a better chance to take antiretrovirals and have the antiretrovirals work."

Sow's garden also received help from the Ministry of Agriculture, which donated seeds, and from the U.S. Agency for International Development, which gave a small grant.

Sitting in his hospital office, Sow waved his arms all about him as he excitedly told this history of the project. Then he stood up and said, "Let me show you!"

In the oppressive heat of midday, he strode around the building, stopping only when he got to the garden's gate, which he pushed open with great flourish.

"Look!" he said. "Look at this!" Before him, for 60 or 70 yards, were row after row of raised wooden beds covered with green stalks of all shapes and sizes—eggplant, tomatoes, turnips, beets, beans, cabbages, mint.

"Onions," he said, pulling a visitor toward them. And as if his visitors didn't fully comprehend how amazing this was, he shouted, "*Onions!*"

His enthusiasm didn't stop with the slender green shoots. "Fantastic!" he said as moved around the beds before pausing in front of old tires in which cucumbers, basil, and mustard grew. "People threw away these tires—can you believe it?" he said. "They can be put to good use in gardens. Look at this!"

Against the walls of the garden, workers had hooked narrow wooden beds sprouting with fresh growth—another additional spot for vegetables and herbs to grow. Not all the beds were filled with soil; some were packed instead with peanut shells, which a local factory had donated to the project. "It's like a mulch—only better," Sow said, digging his hands into the ground-up shells.

The doctor hadn't finished refining his idea. AIDS patients, while greatly appreciating the fresh and nutritious meals, still had so many problems to overcome, he said. The biggest one was not having a steady income.

"These patients are doing very well on their medicine, but they always need money," Sow said. "So I want to make micro-gardening an income-generating activity."

Based on Sow's initial success with the hospital garden, administrators agreed to give him a second plot of land. On it, he plans to give parts of the garden to those living with HIV/AIDS. He said some economists have estimated that each farmer could earn more than US$100 from the project each month. "This would make a big difference in their lives," he said.

But there were indications all around the hospital that the project was already making a huge difference for those who desperately needed nutritious meals.

On one afternoon, Ibnou Gueye was strolling the hospital grounds—a feat in itself. Five weeks earlier, she had arrived at the hospital on a stretcher, unconscious with bacterial meningitis. Doctors saved her life with antibiotic treatment, and then, over the weeks, the food from the garden helped nurture her back to health.

"At home, when I was sick, I stopping eating what they were preparing for me," said Gueye, who learned during her stay that she was HIV positive. "But I've been eating the food from the garden here. The food here is really good for your health."

Gueye walked back to her hospital room. "That's been one of the great things about this garden, with her and my other AIDS patients," Sow said, as he watched her. "They're getting better for many reasons, but one reason is the food from this garden." ■

The HIV/AIDS Epidemic in SENEGAL

a photo essay by Dominic Chavez

Senegal has long been known for its beautiful, pristine beaches. More recently, it has been praised for its model response to the HIV/AIDS epidemic as well. The country's political and scientific leaders have worked together to help keep HIV infection rates in Senegal among the lowest on the continent.

The government of Senegal oversees a public health program for registered sex workers. Clinics provide the women with basic health care and regular testing for sexually transmitted infections, including HIV. Early in its Initiative Senegalese for Access to Antiretrovirals program, the government provided free antiretrovirals to sex workers in need of treatment.

Every afternoon, students from Université Cheikh Anta Diop in Dakar jog down the stretch of a nearby beach and work out together in good-natured mayhem. Targeting HIV education and prevention programs to such young people has been an important part of Senegal's national HIV/AIDS control program.

Senegal's control programs for HIV and other sexually transmitted infections have provided registered sex workers with education, counseling, and condom promotion. This pragmatic approach to working with a key population in the epidemic has helped keep the country's HIV rates relatively low.

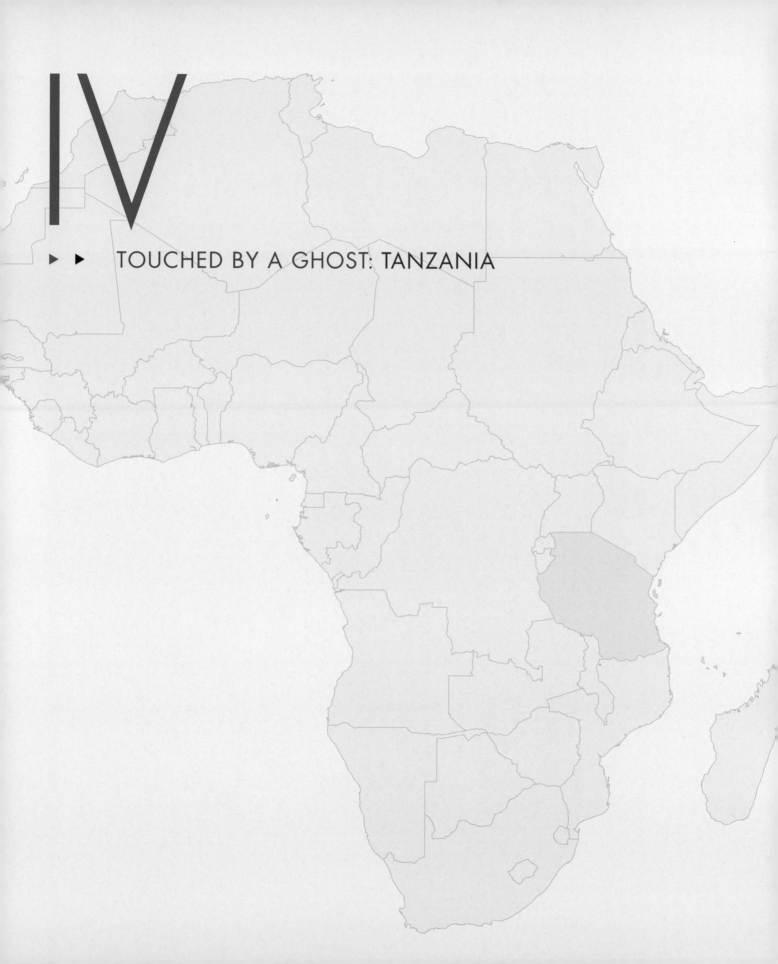

IV

► ► TOUCHED BY A GHOST: TANZANIA

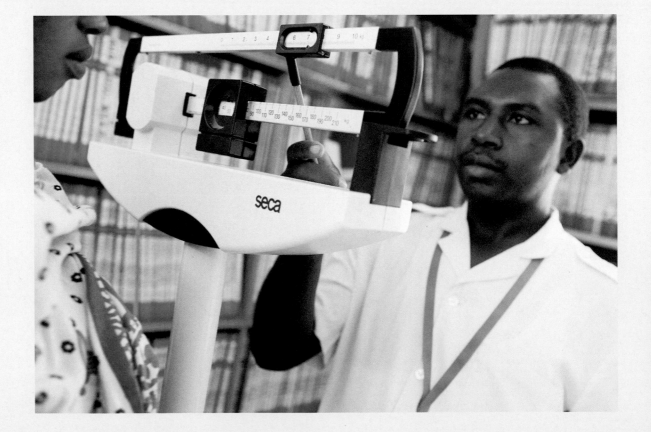

Touched by a Ghost

ONE SUMMER DAY IN 2007, the president of Tanzania, Jakaya Kikwete, sat beside his wife beneath an olive-drab tent. They wore identical white polo shirts and yellow caps with green bills. Although his attire might not have seemed very presidential, his action was: he was launching a new national HIV testing campaign by becoming its first participant.

The president and his wife were having their blood drawn in the hope of inspiring other Tanzanians to follow their example. The public event was part of the launch of TUNAJALI, a five-year, US$56-million initiative aimed at preventing further spread of HIV in Tanzania and providing treatment and care to those already infected. *Tunajali* is the Swahili word for "we care."

The campaign's goals were "to raise awareness among the public and to assure those already affected that we will support them and protect them from abuses," said President Kikwete, who has declared HIV/AIDS a national disaster. "The government will also try to ensure that those affected get the appropriate treatment to enable them to live longer." The U.S. President's Emergency Plan for AIDS Relief, or PEPFAR, and the U.S. Agency for International Development provided funding for the program.

Nearly 1.6 million Tanzanians are infected with HIV. Before the campaign's launch, only a small percentage of the population had been tested. During the six-month campaign, the number of people tested more than quintupled.

Another critical component of Tanzania's response to AIDS has been the National HIV Care and Treatment Program, which began in October 2004 when the government made a commitment to provide free services—including antiretrovirals—to all Tanzanians in need. The program started providing antiretroviral therapy with support from six PEPFAR-funded U.S. partners. By July 2008, out of the estimated 600,000 HIV-infected Tanzanians who qualified for the therapy, 150,000, or 25 percent, were receiving the drugs at 200 sites throughout Tanzania.

Building the infrastructure so critical to the program's immediate and long-term success has been challenging. The AIDS epidemic does far more than cause immeasurable suffering; it also strains health care systems throughout the world. The impact tends to be most devastating in countries whose economies were overstressed before the advent of HIV.

Tanzania, one of the world's poorest countries, had a strained health care system long before AIDS appeared. And its burden has only grown heavier. Each year, more than 100,000 Tanzanians die of malaria. The nation now ranks 14th among the world's 22 countries with the largest tuberculosis epidemics. And Tanzania has only one doctor for every 25,000 people, compared with one for every 400 in the United States.

Dr. Wafaie Fawzi, a Harvard professor, understands well the challenges Tanzania faces. Since 1993, he has headed a collaboration among researchers at Muhimbili University of Health and Allied Sciences, the Dar es Salaam City Council, and the Harvard School of Public Health. Their overarching goal has been to improve the health of Tanzanians living in extreme poverty.

Taking the first letter of each of their names, the collaborating institutions formed the MDH Program in 2004 to support the delivery of high-quality treatment and care to people living with HIV/AIDS in Tanzania. The city of Dar es Salaam owns and runs the health facilities.

The MDH Program has since enrolled more than 63,000 adults and children, including 39,000 patients on antiretroviral therapy. The program, which is funded through a PEPFAR grant, aims first to strengthen the staffing, research, and infrastructure capacity that will be critical to its success.

Once, during a meeting of PEPFAR-funded program representatives, Fawzi learned about a group of HIV outreach workers who had staged a play in an effort to promote fidelity among Tanzanian men. One of the play's central characters was a ghost who quietly stalked, then touched, those who had not been faithful to their partners. The message was clear: those who remained faithful would not be touched by the ghost.

With 6 percent of adults in Tanzania already infected with HIV, Fawzi and his colleagues are working hard to keep the rest of the country from being stalked—and touched—by the spectre of AIDS. ∎

The Challenge and Response in Tanzania

Guerino Chalamilla and Wafaie Fawzi

IN THE EARLY 1980S, YOUNG PEOPLE IN EAST AFRICA BEGAN DYING OF A SEVERE wasting disease, one that reduced them to near skeletons. AIDS had not yet received an official name; East Africans called it "slim disease."

AIDS came early to Tanzania, an East African nation just south of the equator. Since the discovery of the country's first AIDS cases in 1983, HIV has spread relentlessly, affecting people of all ages, in all parts of the country. Approximately 6 percent of adults are now infected—and fewer than 10 percent know their HIV status.

Economic and Social Background

The United Republic of Tanzania was formed in 1964 from the union of two independent countries, Tanganyika and Zanzibar. The republic has a population of more than 38 million people who belong to about 120 ethnic groups. Despite this diversity, Tanzanians share a common language, Swahili.

The country has enormous natural wealth, from the snow-capped Kilimanjaro, to the sandy beaches of the coastal regions, to the gentle shores of Lake Victoria, to the endless national parks. Dar es Salaam, the mainland's commercial capital and major seaport, acts as a gateway for the neighboring landlocked countries of Uganda, Rwanda, Burundi, the Democratic Republic of the Congo, Zambia, and Malawi.

In the early 1990s, following decades of one-party socialism and a slow pace of economic growth, Tanzania embarked on a political and economic transformation. The country now sustains annual economic growth rates that are among the highest in sub-Saharan Africa. In a volatile region, Tanzania is a stable country progressing along a path of democratic governance. It hosts hundreds of thousands of refugees, mainly from Burundi and the Democratic Republic of the Congo, and leads efforts to resolve regional conflicts peacefully.

Despite its economic growth, Tanzania remains one of the world's poorest countries (Table 1). Its economy depends heavily on agriculture, which accounts for more than 40 percent of its gross domestic product (GDP), provides 85 percent of its exports, and employs 80 percent of its workforce. Topography and climatic conditions limit cultivated crops, however, to only 4 percent of the country's land area.

The World Bank, the International Monetary Fund, and bilateral donors have provided funds to rehabilitate Tanzania's outdated economic infrastructure and to alleviate poverty. Long-term growth through 2005 featured a pickup in industrial production and a substantial increase in the output of minerals. Recent banking reforms have helped increase private-sector growth and investment. In 2007, continued assistance from development partners and solid macroeconomic policies supported a GDP growth rate of nearly 7 percent.

The government of Tanzania, under the leadership of President Jakaya Mrisho Kikwete, has been committed to the pursuit of sound, consistent, and predictable macroeconomic policies with low inflation. The government's policies encompass expansions in investments, job creation, exports, and human capital development.

The Burden of HIV/AIDS Disease in Tanzania

The first AIDS cases in Tanzania were diagnosed and reported in 1983 in the northern region of Kagera, which borders Uganda. The rapid spread of HIV soon became apparent and by 1986 all regions of the Tanzania Mainland had reported AIDS

Table 1. Selected Indicators of Development, Health Expenditures, and Outcomes

Indicator	Tanzania	Nigeria	Senegal	Botswana
Human development index ranking, out of 177	159	158	156	124
Human development category	low	low	low	medium
Population (in millions)	38.5	150	12.9	1.8
Population under the age of 15 in 2005	28.9%	55.9%	44.7%	35.6%
Annual population growth (1975–2005)	2.9	2.8	2.8	2.7
Annual population growth (2005–2015)	2.4	2.2	2.3	1.2
Average life expectancy at birth (in years)	51	46.5	62.3	46.1
Under-five mortality rate per 1,000 live births	122	194	136	120
Incidence of tuberculosis per 100,000 people	496	536	466	556
Adult literacy rate	69.4%	69.1%	39.3%	81.2%
Physicians per 100,000 people	2	28	6	40
Gross national income per capita for 2007 using the Atlas method	US$400	US$930	US$820	US$5,840
Population below the income poverty line (% on US$1 a day), 1990–2005 (World Bank, 2007)	58%	71%	17%	28%
Health expenditure per capita (current US$)	US$17	US$27	US$38	US$362

Sources: Gross national income: World Bank. Gross national income per capita 2007, Atlas method and PPP. World Development Indicators Database of July 1, 2008, accessed at *http://siteresources.worldbank.org/DATASTATISTICS/Resources/GNIPC.pdf* on August 21, 2008. Health expenditure per capita (current US$): World Bank. "HNP at a Glance" database, accessed at *http://go.worldbank.org/MALQ9X8AS0* on August 21, 2008.

Note: GNI for Tanzania refers to the mainland only

cases. The epidemic has gradually shifted from the northwestern part of the country to the southern highlands and the eastern coast. Kagera, in the northwestern corner, had the highest prevalence rate in the 1980s and 1990s and yet has since seen a dramatic decrease in its rate. In Dar es Salaam and other southern regions, such as Mbeya and Iringa, transmission rates have risen. The three regions with the highest rates of HIV infection are also ones with major travel routes into and out of the country (Figure 1).

In 2003–04, the HIV prevalence rate in the Tanzania Mainland was estimated at 7.0 percent, with 6.3 percent among males and 7.7 percent among females in the 15-to-49 age group.[1] In 2007–08, a rate of 5.8 percent was found among the same age group.[2] HIV prevalence in urban areas is almost double that in rural areas.

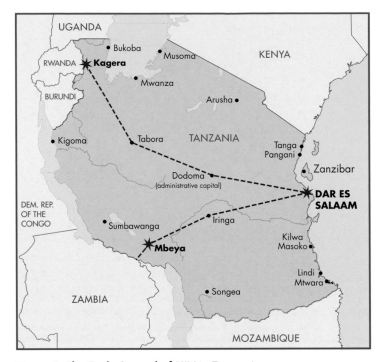

Figure 1. The Early Spread of HIV in Tanzania
The first AIDS cases were diagnosed in the northern region of Kagera. Over time HIV spread along the major highways, possibly by long-distance truck drivers. The highest prevalence rates are now in Dar es Salaam and Mbeya.

Among women, HIV prevalence is 11 percent in urban areas and 5 percent in rural ones. For men, the corresponding rates are 7 percent and 4 percent.

Since the epidemic began in Tanzania in 1983, more than one million have died from the disease. More than 2.5 million adults and children are estimated to be living with HIV/AIDS (Figure 2).

More than 90 percent of those infected do not know their serostatus and so cannot to take full advantage of prevention and care activities. In July 2007, President Kikwete initiated a national campaign to expand and promote voluntary testing for HIV. As encouragement, he and his wife were the first to be tested.

Modes of Transmission

The primary mode of HIV transmission in Tanzania is unprotected heterosexual intercourse, which accounts for an estimated 80 percent of all new infections. Approximately 18 percent of new infections can be attributed to mother-to-child transmission. A 2007–2008 survey reported that 1.8 percent of people aged 15 to 24 years who reported never having had sex were found to be HIV positive.[2] This suggests that they may have been infected through a contaminated blood transfusion, unsafe injections, or traditional practices, including male circumcision or female genital cutting.

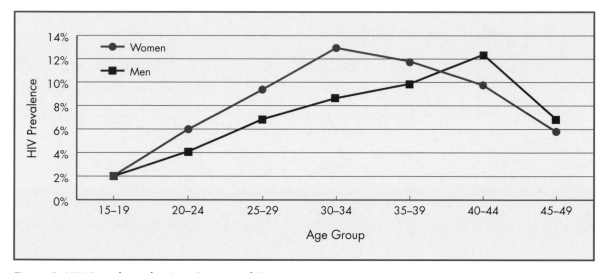

Figure 2. HIV Prevalence by Age Group and Sex

Source: Tanzania Commission for AIDS, Zanzibar AIDS Commission, National Bureau of Statistics, MEASURE DHS. *Tanzania HIV/AIDS and Malaria Indicator Survey, 2007–08*. Dar es Salaam: Tanzania Commission for AIDS, 2008

Although the national prevalence of injection drug users in Tanzania is unknown, reports show the number has been increasing. Surveys also show that the HIV infection rate among drug users is as high as 42 percent. Exacerbating the growing problem is the tendency for new users to skip initial snorting and smoking and to start injecting heroin immediately. Flash blood, the practice of giving a syringe of blood to another injector, and *vipointi*, the practice of injecting a small, measured amount before returning the syringe to another user, have both become common.[3] As a result of the increased number of injection drug users, gender-based violence has risen, with men stealing drugs, syringes, and money from women.[4]

Injection drug use has created an epidemiologic core group for HIV transmission risk. Efforts have begun toward establishing user-friendly voluntary counseling and testing (VCT), HIV care and treatment services, and low-cost or free drug treatment and rehabilitation services for injection drug users. Additional work is needed to promote awareness of the risk of HIV transmission through injection drug use.

The Impact of HIV/AIDS

Tanzania has suffered various manifestations of the HIV/AIDS epidemic, including a lowered life expectancy, a rising infant and child mortality, and a growing number of orphans. Economic impacts include an increased dependency ratio, a reduced growth in the GDP, reduced productivity, and increasing poverty. The epidemic is a serious threat to the country's social and economic development and has direct implications on social services as well. Poverty significantly influences the spread of HIV, which ultimately leads to a loss of economically active segments of society and reductions in income. The human capital loss has serious social and economic impacts in all sectors and at all levels. All too often, the high cost of care and burials falls on already overburdened households.

Reproductive-health–related issues are significant in Tanzania; HIV prevalence is increasing among adolescents and women and risky sexual practices continue despite the scaling up of HIV prevention efforts, including awareness-raising campaigns; the distribution of information, education, and communication materials; and the availability of VCT. Existing education interventions have had only minimal impact on behavior change among adolescents, largely because information on adolescent behavior and their educational needs is so limited. The methods and approaches used have not adequately targeted the specific needs of adolescents.

The government of Tanzania and other stakeholders have demonstrated a commendable zeal in mobilizing resources to scale up the country's response to HIV/AIDS. These efforts have been hampered, however, by a slow absorptive capacity and a poor oversight of funds both among some civil society organizations and in the government ministries, departments, and agencies—a problem that can be attributed to low levels of capacity throughout the government system.

Already weak health care systems are now struggling with the additional burden of HIV/AIDS, which in turn further impedes the provision of quality services. In addition, the health sector has only a limited capacity to roll out the provision of antiretrovirals, both to treat people with HIV/AIDS and to prevent mother-to-child transmission of the virus. Even though the Tanzania Mainland has demonstrated significant achievements in providing antiretrovirals for both purposes, the already overburdened health care system is Tanzania is slowing progress.

A significant rate of HIV infection has led to a twin epidemic of tuberculosis in Tanzania.[5] People with HIV/AIDS are ten times more likely to develop tuberculosis than those who are HIV negative. In a person with latent tuberculosis infection, HIV is a major predictor of advancement from infection to disease. Sixty percent of AIDS-related deaths in Tanzania result from tuberculosis. From 1998 to 2008, the number of tuberculosis cases increased sixfold, overwhelming the capacity of the National TB and Leprosy Programme to deliver effective care. An estimated 52 percent of tuberculosis patients in Tanzania are also infected with HIV. The close link between tuberculosis and HIV has stigmatized people with tuberculosis, which has caused their health-seeking behavior to decline.

Additional challenges brought by HIV/AIDS include the following:

- A serious shortage of human resources, especially in the health sector, to expand testing, counseling, treatment, and care services;
- A high level of national awareness-raising efforts not matched with commensurate positive behavioral changes;
- Difficulty in sustaining current levels of prevention, treatment, and care;
- The need for the nutritional support of poor community members who are infected with and affected by HIV;
- The need to identify and support the increasing number of needy orphans and other vulnerable people;
- The need for accountability and a judicious use of HIV/AIDS resources from the government and development partners; and
- The stigma of HIV/AIDS, which has hindered people's access to prevention, testing, treatment, care, and other support services.

HIV Prevention Initiatives

HIV prevention programs in Tanzania contain messages and activities that focus on several important aspects of behavior change: condom use; monogamy, or limiting the number of sexual partners; and practicing abstinence or delaying one's sexual debut. The programs have also tried to dispel popular misconceptions about how HIV is transmitted, as those misconceptions can place people at risk.

The 2007–08 *Tanzania HIV/AIDS and Malaria Indicator Survey* showed that seven in ten women and three in four men knew that condoms could reduce the risk of contracting HIV during sexual intercourse.[2] Approximately eight in ten women and nine in ten men understood that the risk of HIV could be reduced by limiting sex to one uninfected, monogamous partner. Abstaining from sexual intercourse was the most frequently recognized prevention method; 85 percent of women and 89 percent of men were aware of this method. No major gender differences existed in the levels of awareness of different prevention strategies. In general, women and men between 20 and 39 years of age, urban dwellers, sexually active never-married respondents, and better-educated respondents were more knowledgeable of HIV prevention methods than other respondents.

HIV-Related Stigmatization and Discrimination

Stigmatization and discrimination have played major roles in fueling the HIV epidemic in Tanzania. Stigmatized people have experienced physical and social isolation and have been subjected to gossip, rumors, and name calling, such as *amekwa umeme*—someone so electrically charged they can shock you to death with a single touch. We have also witnessed several instances in which people living with HIV/AIDS have been denied access to such resources as housing and employment.

Stigmatization has proved a stumbling block for prevention-of-mother-to-child-transmission (PMTCT) programs. Women, usually the first in a couple to be tested for the virus, are often blamed for introducing HIV into the family, which in many cases leads to domestic violence, separation, and divorce.

Following mass media campaigns aimed at promoting AIDS awareness in the mid-2000s, the stigma of HIV seems to have diminished significantly. Surveys have found that more than 93 percent of women and men between the ages of 15 and 49 were willing to care for a family member with HIV, and 57 percent of women and two-thirds of men would buy fresh vegetables from a vendor with AIDS. Three in four women and men believed that HIV-positive female teachers should be allowed to continue teaching. Less than half of women and 59 percent of men do not believe that the HIV-positive status of a family member should be kept a secret.

The National and International Response

The National Policy on HIV/AIDS

Government officials have been at the forefront in Tanzania's national response efforts to the HIV epidemic. With technical support from the World Health Organization's Global Programme on AIDS, the government formed the National HIV/AIDS Control Program (NACP) under the Ministry of Health and Social Welfare. Initially, HIV/AIDS was perceived purely as a health problem, and the campaign to respond to the epidemic involved only the health sector through the NACP. The national response consisted of developing strategies to prevent, control, and mitigate the impact of the HIV/AIDS epidemic through health education, multisectoral responses, and community participation.

Unfortunately, the national response has not had the expected impact on halting the progression of the epidemic. Inhibitors to success have included such factors as insufficient human and financial resources, ineffective coordination mechanisms, and inadequate political commitment and leadership.

Some of these constraints are now being addressed. The political commitment and leadership are now strong from the top level. HIV/AIDS has been declared a national disaster and has become one of the government's highest priority development issues. Since fiscal year 2000–01, the government has allocated a substantial amount of funds to fight HIV/AIDS.

The government developed the National Policy on HIV/AIDS with the principal goal of strengthening leadership and providing coordination of the National Multisectoral Strategic Framework on HIV and AIDS. This effort has included the formulation by all sectors of appropriate interventions aimed at preventing the spread of HIV and other sexually transmitted infections, protecting and supporting vulnerable groups, and mitigating the social and economic impact of HIV/AIDS. It also provides a framework for strengthening the capacity of institutions, communities, and individuals in all sectors to help prevent further transmission of the virus.

The prevention and control of HIV/AIDS will depend on effective community-based prevention, care, and support interventions. People living with HIV/AIDS have proved to be a key group in forging the national response to AIDS. With the support of the Tanzanian Commission for AIDS, groups of HIV-infected people established the Tanzanian National Council of People Living with HIV and AIDS, or NACOPHA, in 2007. The role of NACOPHA is to advocate for the rights of people living with HIV/AIDS, to coordinate the activities and strengthen the capacity of its members, and to contribute to the national multisectoral response to the AIDS epidemic in prevention, treatment, care, and impact mitigation as laid out in the 2003–2007 edition of the National Multisectoral Strategic Framework on HIV and AIDS, as well as in the 2008–2012 revision.

Support from the Country's Development Partners

A public expenditure review showed that development partners accounted for nearly 90 percent of Tanzania's total public expenditure on HIV/AIDS in 2005–06. PEPFAR alone accounted for 59 percent of that spending. Total expenditures—including those of the government and donor partners—were expected to nearly double in 2005–06 but actually increased by a little less than half, whereas government recurrent spending nearly doubled. Expenditures committed to HIV continued to grow strongly in 2006–07, with outside donors committing a 77 percent increase above 2005–06 levels. Total expenditure was equivalent to roughly 5.6 percent of government spending in 2005–06 and reached 8 percent of government spending and more than 15 percent of government revenue in 2006–07.

A joint UN Team on HIV/AIDS was established in June 2006. The team comprises officers from United Nations agencies working on the HIV/AIDS epidemic in Tanzania and officially designated by their agency heads to support joint programming. The Joint Team works through four thematic areas that reflect the broad priorities of the national strategic plans of both the mainland and Zanzibar: prevention; treatment, care, and support; impact mitigation; and crosscutting issues/enabling environment. This team is facilitated by UNAIDS under the guidance of the UN Theme Group on HIV/AIDS.

The joint UN Team on HIV/AIDS has developed a United Nations Joint Programme of Support to Tanzania on HIV/AIDS, which covers 2007 to 2010, a period that coincides with the implementation period for the United Nations Development Assistance Framework (UNDAF) for Tanzania. The UNDAF itself was prepared after careful consideration of the poverty reduction strategy documents of the Tanzania Mainland (MKUKUTA) and Zanzibar (MKUZA), both of which focus on economic growth, a reduction in income poverty, improved social services and well-being, and governance. The Joint Programme has been careful to ensure that it is fully consistent and aligned with the UNDAF and government priorities as expressed through MKUKUTA and MKUZA, as well as with the mainland's National Multisectoral Strategic Framework on HIV and AIDS.

VCT was the principal approach to HIV testing in Tanzania. Provider-initiated HIV testing and counseling has been introduced in the health care facilities using the WHO-developed package of interventions to address missed opportunities for HIV screening among patients. Tanzania is currently implementing a national HIV testing campaign that President Kikwete inaugurated in July 2007. On the launch day of the campaign, the president, other top government leaders, members of the community, and representatives of development partners underwent HIV testing. Following the inauguration were campaigns all over the country to open new testing sites and to encourage people, through posters and other media, to pursue VCT. By the end of December 2007, 3.2 million people had already undergone testing, representing 78 percent of the targeted number of 4.2 million people by the end of that year. From 2006 to the end of November 2007, the number of VCT sites had increased from 1,027 to 1,981.

Prevention of Mother-to-Child Transmission

The mortality rate among children younger than five in Tanzania is 122 per 1,000 live births, and HIV accounts for a high proportion of those deaths. In Tanzania, HIV prevalence among pregnant women runs as high as 8.7 percent. Each year an estimated 48,000 children become infected with HIV through mother-to-child transmission, and half of them die before their second birthday. A major challenge to treating those children quickly enough is the difficulty of diagnosing HIV among infants, as rapid test methods cannot distinguish between the presence of circulating maternal antibodies and true infection.

In 2004, the government of Tanzania began offering PMTCT services, though some programs had provided such services in the context of research beginning in the early 1990s. The accepted standard for PMTCT services has included pre- and post-HIV testing and counseling for pregnant women, counseling of HIV-positive women on infant feeding practices and family planning, and the provision of antiretrovirals

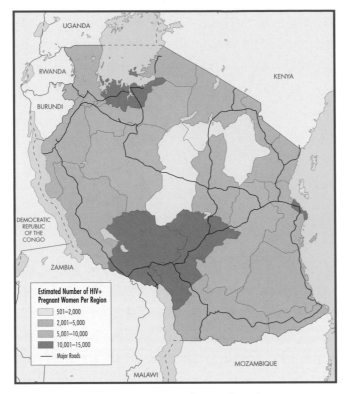

Figure 3. The Estimated Number of HIV-Infected Pregnant Women in Each Region of Tanzania

Sources: U.S. Government Partner Database, 10-30-07; *Tanzania HIV/ AIDS and Malaria Indicator Survey, 2003–04; Population Census, 2002*; antenatal care surveillance data; and *Health Sector HIV and AIDS Strategic Plan, 2008–2012* pregnancy projections

to infected women and their newborns. Additional services—called PMTCT plus—include making antiretroviral therapy, or ART, available to all eligible women identified as HIV positive and to their families; several pilot sites in Dar es Salaam have shown great success.

The percentage of HIV-infected pregnant women who received antiretrovirals to help prevent mother-to-child transmission was still low in 2006 and 2007, at 12.3 percent and 8.2 percent respectively. Efforts have been made to integrate PMTCT into existing community health services as a way to strengthen and scale up programs (Figure 3).

In 2006, an estimated 930,000 orphans and vulnerable children were living in Tanzania, which is 5 percent of the nation's children. The cost of bridging the expenditure gap for these children was estimated to be 37.8 billion Tanzanian shillings (US$31.5 million). Of this amount, 30.7 billion shillings are needed for food and 7.1 billion for non-food items. The number of orphans and vulnerable children is projected to reach 1,044,097 by 2010.

The number of orphans and vulnerable children receiving external support has been increasing. The impact assessment of the Most Vulnerable Children Program implemented by the Department of Social Welfare with support from UNICEF showed, for example, that in 2005 and 2006, nearly 30 percent of surveyed children in the sample districts reported receiving support from the program. The 2003–04 *Tanzania HIV/AIDS and Malaria Indicator Survey* found that 4 to 6 percent of orphans and vulnerable children lived in households that received various kinds of external support.[6] The survey also found that support services were more common in urban areas than in rural ones.

AIDS Treatment and Care

Neither the government nor the international donor community considered HIV/AIDS treatment in Tanzania to be a real possibility until 2004, 21 years after recognition of the nation's first AIDS cases. Before then, any care AIDS patients received came from their individual physicians, with no clear treatment guidelines. Patients bought antiretrovirals through private hospitals and pharmacies.

In October 2004, the government of Tanzania—through the NACP—launched the National HIV Care and Treatment Program. The government made a strong statement of commitment that it would provide free services—including antiretrovirals—to all Tanzanians in need. The program followed the model of having one national treatment guideline, one training curriculum, and one reporting format. This approach has enabled the country to offered a standardized service.

The program started providing ART through 22 sites in 9 of 21 regions with support from six PEPFAR-funded U.S. partners—the Harvard School of Public Health, the Columbia Mailman School of Public Health, AIDS Relief, Family Health International, the Elizabeth Glaser Pediatric AIDS Foundation, and the U.S. Department of Defense. Most of these sites were referral and urban hospitals in major towns, selected because of a high patient demand, the capacity to implement the program rapidly, and the preferences of the U.S. government and other donor partners. The diversity of sites created significant challenges: difficulties in coordination, a duplication of support in some areas, a lack of support in others, and a low cost-effectiveness, all leading to a gap in quality and services between sites.

In meeting these challenges, the government of Tanzania, in collaboration with its U.S government partners, adopted the National HIV Care and Treatment Program concept of regionalization. The intent of regionalization was to facilitate the continued scale up of treatment and care services in a more equitable distribution of services and ensure standardized approaches and effective referrals across a continuum of care. Regionalization entailed a shift from facility-based partner support to one of expanded service delivery across a range of health facilities within a geographic area. Each U.S. government partner has been assigned to support treatment and care sites based on geographic grouping, including all certified medical facilities at all levels in one or more regions down to the district level and where possible to the health center level.

By September 2006 all clinical sites in any given region were working with only one U.S. government partner for support. The initial response has been favorable. Regional and district medical authorities have been appreciative, and facilities have become more efficient in scaling up more cost-effective coverage.

Regionalization has had numerous advantages. It has facilitated equal distribution of partners' support across the country, prevented partner overlap, greatly improved logistics for program rollout and service delivery, and strengthened links among hospitals, health centers, and communities.

Regionalization has further ensured standardized approaches and effective referrals across a continuum of care for each region and district. It has also enabled a more cost-effective approach to training, program management, and supportive supervision. Significant savings have been achieved in training, program management, and supportive supervision, and the cost per patient is expected to drop from the annual average of US$300 in 2008 to less than US$150. Two final advantages have been the sense of ownership and the team building that have developed among region- and district-based stakeholders as they have mapped the various resources and programs.

As of October 2008, of the estimated 500,000 HIV-infected Tanzanians who qualified for ART, only 184,000, or 37 percent, were receiving antiretrovirals at approximately 200 NACP sites throughout Tanzania. The scaling up of ART provision remains a challenge as the NACP seeks to provide treatment in lower-tier health facilities at the community level to reach 500 sites by 2010.

The MDH HIV/AIDS Care and Treatment Program

With support from PEPFAR, the U.S. President's Emergency Plan for AIDS Relief, Tanzania launched an AIDS care and treatment initiative in 2004. The MDH Program, a collaboration of the Muhimbili University of Health and Allied Sciences, the Dar es Salaam City Council, and the Harvard School of Public Health, takes its name from the first letter of each partner institution. The collaboration was a continuation of a

15-year-old partnership that had primarily focused on research and training. With a national treatment and care initiative, the institutions made a decision to embark on service provision in Dar es Salaam City.

The MDH Program, which is fully integrated into the Tanzanian government's plans, provides financial and technical support to three municipalities in the city. Key areas of support have been training, infrastructure development, laboratory capacity building, and the provision of non-antiretroviral drugs, other supplies, essential equipment, data management assistance, public health evaluations, and technical advice. MDH has trained more than 3,000 staff in basic and refresher courses inside and outside the country. Course topics include ART principles, adherence counseling, nutrition, pharmacy logistics management, home-based care, monitoring and evaluation, and good clinical practices.

As of December 2008, the MDH Program has been actively working at all levels of the health care system in 17 public and 14 private health facilities, including hospitals, health centers, and dispensaries. The Ministry of Health and Social Welfare, through the NACP, has assessed and certified all clinical sites to deliver ART. By the end of 2008, an estimated 63,000 patients were enrolled; 39,000 had initiated ART and more than 24,000 were regularly picking up their antiretrovirals.

The central laboratory of the MDH collaboration has played a major role in ensuring quality assurance and control in the district-site laboratories. The central laboratory has also performed viral load assessments and DNA PCR tests for infant diagnosis, tests that are not available at the district-site level. Motorcycles are used to transport specimens and results, a logistical solution that has proved inexpensive, feasible, and sustainable.

The MDH Program has a specific protocol for addressing patient nutritional status. This protocol outlines and identifies specific nutritional problems by appropriate use of anthropometric and laboratory measures for the purpose of appropriate interventions. Multivitamin supplements are now provided in all sites.

The program has also developed successful protocols for tracking patients who miss their scheduled visits and notifying patients whose abnormal laboratory results need immediate attention. MDH has more than 50 tracking team members who devote their time to identifying patients who need follow up. MDH is linked through the network of community health workers in all 63 wards in the region. MDH is also linked with other local nongovernmental organizations—such as Comprehensive Community Based Rehabilitation in Tanzania, Pathfinder International, and PASADA—that provide other social services.

Patients taking antiretrovirals must visit the clinic monthly to pick up their drugs. In addition, several times a year they have a scheduled doctor's examination and laboratory tests to monitor their progress. Factors that impede patients' adherence to scheduled visits include the inability to take off time from work or school, a lack of transportation funds, and long waiting times at the clinics.

To address some of the patients' concerns, MDH introduced double shifts of working hours at its clinics and provided time-block patient appointments. These steps have greatly enhanced patient flow, minimized patients' waiting times at partner clinics, enhanced the quality of care, and increased the number of patients served, despite severe space constraints. Also, to reduce unnecessary overcrowding and long waiting times at the clinics, stable patients who have received antiretrovirals for more than six months with good adherence, fewer opportunistic infections, and a good immune response—defined as CD4+ cell counts higher than 350—now spend no more than 20 minutes by passing through an expedited drug pickup system.

To ensure a treatment and care program of the highest quality, MDH established a quality management program that operates based on a set of patient-care-quality indicators—covering the range of prevention, treatment, and care programs. Quality-of-care data are collected using several methods, such as patient record reviews, exit interviews, and expert external observations. Regular quality assessments and quality-improvement visits are performed using checklists. Quality of care has improved through a combination of different models of supportive supervision, a preceptorship system, technical assistance, system strengthening, and logistical improvements aimed at easing access for more patients. Staff recruitment continues through the government system, thereby ensuring continuity within these positions.

All partner clinics provide HIV-infected people with counseling on behavioral and medical approaches to preventing further transmission of the virus. Discordant couples—in which one partner is infected and the other is not—receive special attention and support. To help reduce the stigma of AIDS and discrimination toward people with HIV/AIDS, a number of community care and support groups for people with HIV/AIDS have sought to mobilize the community and inspire people to seek VCT and services at

MDH sites. All patients receive screening for sexually transmitted infections and safer sex counseling, with an emphasis on constant and correct condom use.

The NACP procures all antiretrovirals for patients in Tanzania and distributes the drugs to each certified facility through the Medical Stores Department. Each site obtains antiretrovirals based on the number of its current patients on therapy and its new patient enrollment rate.

The MDH Program uses standard data collection forms completed at each patient encounter as the basis for its patient monitoring and evaluation system. The data are entered into a database; to evaluate the rate and character of entry errors, data are "double entered." At the laboratory, orders and results are entered into a database before results are issued to the sites.

The MDH PMTCT program operates with guidance from a PMTCT technical sub-committee of the National HIV/AIDS Steering Committee. Services provided include routine HIV testing and counseling, ART, prophylaxis for mothers and children, safer delivery practices, counseling and support for safer infant feeding practices, long-term follow-up care for mothers, and family planning at antenatal clinics and labor wards. As a national policy, all services are now provided for free.

PMTCT indicators have been established at the national level.[7] Most indicators used in Tanzania measure coverage—the delivery of key PMTCT services by health facilities—and uptake—the level of client acceptance of each service. The overall goals of the MDH PMTCT program are to support expansion of the PMTCT services to reach 100 percent coverage in Dar es Salaam and to strengthen the existing system's capacity to provide quality services.

The MDH PMTCT program has sought to improve access to treatment and care services for HIV-positive mothers, their partners, and HIV-exposed and infected infants by strengthening existing referral systems in several ways: improving recording and documentation methods, providing feedback, and enhancing communication through telephone calls, physical escorts, and regular meetings of relevant sectors.

As of September 2008, MDH supported 42 PMTCT sites. By implementing best practices such as testing at labor and delivery, opt-out testing, and male partner involvement, MDH has been able to reduce missed opportunities for counseling and testing and to deliver PMTCT services to a greater number of people. We have started providing the more efficacious bitherapy prophylaxis regimens—a combination of two drugs—and three-drug treatments to eligible pregnant women within antenatal clinics.

The PMTCT program has faced some setbacks because of insufficient space for confidential counseling and testing and a low level of participation by male sexual partners. MDH is therefore making investments in facilitating minor renovations to improve counseling rooms. We are also performing a pilot trial of establishing a family clinic to try to attract more male participation. We are seeking to make antenatal clinics more appealing to men by facilitating renovations and expanding the space available for couple counseling, creating and disseminating male-targeted information and education materials, fast-tracking couples, and employing male staff.

Innovations aimed at improving pediatric enrollment and retention include the training of health workers on the early detection of the signs and symptoms of HIV in children and the establishment of child-friendly clinics. Saturdays now serve as pediatric clinic days, for example, and the waiting rooms contain toys and games.

A major obstacle to rolling out and scaling up services in treatment and care clinics has been the lack of adequate clinical space. PEPFAR funds have been devoted to expanding clinical space in three district hospitals—Amana, Temeke, and Mwananyamala—as well as in nine other facilities. During the summer of 2007, President Kikwete inaugurated the Amana site, while David Mwakyusa, Tanzania's minister of health and social welfare, and Michael Leavitt, secretary of the U.S. Department of Health and Human Services, jointly inaugurated the new clinic at Mwananyamala Hospital. As a result, the number of HIV-infected patients seen daily at the district hospital clinics has more than doubled, from an average of 100 to 250. The additional space has helped decongest the hospital outpatient clinics, enabling health care providers to attend to patient needs better.

Private hospitals have contributed significantly to the HIV/AIDS treatment and care program. In the spirit of public–private partnership, these facilities have participated in the national program. MDH had conducted an assessment of various private clinics in Dar as Salaam before engaging them to identify areas in need of bolstering. The assessment revealed that several issues needed to be jointly addressed. MDH signed a memorandum of understanding with 14 private hospitals and the resulting collaborations have strengthened several areas, including training, laboratory work, data management, and patient tracking.

Conclusion

Home to a flourishing democracy and a prospering economy, Tanzania is well known for its peace and security. Despite their ethnically diverse society, Tanzanians are united by a common language and a sense of community. This unity translates into a strong sense of national identity and a dedication to building a better future for all.

With this national spirit and resilience, Tanzania has made significant progress since its first AIDS cases were diagnosed. President Kikwete has championed the national campaign to bring HIV prevention, treatment, care, and support to the lowest levels of the health care system, and many professionals and community advocates have joined forces to make the program a reality. Much remains to be done, and yet much is possible with strong national and local leadership and the support of the international community.

REFERENCES

1. UNAIDS. *AIDS Epidemic Update*. Geneva: UNAIDS, 2007.

2. Tanzania Commission for AIDS, Zanzibar AIDS Commission, National Bureau of Statistics, MEASURE DHS. *Tanzania HIV/AIDS and Malaria Indicator Survey, 2007–08*. Dar es Salaam: Tanzania Commission for AIDS, 2008. www.ihi.or.tz/docs/TzHIV-Malaria IndicatorSurvey-07-08-PreliminaryReport.pdf; accessed November 4, 2008.

3. McCurdy SA, Williams ML, Ross MW, Kilonzo GP, Leshabari MT. New injecting practice increases HIV risk among drug users in Tanzania. *BMJ*, 2005;331(7519):778.

4. McCurdy SA, Williams ML, Ross MW, Kilonzo GP, Leshabari MT. Heroin and HIV risk in Dar es Salaam, Tanzania: youth hangouts, mageto and injecting practices. *AIDS Care*, 2005;17(Suppl 1):S65–S76.

5. Ministry of Health and Social Welfare, United Republic of Tanzania. *National Guidelines on TB/HIV Management*. Dar es Salaam: Ministry of Health and Social Welfare.

6. Tanzania Commission for AIDS, Zanzibar AIDS Commission, National Bureau of Statistics, MEASURE DHS. *Tanzania HIV/AIDS and Malaria Indicator Survey, 2003–04*. Dar es Salaam: Tanzania Commission for AIDS, 2004.

7. Ministry of Health and Social Welfare, Tanzania. *Prevention of Mother-to-Child Transmission (PMTCT), National Guidelines*. Dar es Salaam: Ministry of Health and Social Welfare, 2007.

Sylvia Kaaya attends to the critical mental health issues that affect people living with HIV/AIDS.

Life Support

JOHN DONNELLY

THE YOUNG WOMAN had just given birth, only to learn that she and her baby were both HIV positive. She was just 18 and had recently moved from her village to Dar es Salaam, where she knew no one besides her husband. So she told him. He said nothing, not one word. The next day, he was gone.

It was 1995, AIDS was shrouded by a conspiracy of silence, and she felt totally alone—alone and with a baby in a rented apartment with no means to pay the rent that was coming due in several days. She fell into despair. She walked to the market and bought rat poison. She would kill herself and her baby.

First, though, she told someone—a nurse counselor. The counselor then sought out the best person she could think of: Dr. Sylvia Kaaya, a psychiatrist. Soon after, the woman was sitting in Kaaya's office.

The woman told her sad tale, then pulled out the bottle of poison. Kaaya stayed her hand, then reassured the young woman she wasn't alone. Kaaya would take her to a support group of other HIV-positive women. It was one of the first of its kind in Tanzania.

"People were just learning about HIV and AIDS, so there hadn't been much in terms of support," Kaaya said, looking back at that moment many years before. "For those in difficult situations, this group was a place where they could really talk about their worries."

The psychiatrist took the young woman to a support group meeting. There Kaaya told the woman's story and asked the members to help her. "One of the women said, 'This is so common. She can stay with me,'" Kaaya remembered. The young woman accepted the offer and moved in, along with her baby.

She no longer had the rat poison. She had left it in Kaaya's office.

Against the Odds

Since 2004, the response to the AIDS epidemic in many of the hardest-hit areas of sub-Saharan Africa has had an all-hands-on-deck feel to it, especially when it has come to treating the virus. But few have delved into—or even tried to understand—the mental health aspects surrounding AIDS.

Kaaya, the department chair of psychiatry at the Muhimbili University of Health and Allied Sciences in Dar es Salaam, has been a pioneer in the field. In a series of research projects examining the links between AIDS and mental health, Kaaya has delved into little-understood psychosocial aspects of the epidemic. "Most people have ignored the mental health implications of AIDS," she said with a shrug.

Even in innovative efforts to stop mother-to-child transmission of HIV during birth, Kaaya found that few programs focused enough on either the physical or mental health of the mother. "The typical approach puts a lot of focus on the infant not becoming infected and not enough focus on the woman bearing the child," she said. "Child survival has increased significantly since Tanzania's independence, but maternal mortality has continued at high levels."

Kaaya was reared in the foothills of Mount Kilimanjaro by a mother and father who ignored the local custom of finding a partner within their village. After her father announced he had found a bride some 25 miles away, his own father asked him, "Why did you have to cross so many rivers to find a wife?"

That was Kaaya's world at root, her place of childhood. Her father would become a well-known economist, leading public and private institutions, including British tea farms; his work would take his family to as far away as Nairobi in neighboring Kenya. But during most of Kaaya's youth she lived in the city of Dar es Salaam, where the family kept a farm that included chickens by the score. Her mother oversaw operations, but the children were never far behind.

"I remember in the mornings before school, we'd have to slaughter the chickens to get them ready for sale," Kaaya said. "We would all get up at five in the morning to slaughter the chickens."

When she was growing up, her parents gave her a stethoscope, a gift that started her thinking about becoming a doctor. She followed that dream to the University of Dar es Salaam, where as a first-year medical student she met her future husband, Ephata, who was then a fifth-year medical student. She wouldn't allow romance to derail her. "We had a six-year courtship," she said. "I had to finish school first."

By then, she had become fascinated by the world of psychiatry. In the early 1990s, after earning a master's degree in psychiatry from Victoria University of Manchester in Great Britain, Kaaya, already married, already with one preschool daughter, returned to her homeland. She became just the fifth psychiatrist in Tanzania, a country with one psychiatrist for every 6.8 million people. (The United States, with 45,600 psychiatrists, has one for every 6,500 people.) Kaaya didn't know it at the time, but she was about to enter fully into the AIDS epidemic.

Meeting the Challenge

In 1994, Kaaya heard about a Harvard research project headed by Dr. Wafaie Fawzi, now a professor of nutrition and epidemiology at the Harvard School of Public Health. Fawzi had started looking at the effects of multivitamins on HIV-positive women. He and his colleagues had already identified 1,800 infected women, more than half of whom had agreed to participate in the study.

Kaaya joined the study to examine the mental health status of the women. After following the women for eight years, she and fellow researchers compiled evidence that showed depression was a silent plague for most of them. Roughly 60 percent of the women were clinically depressed during some period between 1995 and 2003; that meant they had spent at least two weeks with a severe loss of energy or loss of any interest in pleasurable activities, for no apparent reason. Some could not seem to climb out of their depression. Kaaya had to figure out a way to give them a hand.

Such a task might seem too formidable for most; after all, Tanzania, like all developing countries, suffered from a severe shortage of professionals trained in mental health. But Kaaya relished the challenge.

In her first years as a psychiatrist in Tanzania, she saw more than 20 patients a day, taught psychiatry to undergraduates, helped develop a postgraduate training program in psychiatry, assembled curricula for continuing education courses for counselors, and helped run the study on depression in HIV-positive women.

Since then, Kaaya has become more of a manager, overseeing AIDS treatment for much of Harvard's program in Dar es Salaam and the work of faculty and students at Muhimbili. She still counsels and treats about ten patients a week and tries to meet regularly with people in the field. Often, though, she feels she isn't doing enough.

The Big Picture

One afternoon in the summer of 2008, Kaaya visited the Muhimbili Health Information Center, a voluntary counseling and testing center that her psychiatry department started in 2004. The center's six counselors now see an average of 80 people a day. One counselor she knows well is Sister Daphrosa Lingande, who started her job when the center opened.

Lingande noted that the situation has changed dramatically since 2003. "People accept the result when they learn they are positive now," she said. "Before, when there was no medicine, anyone positive would start to cry, 'Oh, I'm going to die.' But they understand the disease better now, and they know what the medicine can do."

Lingande added that counselors have gradually grown wiser in dealing with patients. She started telling Kaaya about how they deal with women who come in alone for an HIV test and learn they are positive.

"I tell them to get the husband to come in," she said. "A common strategy—when they come back with the husband—is to not show you know the wife. You show that

this is the first time you've seen her. Then it will be easier. You say to them, 'Why do you want to test?' Then you say, 'Suppose you are positive?'"

Kaaya nodded knowingly. "There's a lot of passive aggressiveness in our couples' relationships," she said.

"It's true," said Lingande. "But we don't use this strategy only with women."

"You are using these strategies with men as well?" Kaaya asked.

"Oh, yes!" Lingande exclaimed. "Many times a man will come in alone, and because he is afraid to tell his wife, I will tell him to come back with her. I know how to make it comfortable for them. I explain when he comes back, I will pretend not to know him, and the husband will look at you and say, 'Phew!'"

The two women laughed at the kindness behind the subterfuge. To them, it was just yet another example of how the response to the epidemic has changed. For years many HIV/AIDS programs in sub-Saharan Africa focused their efforts almost entirely on women, ignoring male behavior on the assumption that it was too difficult to get men to change. But after 2003, pioneering efforts in several countries aimed at men taking more responsibility for HIV prevention demonstrated that the only way to achieve behavioral change was to target both women and men.

In addition, much of the evolution of AIDS programs, Kaaya believed, was connected in some way to the start of widespread treatment. Before antiretrovirals were easily accessible, for instance, Kaaya found that some patients had been having brief psychotic episodes, tied to their anxiety around the virus. Now, she rarely sees such manifestations of HIV/AIDS.

"Part of the reason could be that people are adjusting better, even though we still have a lot of stigma attached to HIV," she said. "HIV is becoming much more normalized. Now so many people have a relative who has suffered from HIV."

Another reason for the fewer numbers of acute psychotic episodes, she said, might be related to the availability of antiretrovirals. "Some of the psychological impact may be related to the direct effects of the virus and the secondary opportunistic infections that affect the brain, such as meningitis," she said. "With the drugs, we are reducing viral loads and giving immune systems the chance to fight back. That reduces both the primary impact of the virus and the prevalence of secondary infections."

But the changes connected to mental health conditions also include new challenges. Kaaya expects to see more HIV-related dementia as patients live longer.

She mentioned the case of a man who was obsessed with philanthropist Bill Gates. The man, a health care worker, had AIDS-related mania. He wrote long emails to Gates about the need for a revolution in spreading information technology in rural Tanzania. "He asked for grants to get funding to set up Internet kiosks in rural areas," Kaaya said. "It was a big plan, but it was not clear how he would implement it. He would go out and buy many of these old computers, which made his wife concerned."

Co-workers brought the man in to see Kaaya. "He had been on antiretrovirals for three years, along with his wife," Kaaya said. "She continued on the drugs, but he had stopped for a year. He was convinced that traditional medicines would work best. It was heartbreaking—as his mental status improved he had a whole lot of things he wanted to do, he had so many ideas that he wanted to work on, but he never had a chance." The man died six months after he first saw Kaaya.

Peace of Mind

Kaaya sees a connection between dementia and the increasing coordination problems of her aging patients. In one such case, a 55-year-old professional became depressed as he gradually lost the ability to perform simple motor tasks with his hands. "He had many challenges with self-management," she said. "He had difficulty getting dressed, and he later began losing his memory. In the year I saw him, we developed a set of reminders for him."

She said that Tanzania and other African countries with high HIV prevalence rates need to start preparing for such end-of-life issues associated with people with AIDS.

"There will be a huge demand for health care workers who have the skills to deal with dementia in patients," she said. "Now the focus is much more on letting people know their status, encouraging them to access support networks, and helping them adhere to their drugs. But the skill set is different in dealing with memory loss."

She added that mental health professionals will have to train cadres of health workers on how to best address these conditions. The country also will soon need some simple tools to help patients with memory problems. One example, she said, will be to provide patients with pillboxes so they can easily track their daily drug dosages.

Kaaya believes that the country is beginning to scale up to meet the challenge. Tanzania now has 12 psychiatrists, and Kaaya is helping train dozens of university students each year in the discipline of psychiatry. Members of support groups now number in the tens of thousands around the country. One of the leaders in the support group movement has been the young woman who long ago bought rat poison but never used it.

"As a department we've struggled for many years to convince people that HIV has huge mental health care implications," Kaaya said. "We've changed our counseling agenda from giving advice and telling people what to do, to listening and empowering them to move toward healthy actions instead. It's getting much better. Every time I'm reminded of the girl who was thinking about taking rat poison, I say to myself, 'My God, we saved her!' That feels really good." ∎

Guerino Chalamilla, deputy director of the Harvard–PEPFAR program in Dar es Salaam

A Power of Good

John Donnelly

On weekends in years past, Amana Hospital in Dar es Salaam, Tanzania, turned extremely quiet. Workers handled emergencies as they arose. A skeletal staff of nurses would go from bed to bed, doing the best they could.

But starting in late 2004, when the government offered free AIDS treatment, the status quo became untenable. Patients came in ever-increasing numbers. By the end of 2005, the daily clinics were overrun with those seeking treatment, and that meant long lines and long days for people waiting see nurses, doctors, and pharmacists.

Out of disorder, though, came order. Hospital planners viewed Saturdays as part of a plan to overhaul management of patient care. The AIDS treatment program started two shifts on Saturdays for mothers and their children; on weekdays, they switched from one shift to two, morning and afternoon, and gave specific times for appointments. And then they began to train health workers in smaller health centers and antenatal clinics to oversee the distribution of AIDS drugs and to monitor patients. This decentralization greatly increased the numbers of health workers involved in antiretroviral treatment—and greatly decreased waiting times for patients.

The results are in plain view now. On one Saturday morning in 2008, the AIDS clinic was half full of mothers and children sitting in chairs. Nurses called out names, and patients went in to see their doctors. Instead of waiting six or seven hours, patients were now seeing a doctor within an hour of their appointments.

In one office, Dr. Emanuel Maeda, who was seeing a new patient every 15 minutes or so, examined a thin seven-year-old. "How are you feeling today?" he asked the boy, who looked at him glumly. "What's the matter? You're usually so talkative."

His mother said that the boy was unhappy because a nurse had taken blood from him and he didn't like needles. But he would get over it, she added, in part because he knew some of the other children at the clinic, one of the benefits of the Saturday sessions. Children, while waiting their turn, could play outside together.

"On Saturdays, the children play soccer together—in other clinics, during the weekday, they don't have that chance," said the 42-year-old mother of five. "So this is much better. You can find all the children together here. I really like doing this on Saturdays. You get everything done at once—I'm examined, he's examined, we get our drugs, and we're done."

Maeda listened to the boy's breathing, his stethoscope pressed against the boy's chest. "Hmmm," he said. "His lungs don't sound too good. He may have pneumonia. You may have to give him antibiotics as well as antiretrovirals."

The boy and his mother left; he would need an x-ray to confirm the doctor's suspicions.

As Maeda watched them depart, he took a moment to explain that working Saturdays also helped him.

"I really like working with the children," he said. "This way, with the Saturday appointments, I get to see the children over and over. I get to know them—like that boy just in here. He usually is very happy and active, but not today."

Dr. Guerino Chalamilla, the deputy director of the Harvard–PEPFAR program in Dar es Salaam, has been overseeing the change in patient management.

"In the mornings at the hospital, we always had a lot of congestion," Chalamilla said, walking around Amana Hospital. "It was terrible. You could feel the tension. Patients would come to the hospital at five in the morning to be first in line. But now the patient flow is very good. We were able to solve a problem for the patients and for us."

Chalamilla grew up in the south-central Tanzanian town of Iringa, the second of nine children to a father who was a politician and a farmer and to a mother who taught in primary school. He spent a dozen years in Russian colleges and universities, where he specialized in dermatology. In 1998, just shy of his fortieth birthday, he returned to Tanzania and immediately started working in infectious diseases, including managing sexually transmitted infections. Six years later, just as the national AIDS program began, he became field director of HIV/AIDS treatment and care in Dar es Salaam for the Tanzanian government and the Harvard program.

The initiative has grown rapidly. Starting with just a handful of patients in 2004, Chalamilla helped build a treatment program that four years later had 630 staff workers and 63,000 patients, including 39,000 already on antiretrovirals.

Even though the new management practices—especially the decentralization and the double shifts six days a week—have reduced patient waiting times, Chalamilla believes the system could still use much improvement.

At Amana Hospital, one of three district hospitals in Dar es Salaam, he made the rounds not of patients, but of staff, checking in to see how everything was going. One area that bothered him was data entry; workers were still taking notes by hand and then entering the information into computers. He was in the midst of overseeing an overhaul of the system to make it completely electronic.

"It's a real struggle," Chalamilla said, standing in a room filled with stacks of patient files waiting to be updated. "It seems what we really need to do is increase the number of data clerks."

He walked around the outdoor courtyard and poked his head into a room where three people sat huddled around files. They were "trackers," whose job it was to find people who had missed their appointment the day before. Twenty-five people—or roughly 15 percent of the day's patients—hadn't shown up the previous day. Finding these patients was a critical part of the success of the overall program; if they stopped taking their antiretrovirals, then later restarted the drugs, they greatly increased their chances of developing resistance to the therapies.

"It's a very difficult enterprise," said Dr. Ayoub Kibao, the site manager at the Amana AIDS clinic. "Most of the streets don't have names, for instance. We also face difficulties related to stigma, so when we track patients we have to be careful what we say."

Soon, the program would begin to hire community-based health workers also to track down missing patients. This kind of outsourcing was already being felt in smaller clinics, which were beginning to enroll patients of their own.

At the Tabata Refill Site, Dr. Berlina Job, the site manager, reported that the clinic was just starting to get its first AIDS patients. Before, the site had merely administered drugs to patients, but now larger health centers were referring patients who were doing well on their medication to smaller sites like Tabata. In essence, after training health workers at the smaller sites, those who ran Harvard's AIDS program trusted them to oversee treatment of patients whose care was relatively straightforward.

"If patients have been on antiretrovirals for more than six months, and they are stable, we will be getting them," Job said. "We hope to be getting many patients in the future."

The site already had a busy antenatal care center for women; soon it would be adding a laboratory. More than 30 pregnant women sat in rows of chairs waiting to see nurses for their checkups. With each appointment, the nurses would ask the women to take an HIV test.

"We haven't had one who has said no to a test—not for the past several years," said Stella Paul, a public health nurse and counselor. "It's true. They all want to be tested." She flipped through a 2008 registration book, in which the nurses had recorded patients' visits. Every woman had been tested; of the last 170 women, 17—or 10 percent—were HIV positive.

Before 2005, when antiretrovirals weren't widely available, Paul said, many women were reluctant to be tested, as they often saw little reason in knowing their status if they couldn't access therapies to extend their lives. But after the antiretrovirals became available to everyone, not only did women agree to be tested—but many requested it. Suddenly, their reluctance disappeared because they knew that they could become well if they tested positive. The nurses said that while stigma still existed in the community, inside the health center it had dissipated entirely.

One 20-year-old, who was expecting her first baby, said she has tested every year since 2005, when she got married. "I want to know my status," she said. "If I am positive, I would want to prevent my child from being infected. It's as simple as that."

Guerino Chalamilla continues to fine-tune the work of the Harvard–PEPFAR program in Tanzania.

The woman next to her, a 22-year-old expecting her second child, agreed. "I am ready and willing to be tested," she said.

The nurses around her laughed. "All the women feel this way," Paul said. "We are encouraging them. We are improving our services. Things are getting better." ■

Mama Wandoa Mwambu lines children up to receive free mattresses and bed kits in Kigamboni, Tanzania.

The Bridge of Goodwill

JOHN DONNELLY

MAMA WANDOA MWAMBU stood before hundreds of parents and guardians in an outdoor school courtyard in the community of Kigamboni, just a short ferry ride from Dar es Salaam, the capital of Tanzania. She wanted her audience to know what to expect, in an effort to create order instead of chaos.

So she told them that she and her group would be distributing free mattresses and bed kits to the 700 children in the schoolyard; the children were selected either because they had lost one or both parents or because they came from extremely poor families. Each kit included an insecticide-treated bed net, a blanket, a bed sheet, a T-shirt, and a kanga, a wraparound cloth. Mama Wandoa told the adults that it was their job to ensure no one stole these gifts from the children.

One other thing, she said. She told them she would help them as well, if she could.

231 ◀

When Mama Wandoa finished her talk, a half-dozen women surrounded her and began pouring out their woes. One told her she was HIV positive. Mama Wandoa took her by the hand and led her away. The two pressed close, strangers transformed into dear sisters, and Mama Wandoa said she would help, that the woman should find her daughter, and then move to the front of the line.

The woman did as she was told. She returned hand-in-hand with her nine-year-old daughter, and they watched from the sidelines as Mama Wandoa delivered instructions to her boys—a group of young men who had risen at two o'clock that morning to load hundreds of mattresses onto two trucks and who had just unloaded the mattresses in tall stacks in the schoolyard.

"When I was listening to her talk to the big group of us, I felt very happy—almost like I wanted to cry," the woman said, still watching Mama Wandoa. "I could feel that Mama Wandoa loved all of us. We all want to be like Mama Wandoa."

It is not such an unusual sentiment about the woman who would soon be turning 70 years old. The boys in the schoolyard declared they would do just about anything for her. Fellow churchgoers said she had a gift from God. And those working with her at Harvard's AIDS treatment program in Dar es Salaam called her their bridge of goodwill, linking their research and programs to the huge community of people infected with—or even just affected by—the deadly virus.

Mama Wandoa's beginnings foreshadowed none of this. She was born in 1938 in the central Tanzanian town of Singida, the fourth of 11 children to a holy alliance: a pastor father and an evangelist mother. She graduated from secondary school, and in 1960 her parents moved the family to Dar es Salaam. She was just 22. It was an exciting time to be in Tanzania, then known as Tanganyika. The next year, the country was granted self-governance from Great Britain, and Julius Kambarage Nyerere became the new country's first prime minister.

A few years later, Nyerere, who would be known as Baba wa Taifa, or the Father of the Nation, became the first president of Tanzania. One of his major initiatives was to "Africanize" the government ministries by filling them with Tanzanians. Mama Wandoa heeded that call, learned shorthand, and soon was serving in the president's office as a stenographer. She also began to have children, one after the other, eventually stopping at eight. Life as a single mother and in the president's service would be full.

In President Nyerere's office, she rose to become one of his secretaries. Years later, she resigned to work as an instructor for the National Development Corporation, which was formed by the country's parliament to help put together economic ventures between the government and the private sector. She enjoyed her job, but it was only a part of her life. Her children grew up, and some moved out to start families of their own. Still Mama Wandoa's family expanded, as she began inviting outsiders affected by AIDS to come live with her, so she could better care for them.

The spread of HIV had much to do with that expansion. In the early 1990s, the virus became so widespread that it crept into her home, just as it did other homes. The virus snatched away life, but it added to life as well. One day a young man came to her house in Dar es Salaam; someone had told him that Mama Wandoa might be able to help him. He told her that he was HIV positive, and he now felt so overwhelmed that he wanted to kill himself. His girlfriend, he said, had just died in childbirth, and he was left alone to take care of the baby. Mama Wandoa talked him out of committing suicide, retrieved the baby from the hospital, and placed the girl in an orphanage.

That was just the beginning. The virus, she learned, was present every Friday during the deliverance prayers at church.

"The pastor would say to us, 'Come to the front, and we will pray for you.' Many people came and said, 'I have a fever,' or 'I have a headache,'" she said. "But to me those were possible signs they had HIV or AIDS. I talked to them afterward, and told them, 'You need to go for a test.' They would agree."

Most were positive. Some of these HIV-infected men and women began arriving at Mama Wandoa's home to talk some more. She invited some to stay with her. Her house soon became an informal gathering spot for those infected with the virus.

Now retired from her job, she only grew busier. UNICEF asked her to mobilize women leaders to teach them about HIV-related issues. The government asked her to work in an HIV counseling unit. She formed her own nongovernmental organization called the Upendo AIDS Center. Since 2001, it has offered a range of services, including HIV counseling; the facilitating of testing, treatment, and care; and special assistance to orphans and vulnerable children. Mama Wandoa then joined Harvard's AIDS program to coordinate its Community Advisory Board activities.

"People were talking, talking, talking at my house anyway, so I just decided to open a counseling center," she said.

She laughed. "That's how it started," she said. "This is me."

Being Mama Wandoa means many things. One definition is that her house would never be just hers. On one afternoon in August 2008, she sat in an open-air courtyard in the middle of her house amid hundreds of woven plastic bags. A group of young men were filling each bag with the items for needy children, many of them AIDS orphans. Mama Wandoa had joined forces with a Canadian group called Sleeping Children Around the World, which had raised more than $200,000 to distribute 7,000 bed kits and mattresses to children in Tanzania.

One man who had just arrived at the house watched the assembly line from the shadows. Mama Wandoa called him over. "If you find people eating, you wash your hands and eat," she said, smiling. The man nodded in agreement and joined the others in filling the bags.

Mama Wandoa and the Canadians were planning to distribute 700 kits a day in a ten-day marathon. The donor group would arrive the next day, and the distribution would start in two days. But Mama Wandoa faced one big problem: a factory couldn't fill the order for 7,000 blankets, an integral part to the kits.

She started calling competing factories. "We need blankets," she told one person over the phone. "We need 7,000 pieces. Do you have them?"

There was a long pause. She smiled. Apparently, the factory did. She quickly made plans. The factory was a five-hour drive away; she sent a truck immediately to fetch the blankets. Within a day, she figured, it would return with the full load.

Her house was packed with the kits. "This *was* my house," she corrected, laughing, as she pushed open the door to her bedroom. The room was stuffed to the ceiling with the bags. Each room was the same—her home had become a warehouse. She didn't seem to mind, especially not now, not when she had secured 7,000 blankets.

"I'm so happy," she said. "It was really bothering me. I want the kids to get blankets. It is somewhat cold now at night, and they need blankets."

Three days later, she and her boys joined members of the Canadian group to drive two truckloads of bed kits to the Kigamboni schoolyard.

The parents and guardians of the children waited in one area, while the children began lining up near the trucks. Even though the children were remarkably quiet and patient, Mama Wandoa could sense that distribution wouldn't be easy here.

She had two major issues to deal with. One was that there would be a delay in handing out the last 200 mattresses; her two trucks carried just 500 mattresses, and she had had to send one back to Dar es Salaam to fetch the rest. And the second was that a crowd was gathering outside the school after word had spread about the handouts.

Then she noticed a tall boy in line to receive a bed kit. He stood a head taller than almost all the other children. She had pulled him aside earlier and told him he didn't meet the age cutoff of 12 years old. The boy had admitted that he was 13, and he had left the line. But later he had snuck back.

Mama Wandoa pulled him off a second time. He immediately began to weep, and she took him into an empty classroom, shading him from view of the others.

"What's the matter?" she asked.

The boy began to shake and tears fell from his face. "I have a big problem," he said. "My mom died, my father died."

Mama Wandoa Mwambu

He wept and wept, saying, "My God, my God."

Mama Wandoa looked out over the schoolyard, at the lines of children, and said softly, "This is a situation that I have to overlook."

"My God, my God," the boy said.

"I must overlook," she said.

She held his shoulders steady. It took more than a minute for him to stop shaking. He wiped the tears from his face. He wiped them again. She told him to get back in line. He did as he was told.

"My heart hurts for him," she said. "I feel like crying, too."

She didn't, though. Not then. There was no time for that. So she went back to the distribution line, tied the wraps around the children, and told them how wonderful they looked. ∎

The HIV/AIDS Epidemic in **TANZANIA**

a photo essay by Dominic Chavez

In Kigamboni, Tanzania, orphans and other vulnerable children receive free mattresses and bed kits that include insecticide-treated bed nets to prevent malaria. Children are at high risk for malaria in endemic areas, and malaria is a common comorbidity seen with HIV disease. The two infections interact in a lethal cycle; malaria increases susceptibility to HIV infection, and HIV viral load can spike during malarial fevers.

With her house serving as a distribution warehouse, Mama Wandoa Mwambu coordinates the delivery of 7,000 bed kits to orphans and vulnerable children in Tanzania. Mama Wandoa is the driving force behind support services provided to tens of thousands of children through the Upendo AIDS Center, which she founded in 2001.

Treatment of children with HIV poses greater challenges than treatment of adults. Pediatric AIDS drugs are expensive, and they must be constantly reformulated as the child grows. Yet children taking antiretrovirals face an even more daunting test: the reality of lifelong medication and clinical monitoring.

Sylvia Kaaya helps people with HIV/AIDS in Tanzania learn to cope with their infection. The need for psychiatric services for people living with the virus continues to grow, yet Kaaya is one of just a dozen psychiatrists serving the entire country.

V

▶ ▶ THE VIRUS

HIV Variability in Africa

Max Essex

THE HUMAN IMMUNODEFICIENCY VIRUSES ARE CHARACTERIZED BY HIGH RATES OF genomic variation for two major reasons: recombination and the incremental yet rapid accumulation of mutations. Human hosts at the individual and population levels then exert significant selection pressure on rapidly evolving genotypes. The variability and rate of evolution of HIVs create major challenges for biological strategies of intervention, such as drug and vaccine development. This issue is particularly critical in sub-Saharan Africa, which has the world's widest range of HIV variants. This variability may stem not just from the continent's high HIV prevalence rates, but also perhaps from an increased longevity, as the virus appears to have entered the human population from subhuman primates there.

HIV Replication Cycle

HIVs have three major genes—*gag*, *pol*, and *env*—that encode the major virus structural proteins. The *gag* gene encodes a precursor that includes p24, the major core component, and three additional smaller proteins that end up in the core of virus particles.

The *pol* gene encodes a precursor that includes three major components. The first is reverse transcriptase, which transcribes the RNA in the viral genome to make proviral DNA, the form that becomes integrated into the host cell DNA and allows persistence and latency to occur. The second major component of *pol* is the integrase, or endonuclease, which enables the proviral DNA to integrate into the host chromosomal DNA. The third component of *pol*, the protease, cleaves the gag polyprotein precursor to make p24 and the other core components. Because the reverse transcriptase, integrase, and protease enzymes are essential virus-specific components of replication, they provide optimal targets for major classes of antiretroviral drugs.

The *env* gene also encodes a polyprotein, called gp160. The most important component of gp160 is gp120, the glycoprotein that forms spikes at the external surface of virus particles. Gp120 forms bonds with the major cell surface receptor, CD4+, and with the major coreceptors, CCR5 and CXCR4, which are found on the surfaces of lymphocytes and macrophages. The CCR5 coreceptor also appears to be a good target for antiretrovirals.

Neutralizing antibodies function by blocking the bond that forms between gp120 and the receptor or coreceptors. Because of this, immunoselection pressure directed at the regions of gp120 involved in infection may cause a rapid accumulation of mutations. The region of gp120 that most characteristically reflects these changes is called V3, a region of about 36 amino acids.

The HIV genome contains six additional genes that are involved in the activation and regulation of viral synthesis. The RNA is diploid, containing two complete copies of the entire genome. Replication rates can be very high, with up to a million particles per cubic centimeter of blood in advanced infections and in very early stages of acute infection, before the immune response can provide some partial—and temporary—control of replication.

HIV Variation

Genomic variation occurs among HIVs for several reasons. Important factors are the point mutations, insertions, and deletions that occur during the process of reverse transcription to make the DNA provirus from the viral RNA. Mutation rates can be high because the reverse transcriptase lacks the proofreading controls seen with DNA-dependent DNA polymerases.[1,2] More mutations can occur when full-length RNA genomes are transcribed from the integrated proviral DNA. The rates of virus replication may also be high, with 10^{10} virus particles produced each day in an infected individual, and one or more mutations occurring in each virus replication cycle.[3]

Opportunities for even more rapid variation arise when recombination occurs. When two different HIV-1 genomes happen to infect the same cell, the diploid virion genomes released in the next generation may represent two RNA strands of separate parental origin. This in turn generates recombinants when the process of reverse transcription allows switching from one strand to the other. This is particularly noticeable when the same cell might have been infected with parental genomes from two different clades or subtypes, resulting in the generation of intersubtype recombinants. The same process presumably occurs when an individual is infected on two different occasions with virus of the same clade or subtype. In most countries only one subtype of HIV predominates, so many more opportunities occur for intrasubtype recombination. Risk for coinfection is presumably also related to immunity, however, and immunity should be greatest within, rather than between, subtypes. Nevertheless, it is clear that a lack of immunity often allows coinfection with the same subtype.[4]

The constant generation of mutants results in an accumulation of variants that can then be described as a quasispecies or swarm.[5] HIV-1s can accumulate so many mutations that the dominant clone can differ from the parental virus by 1 percent each year.[6]

Along with the generation of variants by either the accumulation of mutations or recombination, a critical aspect of genomic variation is the selection pressure exerted by the host. This is important within a single individual for rapidly emerging variants that show properties such as drug resistance. It is presumably also important at the human population level to determine the relative success of the HIV-1 subtype or circulating recombinant form (CRF) for efficient transmission among people. Phenotypic correlates of viral genotype that enhance transmission efficiency might include the rapid evasion of immune control and the relative affinity of the virus for host cell receptors or coreceptors. The gp120 sequences generally control such properties, which may help explain why envelope sequences typically evolve faster than those of other genes. Furthermore, only a few point mutations in gp120 can rapidly change cell tropism.[7] Selection pressure can also be exerted on non-coding sequences, such as the regulatory region at the long terminal repeats of the virus that determine rates of transcriptional activation.[8]

Classification of HIVs

HIVs are most accurately categorized by determining nucleotide sequences and comparing the sequences using techniques that allow a measurement of genetic distance. Control sequences, used as representatives of different subtypes, are compared to the unknown viruses using sequence alignment methods such as the Neighbor Joining method, Maximum Parsimony, or Maximum Likelihood. Numerous reference sequences are available at the HIV Sequence Database of the U.S. Los Alamos National Laboratory. As nucleotide sequencing became less expensive, such approaches became feasible for use in many laboratories. To obtain the initial sequence, researchers can amplify proviral DNA or reverse transcribed plasma RNA through the use of polymerase chain reaction, or PCR. Other less sensitive procedures, such as the heteroduplex mobility assay, may be used to compare PCR-amplified sequences.

While full-length analysis of viral genomes is most accurate, it is often impractical to analyze more than short stretches of the viral genome. Depending on the information sought, analysis of short stretches may be adequate for categorizing HIV genomes. In geographic regions where recombinants are common, however, the inclusion of many different regions of the viral genome may be required.

Serological techniques have been developed to help distinguish clades or subtypes. These tests' sensitivity for distinguishing subtypes has been relatively low, especially when trying to distinguish subtypes that are only moderately distant from each other. As nucleotide sequencing procedures became less expensive, the serologic techniques rapidly fell from favor.

Two major types of HIVs exist in people: HIV-1s and HIV-2s. HIV-2s have probably infected less than a million people and account for only 1 to 2 percent of all HIV infections. HIV-2s appear to be about 40 percent related to HIV-1s at the genomic level. HIV-2s appear to have entered the human population from mangabey monkeys, which may help explain why they are largely limited to West Africa.[9] It seems likely that several different mangabey simian immunodeficiency viruses, or SIVs, entered the human population in this region (Figure 1).

HIV-2 has spread less efficiently in people than HIV-1.[10] HIV-2 is also less virulent than HIV-1. People infected with HIV-2 are less likely to develop clinical AIDS, at least in the same time it takes to develop clinical AIDS when infected with HIV-1.[11]

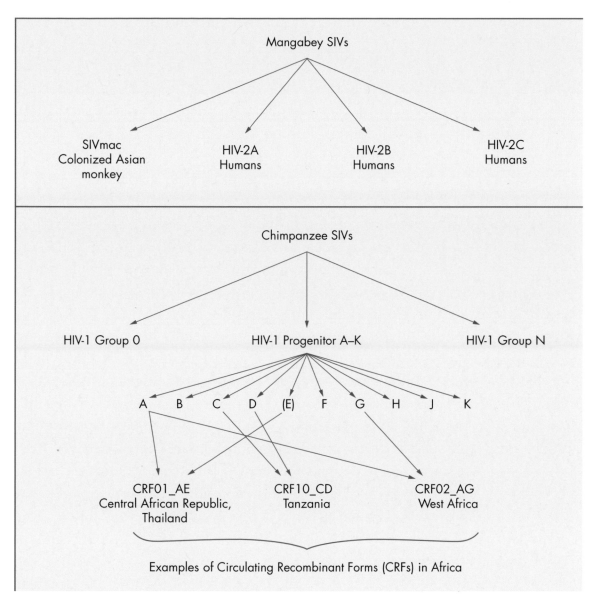

Figure 1. Likely Entry of HIV-1s into the Human Species

Abbreviation: SIV: simian immunodeficiency virus

HIV-1s are initially classified into three groups called the main or major group (M), the outlier group (O), and the non-M/non-O group (N).[12] Only very small numbers of people have been infected with HIV-1 group N or O viruses; nearly everyone infected with HIV-1 has an M group virus. Isolations of the group N and

O viruses are clustered around west–central Africa, in countries such as Cameroon and Gabon.[13,14]

The SIVs that have been isolated from chimpanzees have been more closely related to HIV-1 groups N and O than to group M, which is more common in people.[15,16] Presumably, one or more precursor viruses that are more closely related to the HIV-1 group M viruses also exists or did exist in subhuman primates, but no such precursor virus has been identified. Many other SIVs have been isolated from various species of African monkeys, but most of these viruses are only distantly related to HIV-1 or HIV-2, and descendants of them have not been found in people.[17] SIVs were originally identified in colonized Asian macaque monkeys,[18,19] but it is now clear that they were infected only by exposure to materials from humans or African monkeys, as the SIV/HIV family of retroviruses is not found naturally in subhuman primates of Asian origin.

Within HIV-1 group M, a classification has been established to designate subtypes.[20] Subtypes within group M differ in nucleotide sequence by 20 to 25 percent, with lower rates of divergence in conserved regions such as *gag* and higher heterogeneity in the variable regions of the envelope gp120 gene. At least nine different subtypes have been identified and characterized. They are designated A–D, F–H, J, and K. Two—HIV-1E and HIV-1I—were soon recognized to be recombinants rather than pure subtypes. Only subtypes HIV-1A, B, C, and D have been found in large numbers of people. It is now recognized that B and D are more closely related to each other than first realized—enough so that one could be considered a major subsubtype of the other. HIV-1G has been found in a minority of people in a few West African countries. The others, such as the N and O groups, are rarely found.

The two HIV-1 group M subtypes that are no longer listed as pure subtypes, HIV-1E and HIV-1I, are now recognized to be CRFs. More than 15 CRFs have been described, but only two of these, CRF01 and CRF02, have been found to infect large numbers of people. CRF01 is the virus that was initially described as HIV-1E, or A/E.[21,22] The gp120 envelope of this virus is from a distinct subtype designated E, but no pure E viruses have been found. The rest of the virus is HIV-1A. The CRF02 virus is a recombinant composed primarily of subtype A, with several insertions of G in the middle and at the end of the genome.

The term "strain" is not usually used for HIVs, except to designate an individual isolate from a particular laboratory or source for reference. The high rates of genomic variation in HIVs of infected people are so variable that we must assume the same "strain" would not be found in more than one individual.

Distribution of Subtypes and CRFs

According to UNAIDS, no country outside of Africa has an HIV prevalence rate higher than 3 percent among adults, though several Caribbean nations have rates that range from 1.5 to 3.0 percent.[23] In Asian countries that are sometimes described as having major epidemics—such as China, India, and Thailand—the estimated rates of infection are 0.1 percent, 0.3 percent, and 1.4 percent.[23] Yet most southern African countries have adult infection rates above 12 percent, and the mean for all of sub-Saharan Africa is 5 percent. Within sub-Saharan Africa, rates are highest in southern Africa, lowest in West and Central Africa, and intermediate in East Africa (Table 1).

The distribution of subtypes in the world is also uneven (Table 2). In the Americas and Western Europe, the dominant virus is HIV-1B, and the major routes of transmission are sex between men and injection drug use. Only a small fraction of those infected in the United States have subtypes other than HIV-1B, unless they have traveled to southern continents or had sexual contact with immigrants from regions where other viruses predominate. Rates of infection with other HIV-1 subtypes are somewhat higher in parts of Europe and South America, presumably because higher exchange rates have occurred with people from Africa.[24,25]

The major route for most HIV transmission in Africa is heterosexual sex. In southern Africa, most infections are with HIV-1C.[26] In cities in South Africa, however, Caucasian homosexual men are usually infected with HIV-1B, presumably because of early contact with homosexual men in the United States or Europe.[27] In Central and West Africa, most infected people have CRF02_AG. In East Africa, HIV-1A and HIV-1D are both present in about equal ratios.[28] Tanzania, at the base of East Africa, and Cameroon, at the base of West Africa, seem to have given rise to the largest number of recombinant viruses.[29,30] Tanzania, which has HIV-1A and HIV-1D, is seeing an increase in HIV-1C as well.[31] In countries in the horn of Africa, such as Ethiopia, HIV-1C also predominates.[32]

With two-thirds of all the world's HIV infections in Africa, the subtypes that occur there at high prevalence account for large proportions of the world's infections. HIV-1C,

Table 1. Representative Adult Prevalence Rates in Different Geographic Regions		
Region/Countries	Prevalence	Dominant Subtype
Southern Africa[a]	**16.1**	**C (>95%)**
Botswana	23.9	C (>95%)
South Africa	18.1	C (>95%)
Swaziland	26.1	C (>95%)
East Africa	**6.0**	**A (50%)**
Burundi	2.0	A (55%)
Tanzania	6.2	A (50%)
Uganda	5.4	C (50%)
West Africa	**2.5**	**CRF 02 (70%)**
Burkina Faso	1.6	CRF 02 (>75%)
Nigeria	3.1	CRF 02 (>55%)
Senegal	1.0	CRF 02 (>75%)
Other Representative Developing Countries	**0.4**	**All**
Brazil	0.6	B (>70%)
China	0.1	CRF 07, 08 (>80%)
Thailand	1.4	CRF 01 (>90%)
North America and Europe	**0.4**	**B (>80%)**
Italy	0.4	B (>75%)
Sweden	0.1	B (>75%)
United States	0.6	B (>90%)

[a]Excludes Angola and island countries.

Abbreviation: CRF: circulating recombinant form

Source: UNAIDS. *Report on the Global HIV/AIDS Epidemic.* Geneva: UNAIDS, 2008.

for example, accounts for more than half of the world's infections, and CRF02_AG accounts for another 20 to 25 percent.[26] HIV-1A, HIV-1B, HIV-1D, and CRF01_AE each infect one to four million people and together make up most of the other 25 percent. New CRFs, however, are also emerging in Africa, as they are in China.

HIV-1C also occurs in western India, but HIV-1B is associated with injection drug use in northeastern India.[33] The heterosexual epidemic in Thailand is CRF01_AE, the same virus that occurs in the Central African Republic.[22] Although the initial epidemic among injection drug users in Thailand was HIV-1B, it has slowly transitioned to an epidemic of CRF01_AE.[34]

Table 2. Major Subtypes and CRFs of HIV-1: Transmission Patterns, Percentage of World Epidemic, and Major Geographic Distribution			
HIV-1 Subtype or CRF	Major Transmission Pattern	Percentage of World Epidemic	Major Geographic Distribution
A	Heterosexual	5–10	East Africa
B	Homosexual, IDU	10–12	United States, Europe
C	Heterosexual	50–55	Southern Africa, India, Ethiopia
D	Heterosexual	3–5	East Africa
CRF01_AE	Heterosexual	3–5	Thailand
CRF02_AG	Heterosexual	22–28	West and Central Africa
Others	Heterosexual, IDU	5–10	Africa; Asia, Eastern Europe

Abbreviations: CRF: circulating recombinant form; IDU: injection drug user

Clinical and Biological Differences Between Types and Subtypes

Most geographic regions have only one dominant subtype in a particular population, which makes it difficult to compare epidemiological and clinical outcomes between HIV types and subtypes. A few exceptions occur, such as the female sex worker cohort in Senegal, where both HIV-1 and HIV-2 are present;[10,11] the injection drug user cohort in Bangkok, where HIV-1B and CRF01_AE are present;[34] and in Tanzania, where HIV-1A, HIV-1C, and HIV-1D may all be present at high enough prevalence rates for such measurements.[30,35] In addition, if rapid selection pressure has been exerted on the virus by the population, a given biological property may sometimes vary as much within subtypes as between subtypes.

Despite these limitations, it seems likely that some viruses, such as HIV-1C in southern Africa, are more easily transmissible through heterosexual sex. The rates of saturation or plateau tend to be higher for the countries affected in southern Africa, even though those epidemics started later than the ones caused by other viruses in Africa and elsewhere.[26] It is also apparent that most epidemics of HIV-1B have not spread as effectively as those of the other major viruses except in specific populations in which transmission is more efficient, such as homosexual men and injection drug users. In South Africa, for example, an epidemic of HIV-1B was established in homosexual men, but it never spread at high levels in heterosexual populations. Later, when HIV-1C entered the population, the virus rapidly spread to infect about 20 percent of heterosexual adults.

HIV-2 was already present at saturation levels among Senegalese female sex workers when HIV-1, primarily CRF02_AG, entered the population, enabling a demonstration of the more rapid spread of HIV-1 (Table 3).[10] These differences are most dramatic when mother-to-child transmission rates are compared. HIV-1 transmission rates through breastfeeding regularly exceed 30 percent, but never exceed 2 to 4 percent with HIV-2.[36] HIV-1B was shown to be less efficiently transmitted than CRF01_AE in the same cohort of injection drug users in Bangkok.[34] Mother-to-child transmission was also found to be more effective with HIV-1C than with HIV-1D in the same cohort in Dar es Salaam, Tanzania (Table 3).[37]

Differences in disease development and related parameters have been reported as well. HIV-2 does not cause clinical AIDS in most infected people during the same eight-to-ten-year time period during which HIV-1 causes disease.[11] After clinical AIDS develops in the smaller fraction of HIV-2–infected people who get sick, the disease itself resembles the disease that HIV-1 causes.[38]

Another study in the same cohort of Senegalese sex workers compared time to AIDS in women infected with CRF02_AG, the dominant virus in the population, to a combination of other HIV-1s, including HIV-1C, HIV-1D, and HIV-1G.[39] The CRF02_AG–infected women were less likely to develop AIDS during the same time period. A similar comparison for time to disease in HIV-1–infected adults in Uganda found that HIV-1A–infected people developed disease less rapidly than HIV-1D–infected people.[35]

Development of disease is generally associated with higher loads of virus, generally measured as plasma viral RNA. HIV-2–infected adults tend to have significantly lower levels of plasma viral RNA than HIV-1–infected people.[40] This finding is consistent with the lower rates of both disease and transmission seen with HIV-2. A study in Kenya suggested that plasma viral RNA levels were higher for people infected with HIV-1C than for those infected with HIV-1A or HIV-1D.[41] A similar study in Bangkok found that viral RNA levels were higher for CRF01_AE than for HIV-1B (Table 3).[42]

Table 3. Examples of Biological and Epidemiological Differences Between HIV Types and Subtypes in the Same Population

Property Measured	Viruses Compared	Result	Reference
(1) Transmission			
(a) sexual	HIV-2 vs. HIV-1	HIV-2 less transmissible	[10]
(b) injection drug use	CRF01_AE vs. HIV-1B	HIV-1B less transmissible	[34]
(c) mother-to-child	HIV-2 vs. HIV-1	HIV-2 less transmissible	[36]
	HIV-1D vs. HIV-1C	HIV-1D less transmissible	[37]
(2) Disease Development and Progression	HIV-2 vs. HIV-1	HIV-2 less virulent	[11]
	CRF02_AG vs. other HIV-1s	HIV-2 less virulent	[11]
	HIV-1A vs. HIV-1D	HIV-1A less virulent	[35]
(3) Viral Load	HIV-2 vs. HIV-1	HIV-2 lower	[40]
	HIV-1C vs. HIV-1A and HIV-1D	HIV-1C higher	[41]
	CRF01_AE vs. HIV-1B	CRF01_AE higher	[42]

Abbreviation: CRF: circulating recombinant form

Coinfections and Reinfections

Coinfections can occur with viruses of different types, different subtypes, and within the same subtype. Coinfections with HIV-1 and HIV-2 have been reported, but seem to occur less often than might be expected due to chance alone.[43] While there is no evidence for specific immune resistance against HIV-1 infection for people already infected with HIV-2, in-vitro studies suggest that the chemokines MIP-1α, MIP-1β, and RANTES, when induced by HIV-2, might restrict infection by HIV-1.[44]

The evidence that coinfection can occur with two different subtypes is supported by the large number of intersubtype recombinants that have been identified in sites where more than one subtype is present.[30,45] Studies on actual rates of coinfections in relation to predicted risk for exposure to multiple subtypes have not been reported, however.

Coinfection can also occur with viruses of the same subtype. To the extent that immune responses control HIV replication, it must be assumed that such immune control works best against viruses with similar sequences that encode immune epitopes. Similarly, when most or all immune control has broken down, such as in the advanced stages of disease, coinfections with closely related viruses would be most likely to occur. The high levels of the original virus and the relatively modest differences between some viruses in the same subtype, however, may make those coinfections difficult to detect.

Only one or a few changes in key cytolytic T cell immune epitopes can allow a virus to escape immune control and presumably control against coinfection.[46] While this is usually studied in the context of escape from immune control, it has also been observed to influence coinfection.[4]

Conclusion

HIVs, which have been found in people for just a few decades, have already become highly diverse. The diversity is encouraged by error-prone reverse transcription, high replication rates, recombination, and host selection pressure. The fitness characteristics of some HIV-1s, such as HIV-1C in southern Africa, have resulted in epidemics with high prevalence rates. It is already clear that coinfections with different viruses can occur because of limited immunity between different viruses and escape from immune control. Additional HIV epidemics are likely to occur as new recombinants and variants adapt to human populations.

REFERENCES

1. Lukashov VV, Goudsmit J. HIV heterogeneity and disease progression in AIDS: a model of continuous virus adaptation. *AIDS,* 1998;12(Suppl A):S43–S52.
2. Coffin JM. Genetic diversity and evolution of retroviruses. *Curr Top Microbiol Immunol,* 1992;176: 143–164.
3. Preston BD, Poiesz BJ, Loeb LA. Fidelity of HIV-1 reverse transcriptase. *Science,* 1988;242:1168–1171.
4. Altfeld M, Allen TM, Yu XG, et al. HIV-1 superinfection despite broad CD8+ T-cell responses containing replication of the primary virus. *Nature,* 2002;420: 434–439.
5. Goodenow M, Huet TH, Saurin W, Kowk S, Sninsky J, Wain-Hobson S. HIV-1 isolates are rapidly evolving quasispecies: evidence for viral mixtures and preferred nucleotide substitutions. *J Acquir Immune Defic Syndr,* 1989;2:344–352.
6. Myers G, Pavlakis GN. Evolutionary potential of complex retroviruses. In: Levy JA, ed. *The Retroviridae.* New York: Plenum Press, 1992:51–105.
7. Cheng-Mayer C, Seto D, Tateno M, Levy JA. Biologic features of HIV-1 that correlate with virulence in the host. *Science,* 1988;240:80–82.
8. Montano MA, Novitsky VA, Blackard JT, Cho NL, Katzenstein DA, Essex M. Divergent transcriptional regulation among expanding human immunodeficiency virus type 1 subtypes. *J Virol,* 1997;71:8657–8665.
9. Fultz PN, McClure H, Anderson D, Swenson R, Anand R, Srinivasan A. Isolation of a T-lymphotropic retrovirus from naturally infected sooty mangabey monkeys (*Cercocebus atys*). *Proc Natl Acad Sci USA,* 1986;83:5286–5290.
10. Kanki P, Travers K, Hernandez-Avila M, et al. Slower heterosexual spread of HIV-2 compared with HIV-1. *Lancet,* 1994;343:943–946.
11. Marlink R, Kanki P, Thior I, et al. Reduced rate of disease development with HIV-2 compared to HIV-1. *Science,* 1994;265:1587–1590.
12. Robertson DL, Anderson JP, Bradac JA, et al. HIV-1 nomenclature proposal. *Science,* 2000;288:55–56.
13. Bibollet-Ruche F, Peeters M, Mboup S, et al. Molecular characterization of the envelope transmembrane glycoprotein of 13 new human immunodeficiency virus type 1 group O strains from six different African countries. *AIDS Res Hum Retroviruses,* 1998;14: 1281–1285.
14. Simon F, Mauclere P, Roques P, et al. Identification of a new human immunodeficiency virus type 1 distinct from group M and group O. *Nat Med,* 1998;4: 1032–1037.
15. Peeters M, Fransen K, Delaporte E, et al. Isolation and characterization of a new chimpanzee lentivirus (simian immunodeficiency virus isolate cpz-ant) from a wild-captured chimpanzee. *AIDS,* 1992;6: 447–451.
16. Gao F, Bailes E, Robertson DL, et al. Origin of HIV-1 in the chimpanzee *Pan troglodytes troglodytes. Nature,* 1999;397:436–441.
17. Diop O, Gueye A, Ayouba A, et al. Simian immunodeficiency viruses and the origin of HIVs. In: Essex M, Mboup S, Kanki P, Marlink R, Tlou S, eds. *AIDS in Africa.* 2nd ed. New York: Kluwer Academic/Plenum Publishers, 2002:104–120.
18. Kanki P, McLane M, King NJ. Serologic identification and characterization of a macaque T-lymphotropic retrovirus closely related to HTLV-III. *Science,* 1985; 228:1199–1201.
19. Daniel MD, Letvin NL, King NW, et al. Isolation of T-cell tropic HTLV-III-like retrovirus from macaques. *Science,* 1985;228:1201–1204.
20. Louwagie J, Janssens W, Mascola J, et al. Genetic diversity of the envelope glycoprotein from human immunodeficiency virus type 1 isolates of African origin. *J Virol,* 1995;69:263–271.
21. Carr JK, Salminen MO, Koch C, et al. Full-length sequence and mosaic structure of a human immunodeficiency virus type 1 isolate from Thailand. *J Virol,* 1996;70:5935–5943.
22. Gao F, Robertson DL, Morrison SG, et al. The heterosexual HIV-1 epidemic in Thailand is caused by an intersubtype (A/E) recombinant of African origin. *J Virol,* 1996;70:7013–7029.
23. UNAIDS. *Report on the Global HIV/AIDS Epidemic.* Geneva: UNAIDS, 2008.
24. Couto-Fernandez JC, Morgado MG, Bongertz V, et al. HIV-1 subtyping in Salvador, Bahia, Brazil: a city with African sociodemographic characteristics. *J Acquir Immune Defic Syndr,* 1999;22:288–293.

25. Couturier E, Damond F, Roques P, et al. HIV-1 diversity in France, 1996–1998. The AC 11 laboratory network. *AIDS*, 2000;14:289–296.

26. Essex M. Human immunodeficiency viruses in the developing world. *Adv Virus Res*, 1999;53:71–88.

27. Janssens W, Buve A, Nkengasong JN. The puzzle of HIV-1 subtypes in Africa. *AIDS*, 1997;11:705–712.

28. Rayfield MA, Downing RG, Baggs J, et al. A molecular epidemiologic survey of HIV in Uganda. HIV Variant Working Group. *AIDS*, 1998;12:521–527.

29. Renjifo B, Gilbert P, Chaplin B. Emerging recombinant human immunodeficiency viruses: uneven representation of the envelope V3 region. *AIDS*, 1999;13:1613–1621.

30. Robertson DL, Sharp PM, McCutchan FE, Hahn BH. Recombination in HIV-1. *Nature (London)*, 1995;374: 124–126.

31. Renjifo B, Chaplin B, Mwakagile D, et al. Epidemic expansion of HIV type 1 subtype C and recombinant genotypes in Tanzania. *AIDS Res Hum Retroviruses*, 1998;14:635–638.

32. Abebe A, Lukashov VV, Pollakis G. Timing of the HIV-1 subtype C epidemic in Ethiopia based on early virus strains and subsequent virus diversification. *AIDS*, 2001;15:1555–1561.

33. Halani N, Wang B, Ge YC, Gharpure H, Hira S, Saksena NK. Changing epidemiology of HIV type 1 infections in India: evidence of subtype B introduction in Bombay from a common source. *AIDS Res Hum Retroviruses*, 2001;17:637–642.

34. Hudgens MG, Longini IM, Jr., Vanichseni S, et al. Subtype-specific transmission probabilities for human immunodeficiency virus type 1 among injecting drug users in Bangkok, Thailand. *Am J Epidemiol*, 2002;155:159–168.

35. Vasan A, Renjifo B, Hertzmark E, et al. Different rates of disease progression of HIV type 1 infection in Tanzania based on infecting subtype. *Clin Infect Dis*, 2006;42:843–852.

36. Kanki P, Sankalé J-L, Mboup S. Biology of human immunodeficiency virus type 2. In: Essex M, Mboup S, Kanki P, Marlink R, Tlou S, eds. *AIDS in Africa*. 2nd ed. New York: Kluwer Academic/Plenum Publishers, 2002:74–103.

37. Blackard JT, Renjifo B, Fawzi W, et al. HIV-1 LTR subtype and perinatal transmission. *Virology*, 2001; 287:261–265.

38. De Cock K, Odehouri K, Colebunders R, et al. A comparison of HIV-1 and HIV-2 infections in hospitalized patients in Abidjan, Cote d'Ivoire. *AIDS*, 1990;4:443.

39. Kanki PJ, Hamel DG, Sankalé J-L, et al. HIV-1 subtypes differ in disease progression. *J Infect Dis*, 1999; 179:68–73.

40. Popper SJ, Dieng-Sarr A, Travers KU, et al. Lower HIV-2 viral load reflects the difference in pathogenicity of HIV-1 and HIV-2. *J Infect Dis*, 1999;180: 1116–1121.

41. Neilson JR, John GC, Carr JK, et al. Subtypes of human immunodeficiency virus type 1 and disease stage among women in Nairobi, Kenya. *J Virol*, 1999; 73:4393–4403.

42. Hu DJ, Vanichseni S, Mastro TD, et al. Viral load differences in early infection with two HIV-1 subtypes. *AIDS*, 2001;15:683–691.

43. Travers K, MBoup S, Marlink R, et al. Natural protection against HIV-1 infection provided by HIV-2. *Science*, 1995;268:1612–1615.

44. Kokkotou EG, Sankalé J-L, Mani I, et al. In vitro correlates of HIV-2 mediated HIV-1 protection. *Proc Natl Acad Sci USA*, 2000;97(12):6797–6802.

45. McCutchan FE. Understanding the genetic diversity of HIV-1. *AIDS*, 2000;14(Suppl 3):S31–S44.

46. Borrow P, Lewicki H, Wei X, et al. Antiviral pressure exerted by HIV-1-specific cytotoxic T lymphocytes (CTLs) during primary infection demonstrated by rapid selection of CTL escape virus. *Nat Med*, 1997; 3:205–211.

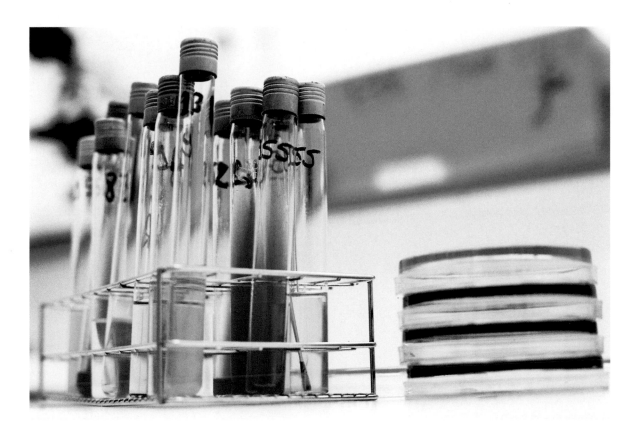

Afterword

WHILE DRIVING THROUGH THE UGANDAN COUNTRYSIDE IN THE MID-1990s, WE ONCE stopped near a small roadside shack, where a dozen men worked together to build coffins. Some of the men planed wood, while others sawed boards or hammered the pieces together into recognizable shapes. Young children played in the workers' midst; older children helped by stacking the finished coffins up against the shack. As we watched coffin after coffin being lifted into the air, we realized we were witnessing the devastation of AIDS on Africa.

The situation seemed nearly hopeless for Africans infected with HIV. By the end of that decade, even as effective drugs were widely available in the developed world, access to those drugs was virtually nonexistent in Africa. At that time, international agencies debated whether providing therapy to HIV-infected Africans was technically feasible, much less sustainable. The resulting silence suggested to many of us working in the trenches of Africa's epidemic that no therapies would be forthcoming.

In this book, we have tried to faithfully record the responses of some of the governments, institutions, and remarkable individuals who decided that taking no action—denying Africans with HIV/AIDS access to livesaving treatments—was unacceptable. They drew a line in the sand, declaring they would treat people in need.

We have worked in the four countries depicted in this book for many years, and we believe their stories help portray a range of responses to the AIDS treatment crisis. Many other African countries have made similar strides; these countries are not singular. We believe, however, that they demonstrate the heterogeneity of the epidemic and illustrate the many factors that can affect the success of an AIDS treatment program, such as the impact of culture, the involvement of national leadership, the strength of the existing health care infrastructure, and the role of international development agencies.

The countries described in this book have demonstrated not only that AIDS treatment is technically feasible in Africa, but also that rapid scale-up is possible. In just a few years, in these four countries alone, hundreds of thousands of patients have received lifesaving drugs. But that's not the only progress. Through this assistance, health care systems have been strengthened to support the complexities of comprehensive HIV treatment and care. Universal access has become the new mantra, and critical statistics on a country's progress toward these goals has become a new report card for international donor agencies.

The cost of antiretrovirals and laboratory monitoring tests has decreased dramatically since the late 1990s—and so have concerns about the financial sustainability of treatment programs. Nonetheless, as we move from the start-up phase of the treatment programs, we must consider the sustainability of lifelong therapy for patients already on the drug regimens—and then remember that many, many more still await treatment.

The nations of southern Africa—Botswana, Lesotho, Namibia, South Africa, Swaziland, and Zimbabwe—carry a significantly higher burden of HIV disease than countries in other African regions. We have been privileged to be able to work in Botswana and to witness the courage and vision of that country's leadership in addressing this crisis. Under the direction of President Festus Mogae, officials initiated the national antiretroviral therapy (ART) program, largely with their government's funds. The national treatment and prevention programs have drawn on their HIV research experience in Botswana to ensure that these programs could achieve the highest quality of care while concurrently setting an important benchmark for the rest of the continent. The African Comprehensive HIV/AIDS Partnerships, or ACHAP, provided unique support by partnering with the government and developing nationwide support for the Botswana treatment program.

The sheer size of Nigeria's population—and the magnitude of the country's impact on the continent—cannot be underestimated. Although the national HIV prevalence rate has now fallen below 4 percent, with the population at 150 million, an enormous number of people still need treatment. While the government of Nigeria, the U.S. President's Emergency Plan for AIDS Relief, and others have made significant dents in reducing the treatment burden, implementing those programs has been challenging.

One critical first step has been to repair and strengthen the health system. Many onlookers have expressed skepticism about the feasibility of implementing treatment programs in Nigeria, not to mention sustaining them. Such an attitude is not new, given Nigeria's history of decades of military rule and its consequences. Yet it has been inspirational to witness the energy and devotion of the thousands of Nigerian health care providers working to save the lives of their fellow citizens. The real sustainability of these programs depends on them and we are optimistic that the proper course is set.

The third country—Senegal, where we have worked since 1985—highlights the critical role that national leadership can play in helping to prevent the spread of HIV. Senegal has been one of the few countries worldwide to demonstrate how prevention measures implemented early can keep HIV infection rates in check. Among the key determinants in the country's success have been widespread HIV education initiatives, control programs for sexually transmitted infections, and the early involvement of religious leaders.

Despite Senegal's relatively low infection rates in the late 1990s, government officials there still tackled the question of whether they would provide HIV treatment to the thousands in need. The nation's leaders declared they could not allow people with HIV/AIDS to go untreated, and Senegal became the first country to establish an AIDS treatment program for patients in need. The government's initial financial commitment represented most of the country's health care budget. We applaud that courage and recognize the importance of the example Senegal has set for other countries in responding to the treatment crisis.

The fourth nation featured in this book, Tanzania, has been able to develop significant health system networks that provide services in a socialist-based model, despite the country's widespread poverty. Tanzania began its ART program in 2004, years later than some other African countries. The nation's excellent reputation among international donors was critical to the robust response that occurred that year, and it was no doubt responsible for the program's dramatic success. In 2005, the government of Tanzania insisted on a regionalization of ART. Among the countries in our book, this approach was unique to Tanzania, but it serves as an important example of how government policy can address disparities in access to treatment. Three years after the regionalization, it is obvious that rural populations in Tanzania have gained better access to treatment as a result. The history of Tanzania's response illustrates well the critical integration of prevention programs with treatment and care.

We had both worked in HIV research in these countries for many years before ART programs began. We had despaired at the high rates of infection and the devastating impact of disease. And although we had worked within our own capacities to develop interventions, we had shared the frustration of our many African colleagues who found themselves unable to treat AIDS patients, and we had watched many people needlessly suffer and die. That has all since changed.

Challenges remain. Many in need still lack access to antiretrovirals. Africans are becoming infected with HIV at faster rates than they are being enrolled in treatment programs. But these countries, in different ways and in varying degrees, have made history. We believe that by telling their stories and celebrating their successes we can offer ideas and inspiration to countries now struggling to start their own HIV treatment programs. Dr. Ernest Ekong, the national clinical coordinator of the Harvard–PEPFAR program in Nigeria, captured it best when he said, "Our ultimate hope is for prevention. But in the meantime, we're grateful to be able to save lives."

Phyllis J. Kanki, DVM, DSc
Richard G. Marlink, MD

Editors and Contributors

Editors

Phyllis J. Kanki, DVM, DSc, is director of the AIDS Prevention Initiative in Nigeria (APIN), principal investigator of the U.S. President's Emergency Plan for AIDS Relief (PEPFAR) program at Harvard, and professor of immunology and infectious diseases at the Harvard School of Public Health. She has spearheaded the longest-standing research collaboration between a Western nation and an African country in the history of the AIDS epidemic. Since 1985, she has worked closely with colleagues in Senegal, a country now heralded as one of the world's greatest success stories in HIV prevention.

A virologist with recognized expertise in the pathogenesis and molecular epidemiology of HIV in Africa, Kanki has also served as principal investigator for several National Institutes of Health research grants on HIV-1 and HIV-2 in West Africa, focusing on such topics as the identification and reduced transmission of HIV-2, cross-protection between HIV-2 and HIV-1, and the various times to disease development for different HIV-1 genotypes.

Since 2000, Kanki has directed APIN, a program she created with a $25 million grant from the Bill & Melinda Gates Foundation. Under her leadership, APIN researchers have modeled their approach to HIV prevention in Nigeria on Kanki's long-term collaboration with Senegal, where HIV infection rates have been kept lower than those of the rest of the continent for more than a decade.

Since 2004, Kanki has also served as principal investigator of Harvard's PEPFAR program. In its first year, this program initiated high-quality treatment and care programs in six sites in Nigeria and five sites in Tanzania. In Botswana, PEPFAR activities have focused on development of the Clinical Master Trainer Program, which provides critical training to health care providers in antiretroviral treatment sites throughout the country, and the establishment of a strong monitoring and evaluation system for the national antiretroviral treatment program.

Kanki has authored or coauthored more than 160 peer-reviewed publications, most of which have been based on studies in West Africa. She coedited *AIDS in Nigeria: A Nation on the Threshold* (Harvard Center for Population and Development Studies, 2006) and the first and second editions of *AIDS in Africa* (Raven Press, 1994, and Kluwer Academic/Plenum Publishers, 2002).

After receiving a doctorate in veterinary medicine from the University of Minnesota School of Veterinary Medicine, Kanki earned her doctorate in virology from the Harvard School of Public Health. In 2008, the University of Ibadan in Nigeria granted her an honorary doctorate and bestowed upon her its Award for Outstanding Contribution to the Development of Public Health in Africa. That same year, she was elected to the Institute of Medicine of the National Academies in Washington, DC.

Richard G. Marlink, MD, is the Bruce A. Beal, Robert L. Beal, and Alexander S. Beal Professor of the Practice of Public Health at the Harvard School of Public Health; executive director of the Harvard School of Public Health AIDS Initiative (formerly the Harvard AIDS Institute); and vice president, technical implementation at the Elizabeth Glaser Pediatric AIDS Foundation.

A medical oncologist and hematologist, Marlink focused his initial research on collaborative clinical trials of new anticancer agents and then antiretrovirals used in HIV infection. Part of the team that initially identified HIV-2, the second AIDS virus, he became involved in laboratory research at the Harvard School of Public Health and in epidemiologic and clinical studies in Senegal. There he helped coordinate studies on the clinical and biologic characteristics of both HIV-1 and HIV-2. Since 1985, Marlink has directed AIDS-related clinical and laboratory training, infrastructure development, and research in Botswana, Brazil, Puerto Rico, Senegal, South Africa, Tanzania, and Thailand. At the Harvard School of Public Health AIDS Initiative, Marlink has been involved in a range of international AIDS projects. In 1996, he helped create the Botswana–Harvard Partnership for HIV Research and Education. Under his direction, the partnership later launched the KITSO AIDS Training Program, which helps prepare Botswana's health care providers to care for those living with HIV/AIDS; the Clinical Master Trainer Program; and the Laboratory Master Trainer Program. Marlink also helped establish the Enhancing Care Initiative in 1998 to improve the clinical care of people living with HIV/AIDS in resource-constrained settings.

Marlink, who earned his medical degree from the University of New Mexico, is the principal investigator of Botswana's first large-scale antiretroviral treatment study, along with other clinical, economic, and basic biomedical studies in Botswana.

At the Elizabeth Glaser Pediatric AIDS Foundation, Marlink helps advance HIV/AIDS treatment and care programs and targeted evaluations in eight sub-Saharan African countries and prevention-of-mother-to-child-transmission-of-HIV efforts in 19 countries and 3,700 sites in the developing world.

Marlink coedited the second edition of *AIDS in Africa* (Kluwer Academic/Plenum Publishers, 2002) and is editor-in-chief of a three-volume book, *From the Ground Up: Building Comprehensive HIV/AIDS Care Programs in Resource-Limited Settings* (Elizabeth Glaser Pediatric AIDS Foundation, 2009).

Contributors

Guerino Chalamilla, MD, is deputy country director for the MDH HIV/AIDS Care and Treatment Program, the Harvard PEPFAR program in Tanzania. The program is a collaboration of the Muhimbili University College of Health Sciences, the Dar es Salaam City Council, and the Harvard School of Public Health. Chalamilla has also served as field director of HIV/AIDS care and treatment at the Amana District Hospital in Dar es Salaam. Chalamilla has more than two decades of experience in clinical work and research, including more than a decade focusing on HIV/AIDS.

Dominic Chavez, an award-winning freelance photographer, has covered a range of domestic and international issues since 1991. From 1997 to 2008, he was a staff photographer at *The Boston Globe,* for which he reported from the frontlines of Iraq and Afghanistan to the war-torn streets of Angola. He has recorded the effects of the ongoing drug war in Colombia and in the United States, and he has documented many health issues facing the nations of Africa.

Among his many photographic essays has been "Lives Lost: A Worldwide Health Crisis," a yearlong effort that *The Boston Globe* launched in 2003 to examine the lack of basic health care in developing countries, which leads to several million unnecessary deaths a year. More recently, Chavez has made the HIV/AIDS epidemic in Africa a specialty; among his projects has been a photographic essay in *AIDS in Nigeria: A Nation on the Threshold* (Harvard Center for Population and Development Studies, 2006).

The recipient of numerous national and international awards, Chavez was named Photographer of the Year in 2000 by the Boston Press Photographers Association for his coverage of Afghanistan, Angola, and Colombia. In 2004 the National Press Photographers Association awarded him first place in its international news stills category for his portrayal of an Iraqi father mourning the death of his son.

John Donnelly, an award-winning writer based in Washington, DC, specializes in international development issues that range from global health to global warming. He is currently vice president and senior editor at Burness Communications in Bethesda, Maryland.

From 1999 to early 2008, Donnelly was a reporter with *The Boston Globe.* He worked for six years in the *Globe*'s Washington bureau, then for three years in Africa, opening the newspaper's first ever bureau on the continent. A highlight of his coverage was his work directing and writing much of the *Globe*'s award-winning "Lives Lost: A Worldwide Health Crisis" series, recounting the stories of people from Appalachia to Zambia who died for lack of basic, simple interventions taken for granted in wealthier settings.

Before joining the *Globe*, Donnelly worked for four years based in Jerusalem and Cairo covering the Middle East for Knight Ridder and the *Miami Herald*. He has also worked for the Associated Press in Vermont and New York City. John spent 2007 as a journalism fellow with the Kaiser Family Foundation, where he worked on a project that examined how Americans are trying to help orphans and vulnerable children in Africa.

Donnelly has won many awards for his work. He was part of the *Miami Herald* team that won the Pulitzer Prize for its coverage of Hurricane Andrew, and he has received individual awards from the Global Health Council, RESULTS, InterAction, and the American Society of Tropical Medicine and Hygiene.

Max Essex, DVM, PhD, is the Mary Woodard Lasker Professor of Health Sciences at Harvard University, chair of the Harvard School of Public Health AIDS Initiative, and chair of the Botswana–Harvard Partnership for HIV Research and Education in Gaborone, Botswana. Essex was one of the first to link animal and human retroviruses to immunosuppressive disease, to suspect that a retrovirus was the cause of AIDS, and to determine that HIV could be transmitted through blood and blood products to hemophiliacs and blood transfusion recipients. With collaborators he also provided the first evidence that HIV could be transmitted by heterosexual intercourse.

Essex's laboratory in Boston conducts research on the virology, immunobiology, and molecular epidemiology of HIV-1. The research is oriented to the evolution of new viruses, both circulating recombinant forms and variants that emerge by accumulation of mutations. The studies are usually linked to questions of vaccine design, disease pathogenesis, drug efficacy, and transmission efficiency.

Essex also maintains a laboratory in Gaborone to support field trials in southern Africa. The research there focuses on chemoprophylaxis to block mother-to-child transmission of HIV, trials to evaluate the safety and efficacy of new vaccine candidates, and trials on different drug regimens for people with HIV/AIDS.

In 1984, Essex and Tun-Hou Lee identified gp120, the virus surface protein that is used worldwide for blood screening, AIDS diagnosis, and epidemiologic monitoring. With collaborators, Essex discovered the first simian immunodeficiency virus, as well as HIV-2. Since 1986, he has developed AIDS collaborations in Senegal, Thailand, Botswana, India, Mexico, and China. In 1996, he helped establish the Botswana–Harvard Partnership for HIV Research and Education, a collaboration between the Ministry of Health in Botswana and Harvard.

Essex holds nine honorary doctorates and has received numerous awards, including the Lasker Award, the highest medical research award given in the United States, jointly with Robert Gallo and Luc Montagnier in 1986. He has published more than 500 papers and nine books, including *AIDS in Asia* (Kluwer Academic/Plenum

Publishers, 2004) and two editions of *AIDS in Africa* (Raven Press, 1994, and Kluwer Academic/Plenum Publishers, 2002).

Wafaie Fawzi, MBBS, DrPH, is a professor of nutrition and epidemiology at the Harvard School of Public Health, where he teaches and conducts research on issues related to the nutrition and epidemiology of public health problems in developing countries.

Since 1993, in collaboration with partners in Tanzania and at Harvard, Fawzi has developed and led research and training initiatives focused on nutrition and epidemiology in relation to infectious diseases, perinatal and child health, and non-communicable diseases. Among his studies are clinical trials that have examined the safety and efficacy of micronutrient supplements on pregnancy outcomes, child health, and immune response and progression of HIV disease and tuberculosis. Research from his team has noted the beneficial effects of periodic vitamin A supplementation to children older then six months of age. In a large trial among HIV-positive pregnant women and in another among negative women, the team reported that prenatal multivitamin supplements resulted in significant reductions in adverse birth outcomes. In other completed clinical trials, multivitamin supplements were shown to be beneficial in significantly slowing disease progression among HIV-infected adults and improving health outcomes among patients with tuberculosis.

Fawzi leads the U.S. National Institutes of Health–funded Harvard–Tanzania Clinical Trials Unit of the International Maternal Pediatric Adolescent AIDS Clinical Trials (IMPAACT) Group. IMPAACT conducts multi-centered research to develop and assess safe and cost-effective approaches to the prevention of mother-to-child transmission and evaluates treatments for HIV-infected children, adolescents, and pregnant women. Fawzi is also country director of the PEPFAR-funded HIV/AIDS Care and Treatment Program in Tanzania, which aims to strengthen capacity for care and treatment of HIV/AIDS, with a special emphasis on operational research and training.

Fawzi has authored or coauthored more than 150 peer-reviewed publications and has mentored more than 30 doctoral students and fellows. He completed his medical training at the University of Khartoum in Sudan and earned his doctorate of public health at the Harvard School of Public Health.

Acronyms

ACHAP	African Comprehensive HIV/AIDS Partnerships
AIDS	acquired immunodeficiency syndrome
APIN	AIDS Prevention Initiative in Nigeria
ART	antiretroviral therapy
ARV	antiretroviral
BHP	Botswana–Harvard Partnership for HIV Research and Education
CRF	circulating recombinant form
HIV	human immunodeficiency virus
IEC	information, education, and communication
ISAARV	Initiative Senegalese for Access to Antiretrovirals
NACA	National Action Committee on AIDS
NACP	National HIV/AIDS Control Program
NNRTI	non-nucleoside reverse transcriptase inhibitor
NRTI	nucleoside reverse transcriptase inhibitor
PCR	polymerase chain reaction
PEPFAR	President's Emergency Plan for AIDS Relief
PMTCT	prevention of mother-to-child transmission of HIV
PNLS	Programme National de Lutte Contre le SIDA (National Program for the Fight Against AIDS)
STI	sexually transmitted infection
UNAIDS	Joint United Nations Program on HIV/AIDS
UNDP	United Nations Development Programme
UNFPA	United Nations Population Fund
VCT	voluntary counseling and testing
WHO	World Health Organization

273

Acknowledgments

THE EDITORS ARE DEEPLY GRATEFUL TO THE SCHOLARLY COAUTHORS OF *A LINE DRAWN in the Sand*—Drs. Guerino Chalamilla, Max Essex, and Wafaie Fawzi—not only for their contributions to this book but also to their longstanding and remarkable contributions to the fight against AIDS in Africa. Our gratitude also extends to two other major contributors who have devoted much of their careers to providing the public with a glimpse into the reality and harsh costs of global health problems—John Donnelly with his words and Dominic Chavez with his photographs.

In 2000, the Bill & Melinda Gates Foundation awarded the Harvard School of Public Health with a $25-million grant to create the AIDS Prevention Initiative in Nigeria (APIN). In partnership with government agencies, universities, and nongovernmental organizations in Nigeria, APIN has been able to develop a significant national HIV prevention program. Without the support of the Gates Foundation, this book—and the ongoing work of APIN—would not have been possible. We particularly recognize Dr. Luke Nkinsi for the important role he has played in ensuring the success of APIN.

For several decades, our work in Botswana, Nigeria, Senegal, and Tanzania has been supported by funding agencies as well as many private donations. The U.S. National Institutes of Health and the U.S. Department of Defense have provided major funding for many of the research, prevention, and treatment programs described in this book. The John E. Fogarty International Center of the National Institutes of Health has supported our training programs in all four countries for more than 20 years, with a legacy of scientists who continue to spearhead critical efforts in Botswana, Nigeria, Senegal, and Tanzania.

Since 2004, a grant from the President's Emergency Plan for AIDS Relief, or PEPFAR, to the Harvard School of Public Health has provided funding for AIDS treatment and care in Botswana, Nigeria, and Tanzania. The impact of PEPFAR on Africa has been historic, and we have felt privileged to be a part of it.

We wish to thank the Harvard School of Public Health AIDS Initiative's International Advisory Council members, particularly Maurice Tempelsman, Deeda Blair, and Bruce Beal, three friends whose tireless support and devotion to our programs in Africa now span several decades.

Professors Michael Reich and Lisa Berkmann championed the concept of this book and its publication through the Harvard Center for Population and Development Studies. Sara Davis, our contact at Harvard University Press, helped us enormously. Dr. Olusoji Adeyi, coordinator of public health programs for the World Bank and former technical director to APIN, contributed his expertise on health economic indicators.

This book was produced on a constrained timeline in order to launch a preview edition at the 15th International Conference on AIDS and STIs in Africa, held in Dakar, Senegal, in December 2008. Our designer, Lisa Clark, contributed her artistic talents and Matt Mayerchak his production prowess. Our thanks also go to Connie Smith, Beth Chaplin, Don Hamel, Steven Fake, Dr. Geoffrey Eisen, Dr. Jean-Louis Sankalé, Michelle Stern, and Erika Fardig for various aspects of the book's development and production. The book's completion would not have been possible without our consulting editor, Paula Brewer Byron. She made major contributions to the book, and her invaluable publishing expertise ensured that the book would capture the histories we wished to recount.

This book attempts to chronicle responses to the HIV epidemics in four countries over several decades. The voices and perspectives of some of these countries' heroes have been included, but many, many others are missing. We acknowledge their contributions, which have altered the course of the HIV epidemic, and we recognize that their continued commitment will determine the ultimate success and sustenance of these HIV prevention, treatment, and care programs.

Photo Credits for Endpapers

Column 1. Festus Mogae, former president of Botswana: *courtesy of the Botswana–Harvard Partnership*; Richard Marlink, executive director of the Harvard School of Public Health AIDS Initiative, with children at Princess Marina Hospital, Gaborone, Botswana: *Phyllis Kanki*; Adetokunbo Lucas, adjunct professor of international health, Harvard School of Public Health and a member of the AIDS Prevention Initiative in Nigeria Advisory Council: *Seyed Jalal Hosseini*; Ernest Ekong, national clinical coordinator for the Harvard PEPFAR in Nigeria: *Phyllis Kanki*; Tanzanian President Jakaya Kikwete and former U.S. President George W. Bush: *Nicholas Kamm/AFP/Getty Images*; newborn in a clinic in Jos, Nigeria: *Dominic Chavez*

Column 2. A patient in Botswana getting his blood pressure checked: *Dominic Chavez*; Phyllis Kanki, director of the AIDS Prevention Initiative in Nigeria (with colleagues Oluwole Odutolu and John Idoko in the background): *Dominic Chavez*; Peter Ekeh at the antiretroviral therapy clinic at Jos University Teaching Hospital in Nigeria: *Dominic Chavez*; Marie Mboup: *Dominic Chavez*; Wafaie Fawzi, director of the PEPFAR-funded HIV/AIDS Care and Treatment Program in Tanzania, placing a ceremonial hood on a doctoral candidate at the Harvard School of Public Health: *Kent Dayton/ Harvard School of Public Health*; from left, former U.S. President Jimmy Carter, William Gates, Sr., co-chair of the Bill & Melinda Gates Foundation, Mimi Gates, Abdulsalami Nasidi, director of special projects at the Federal Ministry of Health in Nigeria, and former Nigerian President Olusegun Obasanjo: *Jeff Christensen/AFP/Corbis*

Column 3. Members of the Inter-University Convention during the early years in Dakar, from left: Richard Marlink, Abdoulaye Dieng-Sarr, Georges Diouf, Tidiane Siby, Souleymane Mboup, Moustapha Sarr, Phyllis Kanki, Magette Diaw, and Anta Ndour: *courtesy of Phyllis Kanki*; former Senegalese President Abdou Diouf (left) with current Senegalese President Abdoulaye Wade: *Pierre Verdy/AFP/Getty Images*; a mother and her child at a clinic in Jos, Nigeria: *Dominic Chavez*; laboratory samples in Senegal: *Dominic Chavez*; Jean-Louis Sankalé (left), senior research scientist, Harvard School of Public Health, and Luke Nkinsi of the Bill & Melinda Gates Foundation at Kuramo Village in Lagos, Nigeria: *Phyllis Kanki*; Festus Mogae, former president of Botswana, with Bill Gates, co-chair of the Bill & Melinda Gates Foundation: *courtesy of the Botswana–Harvard Partnership*; blood samples in Botswana: *Dominic Chavez*

Column 4. Antiretrovirals in a Tanzanian pharmacy: *Dominic Chavez*; Max Essex, chair of the Harvard School of Public Health AIDS Initiative: *courtesy of Max Essex*; Emmanuel Isamade (left), head of HaltAIDS, with HaltAIDS staff and Luke Nkinsi (*far right*): *Phyllis Kanki*; a nurse transports blood samples in Botswana: *Dominic Chavez*; Eyitayo Lambo, minister of health for Nigeria: *Akin Jimoh*